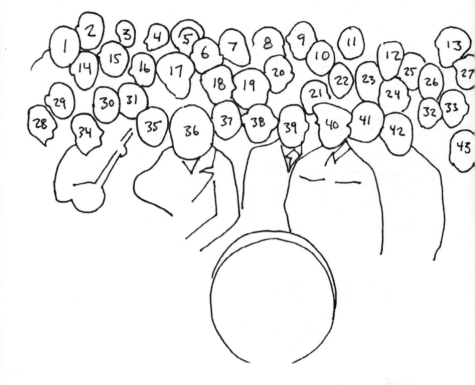

1. Pablo Picasso—(b.1881, d. 1973). Spanish artist and member of the French Communist Party from 1944 until his death

2. William Z. Foster—(b. 1881, d. 1961). American labor agitator and Communist Party USA leader

3. Sidney Webb—(b. 1859, d. 1947). British coauthor of *Soviet Communism: A New Civilization* (1935)

4. Beatrice Potter Webb—(b. 1858, d. 1943). Wife of Sidney Webb and coauthor of *Soviet Communism: A New Civilization*

5. Woody Guthrie—(b. 1912, d. 1967). American folk singer and song writer who wrote the column "Woody Sez" for the Communist paper *The Daily Worker* from May 1939 to January 1940

6. Michael Klonsky—(b. 1943). American educator, leader of the modern small schools movement, and political activist who became a leader of the New Communist Movement in the 1970s

7. Roger Baldwin—(b. 1884, d. 1981). American pacifist and Communist who advocated the abolition of private property; one of the founders of the ACLU (1920)
8. W.E.B. DuBois—(b. 1868, d. 1963). Admitted Socialist who joined the Communist Party USA in 1961; one of the founders of the NAACP (1909)
9. Bill Ayers—(b. 1944). Member of the Students for a Democratic Society (SDS) and well known for his 1960s militant activism; cofounder of the militant Weather Underground (1960); describes himself as a "radical, leftist, small-c communist" (1995)
10. Vanessa Redgrave—(b. 1937). British actress and supporter of Communist causes, including the Worker's Revolutionary Party, the Marxist Party in the 1990s, and the Peace and Progress Party since 2004
11. Bernardine Dohrn—(b. 1942). Wife of Bill Ayers and former head of the anti-Vietnam War radical Weather Underground; formerly an FBI most wanted fugitive
12. Michael Straight—(b. 1916, d. 2004). American novelist, magazine publisher, member of the Communist Party, and confessed spy for the KGB
13. Antonio Gramsci—(b. 1891, d. 1937). Italian philosopher, writer, political theorist, and leader of the Communist Party in Italy; considered one of the most important Marxist thinkers of the 20th century
14. George Bernard Shaw—(b. 1856, d. 1950). Irish playwright, political activist, and avowed Socialist who loved Communism; leader in the Fabian Society
15. Armand Hammer—(b. 1898, d. 1990). Flamboyant American tycoon known for his close ties with the Soviet Union
16. Herbert Marcuse—(b. 1898, d. 1979). German philosopher and student of Hegel and Marx; known as the father of the "New Left" and a member of the Communist-inspired Frankfurt School; immigrated to the United States in 1940
17. Frank Marshall Davis—(b. 1905, d. 1987). African American poet, writer, and political activist; member of the Communist

Party USA; friend of Barack Obama's maternal grandfather in Hawaii and Obama's mentor

18. Anthony Blunt—(b. 1907, d. 1983). British art historian who taught at the University of London and was exposed as a member of the Cambridge Five, a group of spies working for the Soviet Union from the 1930s to the 1950s

19. Angela Davis—(b. 1944). Political activist closely associated with the Black Panthers who ran as a vice presidential candidate on the Communist Party USA ticket in 1980 and 1984

20. Mikhail Gorbachev—(b. 1931). Seventh and last General Secretary of the Communist Party of the Soviet Union

21. Alger Hiss—(b. 1904, d. 1996). American lawyer working for the government in the mid-1930s to mid-1940s; involved in the establishment of the United Nations before the end of WWII; accused of being a Soviet spy in 1948 and eventually convicted of perjury

22. Slavoj Zizek—(b. 1949). Slovenian continental philosopher and critical theorist with roots deep in Hegelianism and Marxism; an avowed Leninist

23. Daniel Ortega—(b. 1945). Current president of Nicaragua and a strong advocate of Socialism, Marxism, and left wing nationalism

24. H.G. Wells—(b. 1866, d. 1946). Prolific British author on politics and social commentary and an outspoken Socialist

25. Donald MacLean—(b. 1913, d. 1983). British diplomat who served as a spy for the Soviet Union in WWII and beyond as a member of the Cambridge Five

26. Guy Burgess—(b. 1911, d. 1963). British intelligence officer and a member of the Cambridge Five spy ring who worked as a double agent against the West in the Cold War and gave NATO military strategy secrets to the Soviet Union

27. Saul Alinsky—(b.1909, d. 1972). American community organizer whose writings reflect the true Socialist/ Communist mode of Karl Marx and are credited with inspiring Barack Obama

28. Harry Dexter White—(b. 1902, d. 1948). American economist in the US Treasury Department who spied for the Soviet Union prior to WWII
29. Miguel D'Escoto—(b. 1933). Catholic priest suspended by the Vatican for his revolutionary activities; Nicaraguan diplomat and supporter of Daniel Ortega's Communist regime; former president of the United Nations General Assembly
30. Maurice Strong—(b. 1929). Canadian businessman and environmentalist who developed an early interest in global warming; proponent of the United Nation's involvement in world affairs; now spends most of his time in the People's Republic of China and is a strong supporter of the Communist Chinese government and lifestyle
31. Kim Philby—(b. 1912, d. 1988). High-ranking British intelligence officer who became a Communist spy, defected to the Soviet Union, and worked as an NKVD (Communist secret police) and KGB operative
32. Friedrich Engels—(b. 1820, d. 1895). German political theorist and philosopher known as the Father of Communist Theory; coauthored *The Communist Manifesto* (1848) with Karl Marx
33. Mick Jagger—(b. 1943). British musician and lead singer of the Rolling Stones; political activist whose lyrics support violent revolution, e.g., "Street Fighting Man"
34. Pete Seeger—(b. 1919). American activist/folk singer who joined the Young Communist League in 1936 and the Communist Party USA in 1942; still admires Communism
35. John Lennon—(b. 1940, d. 1980). British musician and founding member of the Beatles; a peace activist in the late 1960s and 1970s; many of his songs were used as anti-Vietnam War anthems; author of "Working Class Hero"
36. Karl Marx—(b. 1818, d. 1883). German philosopher, historian, political theorist, revolutionary, and Socialist who coauthored *The Communist Manifesto* (1848)
37. Mao tse-Tung—(b. 1893, d. 1976). Chinese political revolutionary who led the People's Republic of China from its establishment in 1949 until his death; his economic

policies and political purges caused the deaths of 75 million people

38. Vladimir Lenin—(b. 1870, d. 1924). Russian revolutionary and Communist politician who led the Bolsheviks into power and headed Soviet Russia during its initial years (1917–1924)

39. Hugo Chavez—(b. 1954). Communist dictator of Venezuela who came to power in 1989; is highly critical of American Capitalism and foreign policy

40. Joseph Stalin—(b. 1878, d. 1953). Marxist revolutionary and dictator of the Soviet Union from 1924 until his death; his economic and political policies and purges caused the deaths of untold millions of people

41. Che Guevara—(b. 1928, d. 1967). Argentine Marxist revolutionary who was instrumental in the Cuban Revolution and the rise of Fidel Castro as Communist dictator of Cuba

42. Fidel Castro—(b. 1926). Leader of the Cuban Revolution and Communist dictator of Cuba from 1956 to 2006

43. Jane Fonda—(b. 1937). American actress, entrepreneur, anti-Vietnam War activist, and Communist sympathizer

Dr. Fred Schwarz's son and daughter-in-law, Dr. John and Rosalie Schwarz, founded **The African AIDS Foundation**. One dollar from the sale of each copy of *You Can Still Trust the Communists (to Be Communists)* will be donated to their foundation, so that together we will provide a better future for the 14 million African children orphaned by HIV/AIDS.

"Let us not be deceived by phrases about 'Man taking charge of his own destiny.' All that can really happen is that some men will take charge of the destiny of the others. They will be simply men; none perfect; some greedy, cruel and dishonest. The more completely we are planned the more powerful they will be. Have we discovered some new reason why, this time, power should not corrupt as it has done before?"

—C.S. Lewis

"All power tends to corrupt and absolute power corrupts absolutely."

—Lord Acton

"Those who cannot learn from history are doomed to repeat it."

—George Santayana

You Can Still Trust the Communists...

to Be
COMMUNISTS
(Socialists and Progressives too)

Fred C. Schwarz   **David A. Noebel**

Published by Christian Anti-Communism Crusade,
PO Box 129, Manitou Springs, CO 80829
© 1960 by Prentice Hall, Inc.
© 2010 by David A. Noebel

First edition published in 1960 by Prentice-Hall. Second
revised edition published in 2010 by Christian Anti-
Communism Crusade.

Printed in the United States of America.

ISBN (10): 0-936163-20-8
ISBN (13): 978-0-936163-20-8

Library of Congress Cataloging-in-Publication Data

Schwarz, Fred C.
Noebel, David A.
     You can still trust the communists : to be
communists, socialists, and progressives too / Fred C.
Schwarz and David A. Noebel.
     p. cm.
Includes bibliographical references and index.
ISBN: 0-936163-20-8
1. Communism. 2. Christianity. 3. Socialism. I. Title.

TABLE OF CONTENTS

PREFACE

by
David A. Noebel

The history of Communism as outlined and exposed in the Harvard University publication *The Black Book of Communism: Crimes, Terror, Repression* should have been enough to warn the West, particularly the United States, that Communism was a bankrupt worldview, a nefarious ideology, and ultimately a death-dealing dead end. Unfortunately, that does not seem to be the case. In spite of Communism's deadly march through the 20th century, with over 100 million slaughtered[1] and hundreds of millions more left persecuted and impoverished, Communism's promise of a future utopia continues to deceive the intelligent, the wealthy, the powerful, and the political.

After Marxism's collapse in Russia, many have falsely concluded that "Communism is dead." However, the philosophy of Marx is very much alive and growing. Today, over one billion people live under a Communist flag in countries such as China, North Korea, Vietnam, Laos, and Cuba. Countless more live in Socialist countries such as India, Libya, Sri Lanka, Venezuela, Bolivia, and Ecuador. And the rest of the world seems intent on sliding further and further to the left under the banner of Progressivism. The Berlin Wall is no longer standing, but the Marxist ideas that built that wall continue to deceive and spread.

After fighting against Communism for most of his life, Dr. Fred C. Schwarz, who passed away in January 2009, would find it disappointing that in 2010 we're faced with an American administration willing to hire the likes of Van Jones[2] and Anita Dunn. Jones is an admitted Communist,[3] and Dunn publicly proclaimed Mao Tse-tung to be one of her favorite philosophers.[4] (According to Jung Chang and Jon Halliday, who wrote *Mao: The Unkown Story*, this so-called philosopher slaughtered 75 million of his fellow Chinese.) Dr. Schwarz would also be shocked to learn about the congressional delegation that traveled to the Communist Cuban paradise to fawn over Fidel Castro and his brother.[5]

But there is history to explain the current situation! The President of the United States has been swimming in radical, shark-infested, Socialist waters for much of his life. In fact, in his book *Dreams from My Father* he acknowledges choosing his college friends from amongst the "Marxist professors and structural feminists and punk rock performance poets."[6]

First, to understand Barack Obama's political philosophy, one must understand something about his *alma mater*. Obama is a graduate of the Harvard Law School. In a recent interview with *WORLD Magazine*, fellow Harvard Law graduate Ted Cruz explained the environment at this institution:

> Understanding Harvard Law School is very important to understanding our president, Barack Obama. He is very much a creature of Harvard Law. To understand what that means you have to understand that there were more self-declared Communists on the Harvard faculty than there were Republicans. Every single idea this president has proposed…has been orthodox wisdom in the Harvard faculty lounge.[7]

Preface

When Cruz was asked why the Harvard faculty tend to lean left, he further explained:

> The Communists on the Harvard faculty are generally not malevolent; they generally were raised in privilege, have never worked very hard in their lives, don't understand where jobs and opportunity come from. If you asked the Harvard faculty to vote on whether this nation should become a socialist nation, 80 percent of the faculty would vote yes and 10 percent would think that was too conservative.[8]

Second, the church Obama chose to attend in Chicago provides further insight into his political philosophy. Obama was baptized in the Trinity United Church in 1988 and remained a member there for two decades.[9] Until recently headed by the Rev. Jeremiah Wright, this church is steeped in Marxism. Under the banner of "black liberation theology," Rev. Wright has been actively promoting the Communist cause in African American communities and in Latin America for years.[10] After ABC News broke a story on some of Wright's more controversial teachings,[11] Obama tried to distance himself from his pastor.

Third, it is no accident that Barack Obama chose Bill Ayers and his wife, Bernardine Dohrn, as mentors in his run for the Illinois Senate. Obama conveniently downplays their relationship.[12] However, it is no secret that the goal of Ayers and Dohrn's Weather Underground Organization (1969-c.1977) was "to create a clandestine revolutionary party for the violent overthrow of the US government and the establishment of a dictatorship of the proletariat."[13] William Ayers was a member of SDS (Students for a Democratic Society),[14] a left-wing student group descended from the League for Industrial Democracy.

Ayers and Dohrn are presently associating themselves with the revolutionary group Code Pink, "a women-initiated grassroots peace and social justice movement working to end the wars in Iraq and Afghanistan, stop new wars, and redirect our resources into healthcare, education, green jobs and other life-affirming activities."[15] Jodie Evans, founder of the organization, was a fund-raiser for Barack Obama.[16] It's important to note that through Code Pink, Evans, Dohrn, and Ayers have aligned themselves with several of America's most prominent enemies, including Osama bin Laden, Mahmoud Ahmadinejad, Hugo Chavez, Hamas, and Saddam Hussein.[17]

Jodi Evans' radicalism is also revealed with her ties to associations like the Rain Forest Action Network (RAN) and the Animal Liberation Front, listed by the FBI as one of the largest domestic terrorism threats in the United States. The FBI reported that these groups "committed more than 600 criminal acts and racked up $43 million in damages over seven years."[18] Obama's political advisors were well informed about Evans' radical ties, but chose to keep her campaign contributions regardless.

Fourth, it is again no accident that Barack Obama chose Jim Wallis as his current spiritual advisor. Wallis, a close friend of the Rev. Jeremiah Wright, was a member of the radical Students for a Democratic Society while a student at Michigan State University.[19] His Sojourners community of fellow-travelers in Washington, DC, believes Fidel Castro's Cuba, Hugo Chavez's Venezuela, Daniel Ortega's Nicaragua, and other revolutionary forces "restructuring socialist societies" are the Communist paradises the United States needs to emulate in order to establish "social justice."[20] We will discuss Wallis later in Chapter 14.

Fifth, Barack Obama placed Michael Klonsky on his official campaign website in spite of the fact that he and his entire staff knew of Klonsky's former membership in the pro-Communist SDS and his leadership position in the New Communist movement.[21] One columnist notes the following:

Klonsky is an unabashed communist whose current mission is to spread Marxist ideology in the American classroom. Obama funded him to the tune of nearly $2 million. Obama, moreover, gave Klonsky a broad platform to broadcast his ideas: a "social justice" blog on the official Obama campaign website....Klonsky's communist pedigree could not be clearer. His father, Robert Klonsky, was an American communist who was convicted in the mid-fifties for advocating the forcible overthrow of the United States government....Klonsky the younger teamed with Ayers, Dohrn, and other young radicals to form the Students for a Democratic Society. It was out of the SDS that Ayers and Dohrn helped found the Weathermen terrorist group.[22]

Sixth, two of President Obama's major political mentors are both avid Communists: Frank Marshall Davis and Saul Alinsky. While in his book *Dreams from My Father* Obama familiarly refers to Davis as "Frank,"[23] there is no doubt he is referring to the admitted Marxist who belonged to the Communist Party USA.[24]

Obama's relationship with Saul Alinsky's radicalism is even more troubling and relevant. Alinsky, who died in 1972, authored the revolutionary work *Rules for Radicals: A Pragmatic Primer for Realistic Radicals*. The primer, in essence, argues to bring every facet of American society under the umbrella of a federal progressive government. Thus, in today's economy, if the private banking sector has a student loan program, Alinsky would socialize or nationalize it.[25] If the private sector has a health program for the citizens of the United States, Alinsky would federalize it. If privately-owned newspapers and magazines show financial difficulty, Alinsky would nationalize them. His aim would be to socialize the whole country slowly but surely, piece by piece, rather than by a one-shot Bolshevik revolution![26] Alinsky explains it this way:

A Marxist begins with his prime truth that all evils are caused by the exploitation of the proletariat by the capitalists. From this he logically proceeds to the revolution to end capitalism, then into the third stage of reorganization into a new social order of the dictatorship of the proletariat, and finally the last stage—the political paradise of communism.[27]

A year after graduating from Columbia University, Obama moved to Chicago to direct an inner city Developing Communities Project, a community organizing effort based on Alinsky's organizing methodology.[28] While a law school student, Obama contributed a chapter related to his experiences as a community organizer in a book titled *After Alinsky: Community Organizing in Illinois.*[29]

Later, at Harvard, Obama was further indoctrinated into Alinksy-style community organizing. Alinsky's "contribution to community organizing was to create a set of rules, a clear-eyed and systemic approach that ordinary citizens can use to gain public *power*" (emphasis added).[30] Barack Obama is an Alinskyite. "Trained by Alinsky's Industrial Areas Foundation [a training school for radical organizers], Obama spent years teaching workshops on the Alinsky method."[31] Saul Alinsky's son, L. David Alinsky, wrote a letter to the editor of the *Boston Globe* in August 2008 acknowledging the effect his late father's model for organizing had on the Democratic campaign in 2008. The younger Alinsky proudly noted, "Obama learned his lesson well."[32]

Immediately after his inauguration, President Obama and his political advisors renamed the community organizing project of the Democratic National Committee from "Obama for America" to "Organizing for America."[33] Today, young Americans in public schools are being challenged to join this organization. An OFA internship application states its purpose is to create a "national internship program connecting students all over the country with our organization on the ground—working to make the change we fought so hard for in 2008 a reality in 2010 and beyond."[34]

Preface

This national internship program is a 10-week course of study that includes reading Alinsky's *Rules for Radicals* as well as the works of Rinku Sen and Zack Exley.[35] Sen is a radical feminist who graduated from Brown University with a major in Women's Studies and was winner of the 2008 Progressive Leadership Award. Exley is president of the New Organizing Institute, a "progressive advocacy and campaign training program focused on cutting-edge online organizing techniques (e.g. writing effective emails, engaging bloggers, leveraging social networks, utilizing video), political technology (e.g. using data effectively, progressive technology infrastructure), and the intersection with field and management of these areas of new organizing."[36] And, until March 2010,[37] Exley ran *Revolution in Jesusland*, a blog promoting "dialogue between the secular left and groups within evangelical Christianity that promote economic and social justice as a matter of faith."[38]

Obama worked for the Marxist organization ACORN (Association of Community Organizations for Reform Now) in Chicago, directing Project Vote, a voter registration drive. During the presidential campaign at a meeting with ACORN leaders, he reiterated his unequivocal support: "I've been fighting alongside ACORN on issues you care about my entire career."[39] In fact, as an attorney, he represented ACORN in a lawsuit against the governor of Illinois involving voter registration.[40] ACORN was born within the confines of Radicalism, Communism, Socialism, and Fabianism. Its founder was Wade Rathke, another member of the radical Students for a Democratic Society and a disciple of Saul Alinsky.[41]

Two more Alinsky disciples, Columbia professors Richard Andrew Cloward and his wife, Frances Fox Piven, also figure prominently in Barack Obama's leftist leanings. Both are members of the Democratic Socialists of America,[42] the US affiliate of the Socialist International, whose roots can be traced to Karl Marx. In May of 1966, Cloward and Piven coauthored an article in *The Nation* titled "The Weight of the Poor." In this article, "they outlined their strategy, proposing to use grass roots radical organizations to push ever more strident demands for public services at all levels of government."[43]

ACORN, Rathke, Ayers, and Obama have prioritized putting the Cloward-Piven strategy into action. "Action" here means, in part, securing grants from the Woods Fund of Chicago for radical organizations like ACORN, Obama's Trinity United Church of Christ,[44] the Annenberg Challenge, and the Arab American Action Network among many others.[45] The Woods Fund primarily gives grants for community organizing. Bill Ayers and Barack Obama served as paid board members overlapping the same three-year period.[46] As an Illinois attorney in the 1990s, Obama successfully represented ACORN in a suit claiming redlining (a practice by which banks loaned money to some communities but not to others, based on economic status).[47] ACORN filed hundreds of these lawsuits claiming racism in lending. One of ACORN's goals was to force banks to make risky loans to low-income and minority customers. This paved the way for banks to package mortgages as investments that were underwritten by government-sponsored Fannie Mae and Freddie Mac.[48] "Nationalizing Fannie and Freddie was not the unintended result.

Forcing every segment of society onto the lap of the federal government where the State makes all decisions is undeniably another guise for Communism—although today it is better known as Neocommunism,[49] Progressivism,[50] Liberal Fascism,[51] Fabian Socialism, Keynesianism, Black Liberation Theology (among others) and is espoused by organizations such as the Congressional Progressive Caucus, the Democratic Socialists of America, and the ACLU, founded by Roger Baldwin, who admonished his fellow Socialists to

Preface

"look like patriots in everything we do"[52] and who told his 1935 Harvard reunion class that his goal was Communism.

In fact, let me quote Baldwin himself so as not to diminish the impact of his stated agenda: "I am for socialism, disarmament, and ultimately for abolishing the State itself as an instrument of property, the abolition of the propertied class and sole control by those who produce wealth. Communism is the goal."[53]

Maxine Waters, a member of the Congressional Black Caucus and the Congressional Progressive Caucus, also openly acknowledged her agenda: "And, guess what this liberal will be all about? This liberal will be about socializing...uh, will be about, basically taking over and the government running all of your companies."[54]

Congresswoman Waters, should meet Jane Fonda, who expressed her goals in similar terms: "I would think that if you understood what communism was, you would hope, you would pray on your knees, that we would someday become communists."[55] She also confessed, "I, a socialist, think that we should strive toward a socialist society, all the way to communism."[56]

Interestingly, Vladimir Lenin said nearly the same thing—"The goal of socialism is communism."[57] Lenin also proclaimed that "[t]he way to crush the bourgeoisie [i.e., the middle class] is to grind them between the millstones of taxation and inflation."[58] Mikhail Gorbachev dittoed Lenin: "I am a Communist, a convinced Communist! For some that may be a fantasy. But to me it is my main goal."[59]

And then there is William Z. Foster's landmark work that no one seems willing to talk about today. In 1932, Foster, a member of the Industrial Workers of the World (Wobblies), the American Socialist Party, and finally General Secretary of the Communist Party USA, wrote *Toward Soviet America* (published by the International Publishers, a Communist propaganda machine). In this book, Foster notes, "The Soviet government, as a Worker's State, is liquidating these classes and the whole system of robbery upon which their rule was based."[60] Foster also boasted that the Soviet Union's second Five Year Plan was "the final liquidation of the capitalist class."[61] *The Black Book of Communism* puts this "liquidation" into historical context with the human toll running into the tens of millions.

Foster says, "In the USSR, as part of the general cultural revolution, religion is being liquidated. Religion, which Marx called 'the opium of the people' has been a basic part of every system of exploitation."[62]

Chapter 5 of Foster's book, titled "The United Soviet States of America,"[63] is nearly prophetic! He insists the journey is "from Capitalism, to Communism, through the intermediary stage of Socialism; that is the way American society, like society in general, is headed."[64] He insists, "The American Soviet government will be the dictatorship of the proletariat."[65] Under such a dictatorship, Republicans, Democrats, Progressives, Independents, etc., will be "liquidated."[66] Left, Right, and everyone between needs to wake up and learn the lessons of history before it's too late! Once the "useful idiots" help the Communists into power, they in turn will be destroyed; if they betrayed their own country once, what could prevent them from betraying the newly established "dictatorship?"

To bring about the communization of America, Foster provides the following scenarios: the State will take over all large factories, mines, and power plants; the State will confiscate all church property; mortgage holders, landowners, and coupon clippers will be abolished; private property will be abolished; women will be liberated from "medieval sex taboos" and State childcare will free her from "perpetual care of her children;" all youth will become part of the Communist Youth League; all education will be placed under a National Department of Education and children will be indoctrinated in "a scientific materialist philosophy;" religious schools will be abolished; God will be banished from the classroom; the great art treasures of the rich will be confiscated and assembled in museums; free medical services, based upon the most scientific principles, will be established; Socialism will deal a mortal blow to crime of every description; the economic system will be bascd upon the principle of planning; Socialism will destroy individualism; Socialism will inevitably produce the intelligent and the beautiful and scientifically regulate the growth of population; Socialism will speed up human evolution by "breeding up mankind."[67]

In 1958, W. Cleon Skousen wrote *The Naked Communist* in which he compiled a list of 45 "Current Communist Goals." All Americans owe it to themselves to read these 45 goals and check off those that already have been fulfilled and those that have not. Among the 45 goals are the following: (1) Present homosexuality, degeneracy, and promiscuity as normal, natural, and healthy; (2) Eliminate prayer or any phase of religious expression in the schools; (3) Discredit the American Constitution; (4) Discredit the family as an institution; (5) Support any socialist movement to give centralized control over any part of the culture—i.e., education, social agencies, welfare programs, mental health clinics; (6) Infiltrate the churches and replace revealed religion with "social" religion. Discredit the Bible and emphasize the need for intellectual maturity that does not need a "religious crutch."[68]

Any reader who seriously wishes to know the full content of the list may visit the website of the Communist Party USA. The red hammer and sickle are prominently displayed along with what must be done to bring about a Communist heaven on earth, including these words: "A better world is possible—a world where people come before profits. That's socialism. That's our vision. We are the Communist Party USA."[69]

To bring this Preface full circle, let me close with words from the world-renowned philosopher, sociologist, and psychologist Slavoj Žižek. In a recent interview with the *New Statesman*, he said, "I am a Leninist. Lenin wasn't afraid to dirty his hands. If you can get power, grab it."[70] This is the same political philosopher (with two PhDs) that the news media has dubbed an "intellectual rock star." In fact, *The Chronicle of Higher Education* made a documentary film on Žižek titled "The Elvis of Cultural Theory" and *National Review* dubbed him "the most dangerous political philosopher in the West."[71]

The *New Statesman* article concludes with this telling link between Slavoj Žižek and today's political reality: "The eminent thinker Slavoj Žižek tells Jonathan Derbyshire why he rejects mainstream political theory, why he supports Barack Obama, and why we need Marx more than ever."[72]

I rest my case!

Dr. Fred C. Schwarz's analysis of the Communist heart, mind, and soul is as necessary today as it was when he wrote it a half century ago! It appears we have learned nothing from history. The former Communist newspaper *Pravda* observed that "the American descent into Marxism is happening with breathtaking speed." The article's author, Stanislav Mishin, assesses America's descent into Marxism thusly: "True, the situation has been well prepared on and off for the past century, especially the past twenty years."[72]

Initially, I had planned to completely update Dr. Fred C. Schwarz's 1960 masterpiece *You Can Trust the Communists (to Be Communists)* for the 21st century. But the more I thought about it, the better it seemed to leave it in his own words. Therefore, I have left most of Schwarz's original words untouched, while adding suggestions for further reading, a bibliography, and a new chapter taken from Dr. Schwarz's papers: "The Heart, Mind, and Soul of Communism."

Preface

Following Schwarz's work, I have added three chapters of my own: "Worldviews of Destruction," "Barack Obama's Red Spiritual Advisor," and "The Socialization of America."

While what you read in this book does not apply to every situation in America today, it applies to enough to make this re-publication necessary. Its historical message alone is worth the read and should warn every American what the future holds if we choose to travel further down this road toward Neocommunism, Communism, Socialism, Collectivism, Statism, Progressivism—call it what you will!

You Can Still Trust the Communists

CHAPTER ONE

Trust the Communists?

by
Fred C. Schwarz

The thesis of this book is very simple. It is that Communists are Communists. I intend to show that they are exactly what they say they are; they believe what they say they believe; their objective is the objective they have repeatedly proclaimed to the entire world; their organization is the organization they have described in minute detail; and their moral code is the one they have announced without shame. Once we accept the fact that Communists are Communists, and understand the laws of their thought and conduct, all the mystery disappears, and we are confronted with a movement which is frightening in its superb organization, strategic mobility, and universal program, but which is perfectly understandable and almost mathematically predictable.

In the battle against Communism, there is no substitute for accurate, specific knowledge. Ignorance is evil and paralytic. The best intentions allied with the most sincere motives are ineffective and futile if they are divorced from adequate knowledge. Consider a mother who has a small daughter to whom she is devoted. For this daughter she is determined to do all that a mother may do. She feeds her a well-balanced diet to build a healthy body; she provides the finest education to develop her mind; she cares for her spiritual well-being, and gives her a lovely home. In the environment of this young girl, there are men who specialize in gaining the confidence of little girls by giving them candy and enticing them into automobiles to molest them. If the mother neglects to give her child the specific information to meet such a situation, she will fail in her duty, and all her loving care will count for nothing when the crisis comes. There is no substitute for specific knowledge.

It is the purpose of this book to give that knowledge. Some of it is a little technical. Some of it may seem a long way from the everyday needs and activities of life. Nonetheless, the information contained is essential to survival.

The statement is frequently heard: "You cannot trust the Communists!" This is incorrect; you can trust the Communists.

They are extremely trustworthy. You can trust a cancer cell to obey the laws of its lawless growth. You can trust an armed bank robber to take the money and try to escape. Similarly, you can trust the Communists to act in accordance with the laws of their being.

When people operate according to clearly defined principles, they are both trustworthy and predictable. While we continue to believe that the Communists think, feel, and believe as we do, the Communist movement is, as Winston Churchill described it, "a riddle wrapped in an enigma." The movements of the heavenly bodies appeared mysterious and unpredictable until Copernicus discovered the governing laws. When we understand the philosophy [or worldview] of Communism, the unifying purpose concealed in their frequently chaotic and contradictory conduct is revealed.

Trust the Communists?

MARXISM-LENINISM

Nikita Khrushchev said, "Anyone who thinks we have forsaken Marxism-Leninism deceives himself. That won't happen till shrimps learn to whistle." We can trust the Communists to practice Marxism-Leninism.

What is Marxism-Leninism? Stripped to its barest essentials, Marxism is the doctrine of the universality of class warfare, and Leninism is the doctrine of the historic role of the Communist Party to consummate the universal class war in world Communist victory. The basic doctrine of Marxism-Leninism is that a state of war exists and that the Communist Party has been created to win this war. The war was originally discovered, not declared, by Karl Marx. It is between two classes of society, which he called the proletariat and the bourgeoisie. The bourgeoisie is the class of property owners, the class that owns the means of production. The proletariat he defined as the class of wage laborers. Between these two classes, Marx claimed to discover a state of war. The bourgeoisie desires profit; the proletariat desires high wages. If wages go up, profits come down. If profits go up, wages come down. Thus, there is a fundamental conflict between these two classes. Marx called this conflict the "class war."

Marx taught that the bourgeoisie is the established class in Capitalist society. It has created the State as an instrument to oppress and exploit the proletariat. In reaction, the proletariat creates the Communist Party to wage war against the State. Thus, the class war manifests itself as war between the Communist Party and the State. With the progress of history, the Communist Party has come to power in Russia, China, and Eastern Europe.[1] The bourgeoisie remains in power in America and her associated allies. Thus, the class war has transferred itself from the national to the international plane. The fundamental doctrine of Marxism, therefore, is that Russia and America are at war; that China and America are at war—not that they could be at war; not that they might be

[17]

at war; not that they will be at war; but that they are at war. This war is historically declared; it is universal; it encompasses every aspect of society; in it there can be no vestige of truce. The Communists did not choose it; they simply recognized it. Their duty is to prosecute the war to total and complete victory.

The weapons of this warfare are not merely the classical weapons of guns, tanks, bombs, and aircraft. The weapons are universal. Education is a weapon; language is a weapon; trade is a weapon; diplomacy is a weapon; religion is a weapon; cultural interchange is a weapon. The Communists view every act and judge every situation as part of the class war. When the Bolshoi Ballet performs in the United States, that is an action in the class war; when a group of American clergymen visits Russia, that is an action in the class war; when the Soviets participate in negotiations for "peace," they fight a battle in the class war. Their participation in the United Nations is part of this warfare. The basic Communist doctrine is, "We are at war!" This is the frame of reference within which every action and thought must be assessed and judged.

It does not take two to make a fight. An idea in the mind of one is enough. Let me illustrate. During the war against Japan, I was a doctor in the Brisbane General Hospital. Brisbane, capital city of the state of Queensland in northeastern Australia, was the headquarters of General MacArthur and the American troops for the advance to the Philippines and Japan. Into the hospital, there came one day a man who told me that he had put his finger down his throat to make himself vomit because the Americans were going to poison him. I looked at him in some astonishment.

"How do you know they are going to poison you?" I asked.

"I saw them watching me as I was having my dinner."

"Why are they going to poison you?"

Trust the Communists?

"I don't know."

I sought for an explanation of his attitude. "Has your wife been running around with the Americans?"

That was the only time he showed any emotion. He became quite indignant and said, "Oh, no, nothing like that!"

"They are not going to poison you."

"Yes, they are."

"I know they're not."

"I know they are."

He was not angry. He was not yelling, shouting, or screaming. He did not have piercing, staring, penetrating eyes. He had none of the external characteristics of insanity. He looked perfectly normal. Nonetheless, I diagnosed him as a mental case and sent him down to the mental ward. However, he was not that bad off, so his wife came in and took him home.

Some days later, an American officer went into a public restroom in Queen Street, Brisbane, and was shot dead with a sawed-off shotgun. His assailant ran away. The police, assuming that the criminal was a man like unto themselves, thinking as they thought, and moved by their motives, investigated without success. They considered the normal motives for murder—robbery, jealousy, revenge, alcoholic fury—but they could not find one clue.

A week later in a suburb of Brisbane, another American officer was killed by the same sawed-off shot gun. This time they caught the assailant. It was the man whom I had treated at the hospital.

He had been working on a baker's delivery van, going from house to house delivering bread to the housewives, handling the money, giving the change, playing with the children. Apparently he was quite normal. But deep down in his conscious and unconscious mind, he believed a lie. He knew the Americans were going to kill him. He wished they were not so determined, but he knew they were. A man must protect himself. He took a shotgun, sawed off the barrel, sawed off the stock, and carried it around with him for self-protection. He walked into the restroom. He saw the American officer. He knew his life was in danger. He pulled out the gun, shot the officer dead, and ran for his life. A week later he repeated the same process. He was arrested, convicted of criminal insanity, and sentenced to an asylum for the insane.

It did not take two to make a quarrel. An idea in the mind of one was enough. Those American officers had never seen the man in their lives. Towards him they had no attitude except goodwill. But he believed that they were bent on his destruction. Suddenly a gun flashed and men died. It does not take two to make a quarrel. An idea in the mind of one is enough.

The Communists believe that they are at war with us. This conviction will never be changed in the slightest degree by any action of the Free World. If tomorrow, the leaders of the Free Nations were to accede to every demand made by the Communist leaders, if they were to neutralize every Strategic Air Command base, if they were to grant the demands on Germany, if they were to neutralize Formosa, if they were to recognize Red China and admit it to the United Nations,[2] if the United States were to withdraw every serviceman and weapon within the borders of the continental United States, the Communists would merely believe they had won massive victories in the class war. A step towards our final conquest and destruction would have been taken. We must either recognize this and defend against it, or ignore it and be destroyed. We have no other choice.

PEACE

Since the Communists are at war, they naturally desire peace. Wherever you find a Communist, you find an advocate of peace. "Peace" is one of the golden words of their vocabulary. They have "peace" movements of every kind; they have peace campaigns, peace prizes, peace conferences, and peace processions. Every Communist is a devotee of peace.

Most people, watching the military preparations of the Communists, noting the enormous percentage of their budget devoted to military objectives, observing their ruthless, brutal repression of any attempt by their captive nations to secure freedom, classify the Communists as blatant hypocrites. This is far from the truth. The Communists are not hypocrites. They are sincerely and genuinely dedicated to peace. If you gave a mature Communist a lie detector test and asked him if he desired peace with all his heart, he would pass with flying colors. They live for peace; they long for peace; they would willingly die for peace.

What is this peace that they desire? During the war against Japan, most Americans undoubtedly wanted peace. Peace was the thought that comforted mothers whose sons were in danger on distant battlefields; peace was the word which sustained wives, lonely and anxious without their husbands; peace was the goal that motivated servicemen who knew the boredom, the loneliness, and the danger of war. Had they been asked to define peace, they would doubtless have described it as the termination of hostilities in the defeat of the enemy by the allies. Under no circumstances would victory by Japan have been termed peace. To the American people, peace meant only one thing—American victory. The Communists believe they are at war. They desire "peace" with all their hearts. But to them, peace is that golden consummation when the progressive force of Communism totally overwhelms American imperialism and climaxes in Communist world conquest. By definition, "peace" is Communist world conquest.

Since this is true, any action that advances Communist conquest is a "peaceful" action. 'When the armies of the

Communist Chinese encompass the Tibetans, robbing them of their land and food, stimulating them to frantic, hopeless revolt, and then massacring them, they are consummating peace. When Khrushchev ordered Russian tanks into Budapest to fire into the apartment buildings, reducing them to rubble, entombing men, women, and children, in his heart he had a song of peace.

The Communists use the word "peace" in their own sense with total sincerity. We interpret it in our sense. We are the victims, not of their hypocrisy, but of our own ignorance.

The Communists are not hypocrites. They suffer from paranoia delusions of an intense sincerity. They are so enmeshed in the delusions of Marxism-Leninism that they are beyond the scope of rational argument and conviction. All observed phenomena are interpreted within the framework of their preconceived conclusions. If they were hypocrites, it would be much easier to deal with them. You can make a bargain with a hypocrite; you can scare a hypocrite. When you are dealing with paranoiacs of highly organized delusional patterns, your sole recourse is to acknowledge and understand these patterns and take appropriate measures to protect yourself against the conduct that results from their delusions.

TRUTH

The Communists invariably tell the "truth," but it is the Marxist-Leninist "truth." Those who believe that the Communists will lie in the interests of Communism are mistaken. In fact, it is not possible for a Communist to lie in the interests of Communism. By definition, if a statement is in the interests of Communism, it is the truth.

Jesting, Pilate asked the question: "What is truth?" Christians believe that God is Truth. Truth is a quality of God Himself. An absolute God created an absolute truth. Truth is. The Communists affirm that this is nonsense. There

Trust the Communists?

is no God; there are no absolutes; everything is relative; truth itself is a relative of the class struggle. Lenin said, "The Communist Party is the mind, the conscience, and the morals of our epoch. Proletarian morality is determined by the exigencies of the class struggle." Truth is a weapon of the class war, and any statement that advances Communist conquest is "true." We can trust the Communists always to say that which will advance Communist conquest. We can trust them always to tell the Marxist-Leninist "truth."

Millions of dollars are being spent on the production of beautiful literature telling this "truth." The truth, according to their literature, is simple: "Where Communism comes to power, everyone is happy, prosperous, and free; America, on the other hand, is the vilest, most evil, most degenerate nation the world has ever seen."

An excellent example of the Marxist-Leninist truth is contained in a beautiful photographic magazine published in English by the Communists in North Korea. Most of the magazine is given over to the portrayal of the radiant happiness and glorious prosperity of North Korea under Communism. Towards the end, however, they present the picture of America. On a page entitled "Massacre Committed by American Brutes," there are six photographs of bodies taken from a mass grave lying side by side upon the ground. Their relatives weep over them. Underneath, is the following text:

Mankind remembers the shocking atrocities the Hitlerites perpetrated in the concentration camps in Majdanek and Oswiencim.

Recently another case of atrocities by the American murderers, which exceeds in its cruelty the atrocities by the Hitlerites, was discovered in Korea.

In a shaft of the Rakyun Mine, Jangyun County, South Hwanghai Province, some 800 dead bodies were discovered.

During their temporary occupation of Jangyun County during the Korean War, the American murderers rounded up miners of the Rakyun mine and the peasants in the nearby villages and put them through severe torture. Then the American devils kicked the tortured miners and peasants into the shaft 100 meters deep.

In the shaft corpses were piled up on top of one another, and the torn pieces of the bodies bore bullet holes and scars made by the bayonets. Many mothers had their babies tied on their backs. The shaft presented a most gruesome scene.

Honest-minded people cannot but hate and condemn the American Imperialist murderers whose lust for blood knows no end.

Funeral services for the murdered took place in the Rakyun mine in the midst of children's crying for their lost fathers, old women wailing over their dead sons. The people's enmity and curses upon the American devils rent the air. 'Avenge us of the American imperialists!' This was the cry of the 800 murdered.

But even at the moment in South Korea, the American murderers are slaughtering our brothers and sisters. This we cannot tolerate.

American cannibals get out of Korea immediately.[3]

This is the Marxist-Leninist truth. The objective truth is, of course, quite different. When the Communists retreated in North Korea, they took with them all the able-bodied personnel to serve as laborers. Those who could not stand the rigors of the northward journey—old men and women, pregnant women, very young children and babies—they massacred and buried in a mass grave if they belonged to the untrustworthy social classes. The advancing American troops time and again found mass graves filled with the bodies of those murdered by the Communists. The Communists merely disinterred one of their own mass graves, and with moral indignation, indicted America for it before the conscience of the world. Their moral indignation was real, not simulated. This is almost incomprehensible.

Hitler worked on this principle: Tell a lie, make it big, repeat it often, and the majority of the people will believe you. The Communists have further developed this concept. Any lie that advances Communist conquest is, by definition, not a lie but the Marxist-Leninist truth. The maturity of a Communist can be judged by the extent to which he can divorce himself from the evidence of his senses and totally identify himself with the verdict of the Communist Party. When confronted with a choice between the evidence of his eyes and the verdict of the Communist Party, the mature Communist will believe with such conviction what the Party has said that, were he given a lie detector test, he would pass with flying colors. He would experience all the emotions associated with truth when he thought of the decision of the Party.

We are astounded when we see evidence of this. An American plane was shot down over Soviet Armenia. The American forces recorded the conversation of the Russian pilots as they shot down the plane. When Mikoyan, visiting America, was confronted with the evidence, he was not confounded in the least. He did not believe it. It was not true. He was a Communist, a Marxist-Leninist. The Communist Party had said that it did not happen, and the verdict of the Party is the Marxist-Leninist truth.

All Communists do not attain this maturity. Many of them would possibly feel a slight element of doubt in such a situation. Final maturity is attained with the ability to identify one's emotions completely with the verdict of the Party.

Communist scientists finally derive their "truth" from the verdict of the Communist Party. Laboratory experimentation is secondary and must be interpreted in accordance with the policy outlined by the Party.

In the late 1940s there arose in Russia a great debate in the realm of Biology. It concerned the question of transmissibility to offspring of characteristics acquired during the life of the parent. Most reputable biologists teach that such characteristics cannot be transmitted.

The Communists attribute this theory to Mendel and Morgan and call it Mendel-Morgan genetics. A Russian biologist, Michurin, developed a theory at variance with this. A plant breeder called Lysenko advocated Michurin's theory.

The biological section of the Russian Academy of Sciences met to discuss this issue. The Foreign Languages Press of Moscow published a full report of the conference under the title, "Proceedings of the Academy of Science on the Teaching of Academician Lysenko." The verbatim speeches of the leading Russian scientists were published. Many of these, on the basis of their long laboratory experience, contended that the Michurin Lysenko school was in error. As scientists, they detailed the evidence on which they based their conclusions.

The issue was resolved very simply. Near the end of the report there is a chapter entitled, "Concluding Remarks of Academician L.D. Lysenko." He reports: "Comrades, the question is asked in a note handed to me: 'Has the Central Committee of the Party adopted any position with regard to your report?' I wish to state that the Central Committee of the Communist Party has read my report and has approved it." (*Prolonged ovation. Great applause. All rise.*)

A strange sequence ensues. The leading Russian scientists, who had opposed the Lysenko position on the basis of their laboratory experience, had a crisis revelation during the night. The following day, they asked permission to make statements. When permission was granted, they rose and indicated that the error of their way had now been revealed to them. They repented of their former service to imperialist biology and dedicated themselves to true proletarian biology.

The cynic may say: "That is easy to understand. They were scared. They knew what would happen to them if they did not agree with the Party line." However, the question goes deeper than that. They were scientists and they were Communists. They were Communists first and scientists second. As Communists they believed the Communist Party to be "the mind of our epoch," the fountain of all "truth." The verdict of the Party must take precedence over the experience of the senses, even in the scientific experiment.

Trust the Communists?

It may be argued that this situation no longer exists, that things have changed. Russian scientists do not all agree with Lysenko now.

The question at issue is not the rightness or wrongness of the Lysenko theories, but the right of the Communist Party to determine scientific truth by edict. That situation has not changed. Russian scientists may have changed their views, but only because they have been permitted to do so by the Party. "Truth" remains the exclusive province of the Party.

RIGHTEOUSNESS

The Communists demand and develop characters of "righteousness," that is, Marxist-Leninist righteousness. In the book, *How to Be a Good Communist*, Liu Shao-chi, President of Communist China [1959–1968] and brilliant theoretical writer says:

> But if sacrifice has to be made for the Party, for class and national liberation, that is, for the emancipation of mankind, for social evolution and for the interests of the greatest majority of mankind embracing countless millions of people, countless Communist Party members will face death with equanimity and make any sacrifice without the slightest hesitation. To the majority of Communist Party members, it will be accepted as a matter of course "to lay down one's life for a noble cause" or "to die for righteousness," if necessary.[4]

What is this righteousness for which they are ready to die? Righteousness is conduct that will advance Communist world conquest. According to this definition, Joseph Stalin was the very personification of Marxist-Leninist righteousness. The many who believe that Khrushchev attacked and condemned Stalin missed the point of his speech entirely. Khrushchev did two things: He described Stalin, and he condemned him. His description depicted a man so vile that most folk took it for condemnation. What he said, in effect, was this: Stalin was a murderer; he was not a reluctant murderer, but an enthusiastic murderer. He enjoyed murder. He got a thrill out of the torture of his own friends. When the Jewish doctors were arrested and accused of poisoning Zdanov, Stalin called in the man responsible for examining them and indicated the type of torture to be given each one. He gave three fundamental rules for getting confessions: "Beat, beat, and beat again." He said: "If you don't get a confession by this date, we will shorten you by a head!"

Khrushchev indicated that Stalin was a stark, raving madman. "When you went in to see him in the morning, he would look at you and say, 'What have you been up to? You have a shifty look in your eye today.' You never knew whether you would leave as his friend or under armed guard to be shot." He presents a picture of a murderer of limitless appetite, a picture of megalomaniacal, sadistic madness. But he concludes by saying: "Don't misunderstand me. Stalin was a good man. He was a Marxist-Leninist. He did these things as a Marxist-Leninist." Khrushchev could have given no higher praise.

How could he justify both description and designation? Let us project ourselves into the stream of history, and look at Stalin in historic perspective. Stalin assumed power when the Communists were a beleaguered garrison and he brought them to the verge of world conquest. It was Stalin who set up their educational program that today is graduating three times as many engineers and scientists as the American program. It was Stalin who became the patron of scientific research. It was Stalin who established their submarine and missile programs that have caused the shadow of impeding death to fall over the life of people in the Free World. It was Stalin who organized the conquest of China. It was Stalin who deceived American and Free World statesmen. Stalin brought Communism to the very verge of world conquest. A few generations hence, when Communism has conquered the world, and regenerate mankind lives in perfect happiness and complete abundance, the name of Stalin, who did so much to bring this to pass, will be honored and revered. His personal idiosyncrasies will be ignored and forgotten. Dead men do not complain. Who worries about last year's fallen leaves? Stalin is the superb exemplar of Marxist-Leninist righteousness.

LOVE

We can trust the Communists to manifest pure, Marxist-Leninist "love." One of the best pictures of Marxist-Leninist "love" was revealed in the boast made by Kliment Voroshilov, [1953–1960] president of Russia, to William C. Bullitt, America's first ambassador to the Soviet Union. At a banquet in Russia in 1934, Voroshilov told Bullitt that in 1919 he persuaded eleven thousand Czarist officers at Kiev to surrender by promising them that, if they surrendered, they, their wives, and their families would be permitted to return to their homes. When they surrendered, he executed the eleven thousand officers and all male children, and sent the wives and daughters into the brothels for the use of the Russian army. He mentioned in passing that the treatment they received in the brothels was such that none of them lived for more than three months.[5]

Voroshilov was merely acting in obedience to the dictates of Marxist-Leninist "love." Believing as he believed, he acted in a truthful, righteous, and loving manner. There he stood, one of history's anointed, entrusted with the destiny of world conquest and human regeneration. There stood a group of male and female animals which he could utilize selfishly by keeping his promise to them and making himself feel good in the bourgeois sense, or which he could utilize for the ultimate regeneration and happiness of all mankind by destroying them. His duty lay clearly before him. As a Communist he had no choice. He was nothing; these people were nothing; the will of history was everything. He saw his duty clearly. To the executioners went all the males, and to the brothels went all the females. The Red Army was strengthened, world conquest came a day nearer, human regeneration a little closer, and Voroshilov had a conscience as clear as spring water and a sense of duty nobly done. He was comforted by an acute awareness of the fulfillment of Marxist-Leninist "love."

Communists believe they have a destiny. Their destiny is to create a new world and regenerate mankind. To do this they must conquer the world, dethrone God, shatter the Capitalist system, and by Communist dictatorship, establish the regenerative environment of Socialism. This new environment will rear the young to perfection.

An inescapable step of their scientific program for the regeneration of mankind is the elimination of the residual diseased social classes following world conquest. A few years ago, the American Communist Party would openly acknowledge that, having conquered this country, they would need to put to death one third of the American people.[6] This is not punishment; it is Social Science. It is not cruelty; it is "love." It is as though the surgeon took the scalpel in a loving fashion to cut away the gangrenous tissue so that the new and perfect might come to maturity.

Communism is applied godless materialism. St. Paul writes:

> Because that, when they knew God, they glorified him not as God, neither were thankful; but became vain in their imaginations, and their foolish heart was darkened. Professing themselves to be wise, they became fools, and changed the glory of the incorruptible God into an image made like to corruptible man, and to birds, and four-footed beasts, and creeping things. Wherefore God also gave them up to uncleanness through the lusts of their own hearts, to dishonor their own bodies between themselves: who changed the truth of God into a lie, and worshipped and served the creature more than the Creator, who is blessed for ever.[7] [KJV]

Trust the Communists?

Emerging from its lair of godless materialism, dressed in garments of science, Communism seduces the young and utilizes their perverted religious enthusiasm to conquer the world. Building on the doctrines of godless materialism, Communism has completely reversed the meaning of our basic moral terms. When we, in our ignorance of this fact, insist on interpreting their phraseology as if they believed the Christian philosophy from which we have derived our basic concepts, we aid and abet them in their program for our conquest and destruction. Once it is known what the Communists believe, there is no difficulty in understanding, interpreting, and predicting their conduct. On the foundation of knowledge, and on that foundation alone, may an edifice of survival be built.

FURTHER STUDY

Chambers, Whittaker. *Witness*. New York: Random House, 1952.

Gairdner, William D. *The Book of Absolutes: A Critique of Relativism and a Defense of Universals*. Montreal: McGill-Queens University Press, 2008.

Joravsky, David. *The Lysenko Affair*. Chicago: University of Chicago Press, 1986.

Klein, Aaron and Brenda J. Elliott, *The Manchurian President: Barck Obama's Ties to Communists, Socialists and Other Anti-American Extremists*. Washington, DC: WND Books, 2010.

Noebel, David A. *Understanding the Times: The Religious Worldviews of our Day and the Search for Truth*. Eugene, OR: Harvest House Publishers, 1991.

CHAPTER TWO

The Recruiting of a Communist

by
Fred C. Schwarz

If there is one question asked more frequently than any other, it is this: Why do rich people, educated people, even religious people become Communists? People say, "I can understand the appeal of Communism to the poor, to the ignorant, to the exploited, and to the oppressed. What I cannot understand is its appeal to the wealthy, the educated, and the religious. Why do millionaires, college professors, and even ministers of religion become Communists?"

The truth is that Communism as such has little appeal for the poor, the oppressed, or the exploited. The basic appeal of Communism is to the educated,[1] and particularly to the student-intellectual.

A survey of leading Communist personalities will soon show that the great majority were recruited as students. While I was in Portland, Oregon, I went to collect my laundry. I mentioned to the laundryman the alarming figures of Communist advance. He had enough intelligence to be alarmed. He said, "We must do something! We must do something!" He thought for a moment and then said, "We must feed them. No man ever became a Communist on a full stomach."

I looked at him and said, "I could mention one or two who did: Karl Marx, Frederick Engels, Vladimir Lenin, Joseph Stalin, Molotov, Bulganin, Kalinin, Mikoyan, Kaganovich, Mao Tse-tung, Chou En-lai, Liu Shao-chi, Chu Teh, Ho Chi minh, Whittaker Chambers, William Remington, Hal Ware." I ran out of breath, but not out of names. Go to any country in the world, take the outstanding Communist figures, and, if they became Communists in a non-Communist country, you will find almost without exception that they embraced Communism as student-intellectuals.

Consider, for example, the Communist Party of China. The chairman, Mao Tse-tung, was converted to Communism at the age of twenty-one while he was the student-librarian at the National University in Peking. The Prime Minister, Chou En-lai, son of a wealthy Chinese aristocrat, was studying at a university in Paris, France, when he became a Communist. Chou En-lai converted the commander-in-chief of the Red Army, Chu Teh, son of a wealthy Chinese, to Communism while he was studying at a Prussian military academy in Germany. Liu Shao-chi, brilliant theorist and apparent heir to Mao Tse-tung, embraced Communism as a young student. The record is the same wherever you go. The sinister truth is that a majority of the students in the world today [1960] are attracted to Communism. Until the appeal of Communism to student-intellectuals is understood, any effort to combat its influence among them is futile.

Following an address at a Baptist school in the South, two students approached me. One was from Mexico, and the other from North Korea. The student from Mexico said, "When I was doing the pre-medical course in Mexico City, 80 percent of the medical students were Communists. They were organized into cells. Their leaders, utterly godless and materialistic, were trained in Moscow.

The Recruiting of a Communist

Actually, it is doubtful that 80 percent of the students were really members of the Communist Party. This would be contrary to the Communist concept of a small, elite group which influences, controls, and exploits much larger groups. However, his statement does indicate the powerful influence of Communism among the students of Mexico. The same thing is true in universities in Central and South America, India, Japan, Indonesia, the Near East, Africa, and, in a measure, in Europe and America. The appeal of Communism to the student-intellectual is extensive and powerful indeed.

It may well be asked why this is so. The second student gave some insight into this. He was a refugee from North Korea. America had opened its arms and its heart and had given him refuge. He was surrounded by love and affection; he was well-fed and well-clothed, an individual protected by the law, significant and important. Despite all this, the ideas the Communists had planted in his mind as a child were still there.

He immediately began telling me all that was wrong with America, and right with Communism. The trouble with America, he said, was the way the bosses exploited the workers, particularly in the South. American prosperity was a bubble that was going to burst into unemployment, depression, crisis, and civil war. He went on to say that in North Korea, they had New Democracy that was bad, so bad that he had to flee from it. But New Democracy was going to develop into Socialism such as existed in Russia that was much better. Socialism would finally evolve into Communism that was very good. Under Communism, human nature would be so perfect that there would no longer be the need for any government whatsoever.

The reality had driven him forth in hunger, nakedness, and terror, but the vision still lived within his mind. This student showed rather clearly certain aspects of the appeal of

Communism to the student mind. Communism utilizes four things to recruit the young intellectual. These are:

1. Disenchantment with Capitalism
2. Materialist philosophy
3. Intellectual pride
4. Unfulfilled religious need

CAPITALIST DISENCHANTMENT WITH CAPITALISM

The first step in the making of a Communist is disenchantment with the Capitalist system. According to the Marxist analysis of Capitalism, depression and war are the inevitable consequences of the Capitalist system. Capitalism is also the creator of vice, crime, and all the evils of society. This has been the great recruiting doctrine of Communism. Whittaker Chambers, author of *Witness*, said that every intelligent person of his acquaintance who became a Communist did so in terms of the Marxist analysis of Capitalism as the creator of depression and war. Once they accepted the Marxist thesis that Capitalism caused recurrent depression and war, it was a short step to the acceptance of the Leninist program for the destruction of Capitalism.

The Marxist analysis, superficially, is very convincing. Marx taught that the Capitalist system does two things: it produces commodities for distribution and it circulates purchasing power or money. In other words, Capitalist society is built upon the production of commodities to be exchanged for money and the distribution of money to secure those commodities. Capitalist society is healthy, according to Marx, when the amount of money available to the people is adequate to buy the commodities produced.

Marx contended that, by the very nature of Capitalism, this balance between goods produced and money available couldn't be maintained for very long. A certain sequence of events is inevitable. The goods produced have a certain money value. That money is distributed in two ways: the major portion is paid out in wages to the workers who manufacture the goods—to the directors, the supervisors, and all the laborers down to the janitor; a smaller portion is retained as profit by those who own the means of production. During the early stages of the industry, the money paid to the owners as profit goes into circulation because new capital goods such as buildings and machinery are necessary. Since these capital goods are produced and are not available for purchase by the mass of the people, the wages paid to the workers producing these capital goods are used to buy consumer commodities. During the period of capitalization, there is usually enough money in circulation to buy the consumer goods produced. But eventually the point is reached where there are enough factories and machinery, and there is no longer need for this expenditure. The profit is then retained and accumulated in bank balances, and the only money circulated is the money paid in wages for producing the goods. Since this is never quite enough to buy the goods produced, production inevitably leads to over-production.

At first this over-production is small and almost unnoticeable, but gradually it becomes more significant. The warehouses of the manufacturer become filled with goods, the inventories of the distributors are complete, and the point is reached where the factory has enough goods on hand to supply the demand for some considerable period. When that point is reached, alternative courses of action present themselves. The manufacturers may say, "Now, the real trouble is that people haven't enough money to purchase these goods. We had better find some way in which people can get more money." On the other hand, they may say, "We have enough goods now. We do not need to make any more for a certain period. We had better cease production until our surplus is used up." The normal process is to follow the latter course and to lay off the workers. When they are laid off, the purchasing power is further reduced, and the situation becomes worse.

According to Marx, this cycle is inevitable. Production leads to over-production that leads to unemployment. This leads to reduced purchasing power, which aggravates the entire situation by accelerating the accumulation of surplus products and leading to further unemployment. The eventual outcome is depression and crisis. Warehouses are filled with goods that the people cannot buy. The economy stagnates and grinds to a standstill.

When this happens, a method must be found whereby purchasing power is once again given to the people that the goods may be bought and the wheels of the economy may begin to roll once again. Historically, one method has always put money in people's pockets without simultaneously creating consumer goods. That method is war. A war breaks out on some pretext or another. Money is found to finance the war; the wheels of industry begin to turn on war production; money is distributed to the people, and the surplus consumer products are purchased. When the surplus is consumed, normal production begins again, and the cycle goes on, repeating itself again and again. According to Marx, therefore, as long as Capitalism continues, there will be recurrent crises of depression and war.

This seems a powerful and convincing argument. It is the more dangerous because it is, like most Marxian arguments, a half-truth. By taking some of the variables in the situation and concentrating on them, it produces conclusions that appear very sound. These conclusions, however, are not necessarily valid, for there are many important factors that are ignored.

In the first place, Marx's argument is merely diagnostic. Even if it is assumed that his diagnosis is accurate, it does not necessarily follow that the treatment prescribed by the Communists is correct. Other groups who accept the Marxian analysis of Capitalism have completely different prescriptions for treatment. Social Credit[2] devotees, for example, say that the problem is not over-production, but lack of purchasing power. Therefore, the amount of surplus production should be assessed periodically and a national dividend declared corresponding to the surplus. This money, given to the people, can be used to buy up the surplus and production will continue.

In the second place, the argument ignores many important factors in distribution. Although this is not a textbook on economics, some of these ignored factors should be mentioned. They are:

1. The dynamic nature of money
2. The role of psychology in the economy
3. The relation of advertising to distribution
4. Consumer credit
5. Continually expanding market
6. People's Capitalism
7. The role of government and legislation

1. THE DYNAMIC NATURE OF MONEY

Money is not static. The same amount of money spent three or four times will distribute three or four times as many goods. There is an intriguing story about a man who wrote a check for a hundred dollars without having any money in the bank. With it he bought a certain article. The man from whom he purchased the article took the check and, without cashing it at the bank, used it to purchase certain goods. These he sold for one hundred and twenty dollars, making a profit of twenty dollars on the deal. The person to whom he gave the check did likewise. This happened ten times, each person making a profit of twenty dollars, before the check finally reached the bank where it was dishonored. The ten people who had handled it got together and decided that to avoid trouble, each of them would contribute ten dollars to cover the check. This was done; the hundred dollars was paid; and each of them was richer by ten dollars. This story simply illustrates that the question of credit and rate of circulation must be considered.

2. THE ROLE OF PSYCHOLOGY IN THE ECONOMY

Suppose everyone is persuaded that a depression is coming and decides not to buy another automobile for twelve months. The result would be an immediate depression in the automobile industry with all the consequences that follow. It is quite obvious that the psychological attitude of the people has a tremendous bearing on the economic situation of a country. This is an aspect of economic theory to which Marx gave little attention.

3. THE RELATION OF ADVERTISING TO DISTRIBUTION

The question of the psychological outlook of the consumer naturally leads to the question of advertising and its role in distribution. During the recession in 1958, this factor was understood more completely and a campaign started urging people to buy. The recession did not develop into a depression. The Marxist cycle was broken.

Marx himself cannot be blamed for his failure to consider the role of advertising, as the advertising industry was not in existence during his lifetime. But the followers of Marx are culpable in this respect.

4. CONSUMER CREDIT

An outstanding development of modern Capitalism is consumer credit. Goods are purchased not with money presently owned, but by a promise to pay in the future. This has become such a large factor in the economy that any analysis that does not consider this is obviously fallacious.

5. THE CONTINUALLY EXPANDING MARKET

Human aspirations are limitless, and under a free economy these form a continually expanding market. A large percentage of American industry now produces items that did not even exist a few years ago. The vast electronic industry, for example, has been a very recent development. The double-car garage is now as normal to the modern home as the faucet with running water. Soon the motorboat will be the routine companion of the car.

6. PEOPLE'S CAPITALISM

Possibly the most devastating repudiation of the Marxist doctrine is the development of people's Capitalism within the United States. Marx foresaw the wealth of the community being concentrated in fewer and fewer hands. The class owning this wealth he called the bourgeoisie, and the natural forces within Capitalism would constantly diminish the number of this class.

Contrary to the expectations of Marx, the ownership of American industry is constantly enlarging. There are now nearly as many stockholders in the United States as there are members of organized labor. It is quite conceivable that in a short period, the number of stockholders will exceed union membership. The profits received by the vast majority of these stockholders are utilized for purchasing.

This renders the whole argument of the "class war" ridiculous. Nothing does such damage to the principles of Marxism as the development of worker ownership in American industry. Proletarian stock holders certainly make the concept of universal class war somewhat ludicrous.

7. THE ROLE OF GOVERNMENT AND LEGISLATION

Finally, the Marxist analysis ignores the role of government and legislation in relation to the economy. The anti-trust laws have restrained the development of monopolies within the American economy. Whatever the individual viewpoint of the role of government in economic affairs, it is a factor that cannot be ignored.

In spite of the foregoing, the Marxist analysis has convinced many people. It would be a simple matter to go before any inexperienced student group and, taking them unprepared, convince practically every one of them that the Marxist argument is sound. This is what the Communists have done. Students throughout the world are being taught as a basic principle that the Capitalist system is evil and the creator of depression and war. Disenchantment with the Capitalist system is the first step in the conversion of a student-intellectual to Communism.

If the situation is considered objectively, it will be seen that there is much to be said in support of Capitalism. The Capitalist system has produced more goods, provided a more equitable distribution, and maintained a higher level of personal freedom than any other system in the world.

The Korean student who spoke to me said, "Of course, in America there is far more freedom than anywhere else."

"That's interesting," I replied. "How did the American people get that freedom?"

He looked at me, puzzled.

"Let's think about it for a while," I said. "The freedom in America has a material and a spiritual foundation. The material foundation is the efficient production of goods in quantity and their extensive distribution is so that most people have the material requirements of freedom—sufficient food, shelter, clothing, transportation, and other necessities. The material system within America has produced more food, clothing, and shelter per individual than any other system. Add to this material abundance the spiritual concept of man as the child of God, created, loved, redeemed, infinite in value, and possessed of certain inalienable rights. The result is this freedom you admire."

Then I asked, "What is the material system that has produced these goods in such quantity and distributed them so widely?"

"I don't know," he replied.

"You most certainly do know. You have been telling me for half an hour how bad it is. It is the Capitalist system. Did it never occur to you that maybe the Capitalist system that you abhor so much stands in causal relationship to the freedom you cherish so highly?"

He was lost. This had not been part of the closed circle of argument that he had heard. His arguments were all worked out and complete. These new ideas came in and shattered the symmetry and perfection.

The idea of collective ownership fascinates some people, but its benefits are a mirage. The story is told of a visitor to a Russian factory who asked the workers, "Who owns this factory?"

"We do," they replied.

"Who owns the land on which it is built?"

"We do."

"Who owns the products of the factory when they are made?"

"We do."

Outside in the corner of a large parking lot were three battered jalopies. The visitor asked, "Who owns those cars out there?"

They replied, "We own them, but one of them is used by the factory manager, one is used by the political commissar, and the other is used by the secret police."

The same investigator came to a factory in America, and said to the workers, "Who owns this factory?"

"Henry Ford," they replied.

"Who owns the land on which it is built?"

"Henry Ford."

"Who owns the products of the factory when they are made?"

"Henry Ford."

Outside the factory was a vast parking lot filled with every make and variety of modern American automobile. He said, "Who owns all those cars out there?"

They replied, "Oh, we do."

You may take your choice, but personally, give me the automobile.

The concept that Capitalism is inherently evil and collective ownership inherently good is contradicted finally by one unanswerable fact. Wherever Communism is in power, the people flee by the millions. They leave everything they love, and they flee to loneliness and the unknown to escape the horror of life under Communist rule.

On the other hand, when all the evils of the Capitalist system have been admitted, the fact remains that every year multiplied thousands risk their lives, not trying to get out of America, but trying to get in. They swim the Rio Grande River. Their goal is not to live at America's highest standard, but to live at her lowest. On a comparative basis, the economic system of competitive free enterprise has produced abundance and liberty and is a magnet to the less fortunate.

Many students, however, have a sense of shame concerning Capitalism. They have been convinced by Communist arguments that the Capitalist system is evil, that it has failed, and that it must be replaced. Once convinced of this, a student has taken the first step toward becoming a Communist.

MATERIALIST PHILOSOPHY

The second factor in the creation of a Communist is materialist philosophy. The student-intellectual is taught that there is no God; that matter in motion is the sum total of all being; that each individual is a body in which a stomach secretes gastric juices, a liver secretes bile, and a brain secretes emotion and thought. There is no soul; there is no spirit; there is no heaven to gain, no hell to shun. A new scientific age has been born, and the need for God has been abolished. The modern outlook is materialism.

Speaking at a university, I outlined these basic materialist beliefs of Communism:

1. Godlessness
2. The material nature of man
3. The environmental nature of man's intellectual and so-called spiritual qualities

A woman jumped to her feet and said, "Why, I hear these things taught in this university every day. The professor of psychology goes to the board and draws a diagram. He says, 'You are only a machine. You are no more and no less. You are a pattern of conditioned behavior. The machinery of your body is very complex. Indeed, your brain is so complex that it gives the impression of freedom, choice, and volition. But actually, you are as automatic as an automobile. You have no soul, you have no spirit, and, in the last analysis, you have no mind.' He laughs at God and he laughs at morality."[3]

That man is not necessarily a Communist. He may even consider himself an anti-Communist. But every student who believes what he teaches will find the Communist program logical and appealing. For Communism carries this teaching to its logical conclusion.

Communism says that every characteristic and attitude of the human personality emerges from the brain. The brain is formed by the accumulation of experiences in the form of conditioned reflexes. The environment that is predominantly economic provides these experiences. What we think, what we feel, what we believe, whom we love, and whom we worship merely reflect our economic environment.

You Can Still Trust the Communists

Once you accept this, it follows, as night follows day, that if you can completely control the environment, you can generate the mind and character you desire. Thus, Communism becomes a program for scientific, materialistic regeneration.

This program for regeneration opens a wonderful vista for the human mind. The Russian Communists already claim to have successfully regenerated many people. One book they have published is entitled *Peoples Regenerated*. They claim they will produce perfect people with perfect bodies, perfect minds, and perfect characters, living together in perfect happiness. This is to be done by scientific means.

The first step in the program is to realistically face the scientific needs. The present environment is Capitalistic and evil, it creates degenerates, criminals, and sundry vicious characters. While this environment continues, human nature cannot be changed. To try to persuade people to be different while they live in an environment that determines how they act is fatuous nonsense. It is like trying to dry the baby while he is still lying in the bath water. To be successful, you must take him out of the water first. Similarly, if man is to be changed, he must be removed from his Capitalistic environment. To do this, the Communists must conquer the world and utterly destroy the Capitalist environment. Capitalism will then be replaced by Socialism, which is built not on profit, greed, and self, but on service, cooperation, and others.

In the new environment of Socialism, the babes will receive new experiences that will condition them to unselfish, voluntary service. The babes will grow to children, the children to adolescents, and the adolescents to adults. How different things will be! Everyone will work because he loves to work. Everyone will give because it is better to give than to receive. The hand of none will be raised in anger against his brother. No longer will there be need for a police force, for there will be nothing for the police to do. There will be no income tax to pay, because people, working willingly, skill-fully, and creatively, will produce total abundance, but will partake merely to the extent of their limited needs. All that mars the happiness of man will be gone forever. Vice, crime, famine, pestilence, and war will be merely words from a forgotten past, while abundance, brotherhood, and mutual, cooperative service will bind lives together in the golden day of Communism that has dawned upon the earth.

Frequently after depicting this promise of Communism, I am accused of making it appear too attractive. This is exactly the way it appears to the student. That is why student-intel-lectuals join the Party. This is just how Communism is pre-sented to them, and on their materialist foundation, it is logi-cal. Liu Shao-chi, in his book *How to Be a Good Communist*, writes:

> What is the most fundamental and common duty of us Communist Party members? As everybody knows, it is to estab-lish Communism, to transform the present world into a Communist world. Is a Communist world good or not? We all know that it is very good. In such a world there will be no exploiters, oppres-sors, landlords, capitalists, imperialists or fascists. There will be no oppressed and exploited people, no darkness, ignorance, backward-ness, etc. In such a society all human beings will become unselfish and intelligent Communists with a high level of culture and tech-nique. The spirit of mutual assistance and mutual love will prevail among mankind. There will be no such irrational things as mutual deception, mutual antagonism, mutual slaughter and war, etc. Such a society will, of course, be the best, the most beautiful and the most advanced society in the history of mankind. Who will say that such a society is not good? Here the question arises: Can Communist society be brought about?' Our answer is 'yes.' About this the whole theory of Marxism-Leninism offers a scientific explanation that leaves no room for doubt. It further explains that as the ultimate result of the class struggle of mankind, such a society will inevitably be brought about.[4]

It is on the foundation of materialism that this scientific program for human regeneration is built.

There are, of course, one or two unpleasant steps on the way to this glorious goal. One of these is the problem of dealing with those who populate the world when the Communists conquer it. These people, formed in the old environment, will think, feel, love, and worship in an established pattern. If they are allowed to raise their young, they will reproduce in them their own qualities, and the Communist aim of generating new characters and perfect human society will be thwarted. Obviously, therefore, they cannot be allowed to remain where they are.

Some of them will be segregated and used to do some useful work until they die. Some of them can be re-educated in re-educational institutions, namely, the labor hospitals. The disease of Capitalist character, according to the Communists, is determined by the false labor relationships of the Capitalist system. In Capitalist society, labor is associated with profit or reward, whereas labor should be its own reward. The unfortunate victims of Capitalist society will be taken in their diseased state and put into Communist institutions of pure labor. There they will rise in the morning to labor and will go to bed at night weary and exhausted with never a thought of any reward. The therapeutic benefits of labor will cure them of their grievous Capitalistic disease. The Communists consider themselves humane in the extreme for providing these therapeutic institutions of labor to regenerate diseased Capitalist mankind. It is our bourgeois ignorance that causes us to classify them as "slave labor camps."

It is only the young, however, who merit the curative process. The older members of the diseased classes who are established in their ways must obviously be destroyed. This the Communists believe to be their duty. Such people would not be happy in the new environment. It is kindness to destroy them—a type of social euthanasia.[5] The Communists have no conscience about it because, according to their materialist philosophy, it is but a step towards the glorious goal of the regeneration of all mankind. This step may seem a little unpleasant if bourgeois sentimentality persists, but it is quite necessary to the process of regenerating mankind.

The record of Communism is one of recurrent fratricide and genocide. Their contempt for individual human life has known no bounds. Whether the life to be sacrificed was that of friend or foe appears to have been immaterial. The Communist Party of Russia devoured its own creators. Stalin put to death a majority of the original Bolsheviks. The Communists destroyed not only landlords and Capitalists, but peasants and workers, Kalmucks and Baits with equal ferocity. In spite of knowing this, the allegiance of many educated, apparently cultured American Communists, has not been shattered. Many people are amazed that they do not turn from Communism in loathing and repulsion when confronted with its unutterable barbarism, brutality, and intellectual prostitution.

To the dedicated Communist, however, these are but the temporary necessary sacrifices that the glorious future demands. To wipe out the residual Capitalist debris is not murder, but social science. Since any individual man is a mere historic accident, an evolved beast, it is stupid to regard him as of infinite value. It is the species and the class that are important. The Capitalist class has been rejected by history and must be destroyed.

Capitalism in America has developed to a greater degree than Capitalism in many other countries. Therefore, the number infected by the Capitalist virus is larger than in other lands. A greater program of elimination will thus be needed. It is probable and natural that, should Communism prevail in America, a program of class liquidation will ensue that will dwarf similar programs in other countries.[6]

To those Capitalists who can regard the triumph of Communism with equanimity, I would ask the question: What will be your attitude when you and your family face destruction because of your membership in the historically rejected Capitalist class? As the wide-bore revolver with the soft-nosed bullet is placed at the nape of your neck to shatter your pattern of Capitalistically conditioned reflexes into a bloody oblivion, will you be able to comfort your dying hours with the thought that you are dying in a good cause, in the interests of the scientific regeneration of the animal species *homo sapiens* and the birth of the classless society?

INTELLECTUAL PRIDE

A third factor in the making of a Communist is intellectual pride. The student of eighteen or nineteen years of age is beginning to feel the freedom of his new intellectual environment. He is just beginning to realize how little his parents know. For sixteen or seventeen years, the truth of their backwardness and ignorance passed him by, but now the light is dawning. He has come to realize the sordidness of the traditions of his own country and to discover that national heroes, even men like Washington and Lincoln, were motivated by personal, selfish greed. Becoming disenchanted with his family and national heritage, he is ripe for conversion to Communism. Convinced of his intellectual brilliance, he sees himself as master of the situation, as one who is entitled, because of his superior intelligence, to be the executive of the great program for the regeneration and perfection of all mankind. Mankind certainly needs changing, and he is just the man to do it.

UNFULFILLED RELIGIOUS NEED

The fourth factor in the making of a Communist is unfulfilled religious need. "Man shall not live by bread alone."

The Recruiting of a Communist

Life needs a purpose. Man is born with a heart to worship God, to reach out for something bigger and beyond himself, to seek some noble vision for which to sacrifice, some purpose for which to live and die. When denial of the existence of God deprives him of his natural fulfillment, Communism provides a substitute. It gives him a sense of purpose and destiny, gives meaning to life, and provides a motive for sacrifice.

People are mystified when a man born to great wealth and social position becomes a Communist, spends his fortune for Communist purposes, and even goes to jail in the interests of the Communist cause. To many people, this does not make sense.

Let us try to put ourselves in his position. As a child he has the finest tutors. He is very intelligent. Very early in life he learns that there is no God, that the idea of God is for dull and second-rate minds, and that he, in the purity and perfection of his intellect, has no need for God. He accepts the Darwinian hypothesis concerning the origin of man, and the Marxian hypothesis concerning the origin of civilization, culture, morality, ethics, and religion.

As a young man he sits on the mount of learning and watches the progress of the animal species from the jungles via savagery and barbarism to civilization. He watches the productive forces as they operate on the human species, dividing it into nations and classes, creating cultures, civilizations, moral codes, educational and political institutions, and religious faith. He sits above it all and beyond it all. He is lost in lonely isolation. Life is devoid of meaning, purpose, and objective. Yet he is a young man with all the idealism and emotional urgency of youth. Where can he find fulfillment? Some seek it in the sporting life, some in the life of a playboy. These outlets have little appeal for him.

Suddenly he hears a whisper on the breeze that history in the goodness of its heart is calling unto itself a few of its finest and its best—superior intellects, courageous characters with an insight into its mind and its purpose, and a knowledge of historic law and historic will; that it is uniting them into its finest organization and giving them the destiny of conquering the world and regenerating mankind. It comes as a vision of glory. It sets a song singing in his heart. It puts stars before his eyes. It leads him forward to live and, if necessary, to die in the Communist cause. In it he finds a religious refuge for his godless and unbelieving heart.

Communists are not born; they are made. They are being formed constantly on the campuses of the world. As long as youth is disillusioned, materialistically orientated, and spiritually unfulfilled, there will be no dearth of Communist recruits. Herein lies our greatest challenge.

The Recruiting of a Communist

FURTHER STUDY

Bethel, Tom. *The Noblest Triumph: Property and Prosperity through the Ages*. New York: St. Martin's Press, 1998.

Horowitz, David. *The Professors: The 101 Most Dangerous Academics in America*. Washington, DC: Regnery Publishing, 2006.

Klein, Aaron and Brenda J. Elliott. *The Manchurian President: Barack Obama's Ties to Communists, Socialists and Other Anti-American Extremists*. Washington DC, WND Books, 2010.

Novak, Michael. *The Spirit of Democratic Capitalism*. New York: Madison Books, 1990.

Richards, Jay. *Money, Greed, and God: Why Capitalism is the Solution and Not the Problem*. New York: HarperOne, 2009.

Skousen, Mark. *The Making of Modern Economics: The Lives and Ideas of the Great Thinkers*. New York: M.E. Sharpe, 2009.

Sowell, Thomas. *Intellectuals and Society*. New York: Basic Books, 2009.

CHAPTER THREE

The Molding of a Communist
Communist Party:
Origin and Organization

by
Fred C. Schwarz

The achievements of Communism are unprecedented in the annals of human history. The Communists have repeatedly achieved the impossible. They have made idiots of every expert. Any man who had predicted twenty years ago the situation that exists in the world today would have been laughed to scorn. How have they done it? What force has been let loose upon the world?

The achievements of Communism are the achievements of organization. The Communist Party was formed, not on a principle of economic doctrine or philosophy, but upon a principle of organization. Communism is the great illustration of the truism that organization will inevitably conquer disorganization and spontaneity.

ORIGIN

Karl Marx and Frederick Engels were the authors of the basic philosophic and economic Communist doctrines. They lived and wrote from about 1840 to 1890. During their lives, many movements were formed to advance Marxist teachings. A Marxist party was finally formed in Russia under the name of the Social Democratic Labor Party. The individual largely responsible for its formation was a man called Plekhanov.

In 1903, a conference of the Russian Social Democratic Labor Party was held in Brussels, Belgium. The police, objecting to this international gang of racketeers and revolutionaries meeting in their fair city, asked them to move, whereupon they went across to London the historic haven of refugees. This congress in 1903 is one of the significant events in world history.

A young man named Vladimir Ilyich Lenin came to the congress with very definite ideas about the type of organization that was necessary to achieve basic Marxist objectives. Lenin desired a party organized on military lines composed of professional revolutionaries subject to maximum discipline and indoctrination. He desired a party of total obedience and submission that would operate with a single mind and will. At the congress, he introduced a motion to implement his ideas concerning the nature of the Party. He moved that no one be accepted as a member of the Party unless he served in a disciplined capacity in one of the Party organizations. A man could not come and say, "I approve of the doctrines, the aims, and the methods of your Party. I'd like to join. I'll pay my membership dues. I'll abide by the rules. Sign me up." This was not the way it was to be done. Lenin declared that if a man wished to join the Party, he should first link up with one of its working units. The Party operated through multiple local organizations. Some of these units met in neighborhoods, others met in factories, while still others met in the military forces. Having joined one of these units, the individual could prove himself by working within it in a disciplined, obedient fashion. Only in this way should he come into Party membership.

Lenin's motion was opposed by Martov, who approved the idea in principle, but who thought it a little too extreme. He pointed out that there were certain important individuals who would be embarrassed if they had to serve in a humble, disciplined capacity in one of the Party organizations—such people as, members of the aristocracy, important business-men, leading government servants, and university profes-sors. Many of these people approved of the Party and were willing to support it, but they would be embarrassed if they had to join a street corner group and engage in its activities. Therefore, he suggested a special clause that would allow general membership for special people who could come into membership without joining one of the working units.

Lenin, however, stood firm, insisting that they did not want such people. They needed a party of unity, discipline, and obedience, with every member under observation and control. Those unwilling to join on these conditions could become sympathizers and helpers, but they must remain on the outside. The Party wanted no member who was not totally subject to Party discipline.

The vote was taken and Lenin obtained a majority. The Russian word for majority is akin to "Bolshevik" and the word for minority is akin to "Menshevik." The followers of Lenin became known as the Bolsheviks, and those of Martov were known as the Mensheviks.

It was a seemingly unimportant difference of opinion con-cerning Party membership, but the division that it caused has become the determinant of the destiny of the world. Neither Lenin nor Martov realized its depth and significance. They held unity conferences periodically, but there were quarrels and the division widened. In 1917, the split became formal and final. In that year, Lenin returned to Russia from exile in Geneva, Switzerland, after the revolution that had over-thrown the Czar, and renamed the Bolshevik segment of the Russian Social Democratic Labor Party the Communist Party of Russia. From that tiny fragment, the entire Communist movement has developed.

You Can Still Trust the Communists

There has never been any growth like that of the Communist Party in the history of mankind. Some measure of its growth is revealed by the fact that, in one generation, the Communists have conquered more people than Christians have even told about Christ after nearly two thousands years. Some measure of their progress is indicated by the fact that today there are five children in school learning in detail the godless doctrines of Communism for every one child in school learning anything about Christ. The success of the Communist Party has been due to the ceaseless activity of this Leninist organization.

The first step is the recruitment of intellectual elites to be the core of the Communist Party. The idea is not to recruit great masses of people. The concept is that of a disciplined and dedicated minority who conquer the masses by reason of their superior knowledge and organization. Some of the influences that lead to the recruitment of the intellectual have already been discussed. It is no light thing to join the Communist Party. The membership price is very heavy. It is yourself. Everything you are and everything you hope to be is given utterly to the Communist Party. Some idea of the concept that the Communists have of their role and destiny is given by the speech of Joseph Stalin on the death of Lenin.

> Comrades, we Communists are people of a special mould. We are made of a special stuff. We are those who form the army of the great proletarian strategist, the army of Comrade Lenin. There is nothing higher than the title of member of the Party whose founder and leader was Comrade Lenin. It is not given to everyone to be a member of such a party. It is not given to everyone to withstand the stresses and storms that accompany membership in such a party. It is the sons of the working class; the sons of want and struggle, the sons of incredible privation and heroic effort who before all should be members of such a party. That is why the Party of the Leninists, the Party of the Communists, is also called the Party of the working class.

The Molding of a Communist

Departing from us, Comrade Lenin adjured us to hold high and guard the purity of the great title of member of the Party. We vow to you, Comrade Lenin, that we will fulfill your behest with credit.[1]

In his book, *How to Be a Good Communist*, Liu Shao-chi, [former] President of Communist China, outlines the qualities demanded of a Communist.

Whether or not a Communist Party member can absolutely and unconditionally subordinate his personal interests to the Party's interests under all circumstances are the criterion with which to test his loyalty to the Party, to the revolution and to the Communist cause.

To sacrifice one's personal interests and even one's life without the slightest hesitation and even with a feeling of happiness, for the cause of the Party, for class and national liberation and for the emancipation of mankind is the highest manifestation of Communist ethics. This is a Party member's highest manifestation of principle. This is the manifestation of the purity of proletarian ideology of a Party member.[2]

The demand is for absolute and unconditional subordination of personal interests to the Party's interests under all circumstances. The Communist must not only be prepared to die for Communism, but he must feel happy while he is dying. Lenin defined Communists as "dead men on furlough." The Communist dies to self, and gives the Community Party his life.

ORGANIZATION

The principle of Communist Party organization is known as "democratic centralism." The Party, at the base, is made up of local units, each containing a small number of people. This unit may be called a cell, a club, or any innocuous name. It may be a neighborhood group, a factory group, a school group, or a nationality group. Each local group elects a representative to a district council, which coordinates the actions of the local units. This election of representatives is the democratic aspect of the organization. However, the local unit may not instruct its representative how to vote at the district council. Once elected, he is responsible to the district council, not his local group.

When the district council meets, each issue is openly debated with arguments for and against, until the vote is finally taken. When the vote is taken, a change comes over the situation. Once the vote is taken, the decision is unanimously binding on every member of the committee. Back they go to their local units to carry the verdict to them. They may not go back and say, "This is how the committee voted, but personally I was against it." They must present the verdict enthusiastically and with conviction. The decision of the district council is binding on every member of the local group. No decision can ever be appealed below. Under special circumstances, it can be appealed to a higher committee.

In a similar fashion, the district committees elect representatives to a higher committee. The decisions of that higher committee, once made, are unanimously binding on every member, and binding everywhere below it, with a possibility of appeal above. Finally, the Central Committee of the Party is reached. From the Central Committee there is elected the executive of the Central Committee, known as the Presidium, formerly called the Politburo. With this committee the ultimate is reached. Since decisions made at each committee level are unanimously binding everywhere below it, decisions made by the top committee, the Presidium of the Central Committee, are absolute and final. There is no possibility of appeal. Their decisions carry the character of absolute truth.

The members of this Presidium are tried, proven Communists. They have worked their way up by hard, dedicated service. They are long established in the principles of Communist discipline and obedience and they observe unfalteringly the principle that the majority vote is final and absolute. Before the vote is taken, they may oppose a proposal vehemently, but once the vote is taken they must believe, with their whole heart, that the majority decision is right. No vestige of conscientious objection remains. As a united body they report to the Central Committee. The Central Committee hears the report, is instructed in the reasons for it, and unanimously approves it. From the Central Committee, the delegates go down to the next committee level where the same process is repeated. The report is given, unanimously approved, and processes to work it out are established. In this way, a decision reached at the top committee level becomes binding on every member throughout the entire organization.

Periodically, we see evidence of what appears to be fundamental division within the Communist Party. Leading Communists are suddenly hurled from their seats of power. They plunge into the abyss of shame, disgrace, and frequently, death. When we hear of quarreling in the top ranks of Communism, we smile happily and wait for the split to come and for Communism to disintegrate. But our hopes are always doomed to disappointment because we do not understand that quarreling at the top level of Communism, leading to the disgrace of high-level Communists, is not an evidence of division, but a proof of unity. It is not a manifestation of weakness; it is a sign of strength.

Historically, this is quite easy to prove. In 1924, Lenin died. He left the destiny of world Communism in the hands of a Politburo of seven men. All were Communist world figures, each of them utterly dedicated to the Communist cause. All of them had given a lifetime of service to Communism, had forsaken home, family, and fortune, and had undergone hardship and suffered imprisonment and privation for the sake of Communism. When Lenin died, they turned on one another in an orgy of mutual destruction. When the final record was written, Stalin had emerged victorious and the other six died violent deaths. According to our customary interpretation, the Communist Party should have been rent asunder and have shivered into fragments. In actual fact, the very reverse took place. It acquired a monolithic unity and strength and went ahead to conquer well nigh half the world.

This seems incomprehensible because the principle of democratic centralism has not been understood. According to this principle, the decision of the Presidium is absolute. If that committee votes that one member is a traitor, he must believe that he is a traitor, he must confess that he is a traitor, and he must welcome his own execution. For his mind is the mind of the Party, and his life belongs to the Party. The willingness of the top Communist leadership to act in this way is an evidence of unity and strength, not of division and weakness. It reveals their total dedication and devotion to the party.

When Lenin died, the great name in Communism was Leon Trotsky. The name Trotsky was linked with that of Lenin throughout the chancelleries of the world as the author of the Communist revolution. Most people expected Trotsky to assume power. Trotsky was a great orator, a military genius, a brilliant philosopher, historian, and author.

But Trotsky had joined the Bolsheviks only in 1917. He was more or less a "Johnnie come lately." In 1903, he had been called "the dagger of Lenin," and was Lenin's spokesman. In 1905, when revolution broke out in Russia, Trotsky was the chairman of the Petrograd Soviet. When the revolution failed, he was arrested and brought to trial. He made a great oratorical defense of the right of revolution, but was convicted and sentenced to a lifetime Siberian exile. Czarist treatment of political prisoners was benign and compassionate compared with the treatment meted out by the Communists. He escaped shortly after he arrived in Siberia, and went into European exile.

The Molding of a Communist

Between 1905 and 1917 Lenin and Trotsky quarrelled constantly about points of doctrine. Lenin led the Bolsheviks; Martov led the Mensheviks; and Trotsky led an intermediate group trying to conciliate the Bolsheviks and the Mensheviks. Trotsky called Lenin the exploiter of the worst elements of the proletariat. Lenin called Trotsky a compromiser without principle.

Lenin returned to Russia in April 1917 and formed the Communist Party from the Bolshevik segment of the Russian Social Democratic Labor Party. Trotsky arrived in May from Nova Scotia, Canada, where he had been interned. He was met at the railway station by cheering throngs and made a speech in line with the policies of Lenin. In July, 1917, he joined the Bolsheviks. When the July revolution was a failure, Trotsky was arrested and Lenin went into hiding. However, influences were brought to bear for Trotsky's release. He was re-elected chairman of the Petrograd Soviet and chairman of the Military Revolutionary Committee. As such, he was official military head of the Communist revolution. Following the success of the revolution, he was Foreign Minister and creator and Commander-in-Chief of the Red Army. He was leader of the Red Army while it defeated the armies of intervention. He was a member of the Politburo until 1924.

Trotsky had a great name and a great popular following. He was a hero to the Red Army. But the fact that he had a great name was unimportant. The fact that he was Commander-in-Chief of the Red Army and its idol was also unimportant. The only important thing was the vote he could get in the Politburo of the Communist Party after Lenin's death. Trotsky received practically no votes at all, for Zinoviev, Kamenev, and Stalin formed a triumvirate to keep him out of power. The death of Lenin was followed by an interregnum of collective leadership. Trotsky was expelled from the Politburo, dismissed as Commander-in-Chief of the

[63]

Red Army, and exiled from Russia. He could have taken the Red Army and turned it against the Communist Party, but he refused to do so. The Communists have a name for the act of using military power for political purposes. They call it "Bonapartism." Trotsky scorned Bonapartism. He said, "History has given one instrument only for the fulfillment of its purpose. That instrument is the Communist Party." When he was escorted to the Turkish border, he made them push him across. He wanted it on record that he had not left Russia of his own volition.

He settled eventually in Mexico City where he organized and wrote. He formed the Fourth International. His name, meanwhile, had become the synonym of evil and hatred within the Communist empire. The word "Trotskyite" was the vilest curse word their tongues could find. Finally, a young man who wormed his way into the Trotsky organization awaited his opportunity to assassinate him. When that moment came, he took a short-handled ax, the kind used for mountain climbing, and crashed it through the skull and into the brain of Leon Trotsky.

Trotsky had the greatest reputation in Russia on the death of Lenin. But Trotsky was voted out by the Politburo, and his fame availed him nothing. According to the principle of democratic centralism, the decision of the Politburo is final and absolute.

The men who caused Trotsky's overthrow in the Politburo were Zinoviev, Kamenev, and Stalin. Zinoviev and Kamenev had been Lenin's lifelong collaborators and coworkers. They were brilliant writers with famous names. Zinoviev was in charge of the Leningrad Soviet organization and head of the Communist International. Kamenev was President of Soviet Russia. Stalin did not have the brilliance or the oratory and writing skill of the other two, but he was Secretary of the Politburo and the Party. As secretary, he was the man who appointed all the provincial officials. He was the bureaucrat par excellence. Suddenly, to their amazement, Zinoviev and Kamenev found themselves isolated in the Politburo. They were expelled from the Politburo and from the Communist Party. They humbled themselves, confessed their sins, and pleaded for readmission to the Party as ordinary members. Their request was granted. Thus, began the mad, recurring cycle of confession, expulsion, and readmission, until finally, in the great Stalinist purges of 1936, they stood up and said, "We are unfit to live. We have betrayed the working class. Please take us out and shoot us." Stalin hastened to grant their last request.

The rise of Stalin to complete power was unnoticed until accomplished. It was widely anticipated that the mantle of Lenin's power would finally rest on the capable shoulders of Nikolai Bukharin. Bukharin was a brilliant Communist theorist, author of *The ABC of Communism*, head of the Communist International after the decline of Zinoviev—a man of the caliber of Lenin himself. When the vote was taken, however, Stalin was victorious by a majority of four to three. Once the vote was taken, it was binding on all seven members of the Politburo. Unanimously they went down to report the verdict to the Central Committee, and finally, the vote at the top became the belief and the marching orders of the entire Communist Party. There is no way whereby quarreling among the leadership can transfer itself to Party membership.

Stalin was then in complete power. He appointed those whom he approved. As secretary of the Politburo, he was in charge of calling meetings and determined the agenda of those meetings. From 1929 until his death in 1953, his power remained absolute.

The rise of Stalin to personal and absolute dictatorship was not due to the qualities of his personality, but due to the nature of the Communist Party structure. An accepted Communist principle is that every member is subject to

Party discipline. This is a euphemism for the reality that every member is under constant, personal, intimate supervision. The organized instrument to administer Party discipline was called the Orgburo. Associated with it was the internal Party police. Individuals rose to great heights of administrative power within the Communist Party, yet the secret police supervised their lives in minute detail. Their telephone calls were monitored. Their individual interviews were recorded. Their papers, both personal and public, were at the disposal of the secret police who possessed a key to the safe of every official. The only Communist official to whom this did not apply was the number one man, Joseph Stalin. To him, the secret police reported, and from him, they took their orders.

Thus, every member of the Politburo, powerful as he was, was isolated from all other members. There was no possibility of the prior consultation necessary if united and planned action was to be taken at a Politburo meeting. If two members should meet and Stalin should become suspicious, they could quickly be arrested and thus prevented from reaching the next meeting. In this way, each meeting of the Politburo was under the complete domination of Stalin. All other members in attendance were isolated from each other, and Stalin himself gave them the information on which their decisions were to be made. In this manner his power became limitless.

His achievements are unbelievable. Khrushchev recounts them in detail in his speech attacking the cult of personality and outlining the "mistakes" of Stalin, but he does not clearly indicate how Stalin did it. He tells us, for example, that Stalin put to death the military leaders of Russia who were the idols of the armed forces. He tells us that Stalin caused to be arrested and shot for treason 70 percent of the Central Committee that elected him to power in 1934—98 members out of 137. He tells us of entire nationalities that Stalin destroyed. He relates how, during the war, Stalin sat in an office with a globe in front of him and gave specific orders to the military commanders in the field. In one operation alone, because of Stalin's ignorance and his refusal to heed the plea of the commanders in the field, hundreds of thousands went to their deaths.

Khrushchev tells us what Stalin did, but he does not explain what gave him the power to do it. How does a man put to death the majority of the military commanders? How does he put to death the majority of the leaders of his own political party?

Khrushchev gives an indication when he says. "Different members of the Politburo reacted in different ways at different times." To understand this statement, we must understand the situation that existed. The Politburo was made up of seven men, each of them all-powerful within his administrative department, but each of them under constant, hourly surveillance. The internal Communist secret police checked everyone they met, listened in on every phone conversation, had a key to every safe, read every document, and reported everything they did to Stalin. Two of them might desire to confer on some question to come before the Politburo. They could not do it. If Stalin heard of their meeting, he would have them arrested before the next session of the Politburo was called. Thus, each of them came to a Politburo meeting completely unaware of the attitude of other members. Not one of them had any idea how the others were going to vote. If a man voted against Stalin and the motion was defeated, his life was ultimately forfeited. This was the end result of the all-or-nothing law of Communism. Only when this situation is clearly visualized can we understand why the other members of the Politburo were powerless to halt the cataract of Stalinist criminality. Only in the light of understanding Communist organization does Khrushchev's plaintive plea—"Different members of the Politburo reacted in different ways at different times"—become significant.

Stalin occupied a position of limitless power from which he operated as a tyrant unequalled in the annals of history. But it was Communism, not Stalin, that was responsible for his tremendous power. It was the organizational structure of Communism that projected him to his all-powerful position.

Communist organization remains the same. It has not changed. The events following the death of Stalin recapitulate minutely the events following the death of Lenin. Multitudes of people stand up and say, "Ah, but there is a difference! Stalin used to execute those he expelled, but Khrushchev does not." Such people have no knowledge of history. Lenin died in 1924. Stalin came to total power in 1929. The expellees from the Politburo were not executed until 1936. In the meantime, they were frequently given jobs appropriate to their abilities in distant areas. The same thing has happened since Stalin died. Immediately after the death of Stalin, there was a period of collective leadership followed by the emergence of Bulganin and Khrushchev. Bulganin was eventually overthrown and appointed to some minor position. Today [1960], at the top is the all-powerful Khrushchev, projected by the Communist Party to leadership of the Communist movement throughout the world.

Those who prate on the importance of public opinion within Russia, and proclaim the power of the Red Army, are ignorant of the political facts of life in Communist countries. All power resides in the Communist Party. Some time ago a name frequently in public discussion was that of Zhukov, Commander-in-Chief of the Red Army, friend of President Eisenhower. Our pundits advised that President Eisenhower and Zhukov meet and negotiate. They pointed out that the Red Army was a very powerful organization and claimed that Zhukov as its Commander-in-Chief was the real power in Russia. Let Zhukov and President Eisenhower get together and they could iron out the problems of the world.

The Molding of a Communist

In truth, Zhukov's position as Commander-in-Chief of the Red Army gave him no more power than if he had been the head of the Boy Scouts. All power is in the Communist Party. The Communist Party is a unified, disciplined party. The man at the top has all authority. From its membership, one disciplined man is taken and made Commander-in-Chief of the Red Army. In his administrative position, within the army, he is very powerful. But as a Communist, he is totally subject to the orders that come down from the top of the Communist Party. Similarly, other men are selected to fill all significant governmental, educational, cultural, and religious positions, but each of them owes complete obedience to the head of the Party.

The difference between the State and the Party is rarely understood. The head of the Russian State may be an insignificant individual. When Stalin was all-powerful within Russia, while he was putting to death the majority of the officers of the Red Army, the majority of leading Communists, and the majority of industrial managers, he was merely Secretary of the Communist Party. When it was necessary for him to meet with President Roosevelt in the capacity of chief of the Soviet State, he appointed himself to that position. When he thought it advisable, he appointed himself Commander-in-Chief of the Red Army. But his power never depended on his being President of Russia, or Commander-in-Chief of the Red Army. His power was derived from his position as head of the Communist Party.

For the Communist, the Party becomes the very voice and breath of God. The statement by Nikolai Bukharin before his execution is most revealing. He said,

> Comrades, I feel it is my duty to make the following statement. You all know that for three months I would say nothing. Suddenly I changed and confessed to everything of which the Comrade Prosecutor accused me. Why the change? I think you are entitled to know. As the moment of death approaches and one goes out into the

great loneliness, the thought of going out alone, unforgiven, apart from the Party in which I have lived and which to me has been life itself, was a prospect I could not face; and, if by some miracle I should not die, life outside the Party would to me be worse than death itself." There is something frightening about a movement that can evoke such devotion in one it is about to destroy.

The curse of Communism is that by the Party it creates, it takes the idealism of its young recruits and uses it as an ultimate instrument of dictatorship, tyranny, and genocide. Their intelligence is prostituted, their idealism debauched, and they are molded into intellectual robots of unquestioning obedience and frightening efficiency at the disposal of the dictator of the Party.

FURTHER STUDY

Pipes, Richard. *Communism: A History*. New York: Modern
    Library, 2001.

CHAPTER FOUR

The Communist at Work
Communist Fronts
and Captive Organizations

by
Fred C. Schwarz

The Communists have never aimed at the conversion of great masses of people to Communism. Their whole concept is that of a small party, compact, mobile, disciplined and dedicated, consisting largely of an intellectual elite. It is the task of this small group to utilize scientifically the social forces that move and direct the masses of the people so that the Communist Party may come to power over them, and impose forcibly, the Communist program. The program of Communism, then, is to recruit into the service of the Party great numbers of individuals, most of whom are unconscious that they are serving the Communist purpose.

Frequently it is asked, "How do you tell a Communist?" It is not always easy. If a Communist does not wish to reveal his Communist membership, it may be difficult indeed to establish the fact that he is a Communist. One test that may give valuable information could be called the "word test." There are certain words in rather common usage that mean one thing to people in general, and something entirely different to the Communists. If such a word is introduced into conversation, a person's position may be indicated by his interpretation of that word.

One such word, for example, is "sectarian." To most people, this word is primarily associated with religion. To the Communist, however, it means quite another thing. The term "sectarian" would be applied to a Communist who publicly advocates Communism and thereby isolates himself, instead of joining an organization and working hard for its objectives so that he can finally use that organization for Communist purposes, thereby multiplying his own power many times.

Lenin clearly discusses sectarianism in his remarkable book, *Left-Wing Communism: An Infantile Disorder*. The book was written as a textbook to direct the Third International or Comintern that had been organized in 1919 to work for world revolution. It is directed primarily against a group of enthusiastic, young German Communists. The position they took was that they were Communists and proud of it. They wanted the whole world to know. They disguised neither their objectives nor their methods. With their goal clearly in view they marched towards it, spurning compromise and deceit. Whatever the difficulty or danger, they neither turned nor flinched. They would die for Communism, but they would not cooperate with their enemies or compromise their principles.

Lenin turned upon these young enthusiasts, whom he called Left-Wing Communists, the full power of his invective that both his friends and enemies acknowledge as considerable. Although he did not believe in God he said, "God Himself has ordained that the young should be stupid." He ridiculed their unwillingness to indulge in compromise and deceit. He stated that they had accepted the limitations imposed by the bourgeois enemy. Compromise and deceit were very powerful instruments in the Communist program. He pointed out that a speaker openly advocating Communism was isolating himself from the great majority and limiting himself to a handful of rabid followers. True Communist strategy was to discover an issue that was important to a large number of people, to focus upon it, and to rally to it a large popular group. The test of their Communist caliber was the skill they showed in directing the people thus rallied into the service of the ultimate Communist purpose.

In illustration of this principle, Lenin gave specific instructions to members of the Communist Party of England to join the British Labour Party if they could, and to work for Henderson, who was the Labour candidate for Prime Minister at that time. He said:

> At present the British Communists very often find it hard to approach the masses and even to get a hearing from them. If I come out as a Communist and call upon the workers to vote for Henderson against Lloyd George, they will certainly give me a hearing. And I will be able to explain in a popular manner not only why Soviets are better than parliament and why the dictatorship of the proletariat is better than the dictatorship of Churchill (disguised by the signboard of bourgeois "democracy"), but also that I want with my vote to support Henderson in the same way as the rope supports a hanged man.[1]

To be sectarian, then, is to operate in isolation instead of utilizing the great social forces that activate large groups of people. Sectarianism ranks high in the list of cardinal Communist sins.

The Communist formula for effective action is a simple one. It may be summed up thusly: Discover what people want, promise it to them, and go to work to get it for them that you may come to power over them. This is the Communist program of action in any situation.

In Marxist schools, the Communists study the groups that compose a given society. They study the emotions of each group, their longings and their grievances, and they devise a program to exploit these ambitions and resentments.

They believe that each group of people is so short sighted and so selfishly motivated that, provided you are working in the interests of their most pressing desires in the immediate environment, they will pay no attention to what you are promising and promoting at a distance.

The Communist is not at all disturbed by the fact that he may be working simultaneously for two groups with conflicting interests and objectives. This is not inconsistency; it is the application of science.

The Communists have one objective—to come to power. They will do whatever is necessary to achieve this goal. In the economic realm, for example, they have no consistent economic program from country to country. Communist economic policy is to find out what any group wants and promise it to them. Classical Marxist economics advocated the collective ownership of land, but the Communists came to power in Russia and China by the reverse policy of the distribution of land, by making everybody a little Capitalist. Communist policy is to do whatever is necessary to advance the Communist Party's drive to dictatorial power.

Speaking at a girl's school in Dallas, Texas, I outlined the Communist formula for advance: Find out what people want, promise it to them, and go to work to get it for them in order to come to power over them. One girl asked the very natural question; "If Communists promise people all sorts of things but do not fulfill their promises when they come to power, why are they not thrown out?" I replied, "If I get into this room by promising you girls that I have a lotion that will make each of you very beautiful, and if, as soon as I get in here, I pull out a machine gun and train it on you, why don't you throw me out?" Communism is, in essence, the fulfillment of the dearest ambitions of the populace, and retaining power by the efficient use of force.

The Communists go to the working man and promise him higher wages, shorter working hours, and better conditions.

The Communist at Work

They approach the employer with the glittering prospect of industrial peace, good trading relations, and higher profits. To the Negro they promise first-class citizenship. They will strive so that he may live where he wants to live, work where he wants to work, and marry whom he wants to marry. They promise the opponents of the Negro that they will keep the Negro where he belongs. To the Jew the vision they present is that they will end anti-Semitism for all time. To the Arab they vow that they will eliminate the Jews. They tell the Christian of glorious religious freedom and Christian revival under Communism. Their promise to the Hindu is to aid in the conversion of every Christian and Muslim to the Hindu religion. The Muslim is lured by the promise of assistance in promoting the cause of Islam.

Their program of deception is often successful for two reasons. In the first place, as far as people can observe in the local situation, the Communists are sincere and keep their promises. It is a characteristic of Communist conduct to work hard and sacrificially for the immediate needs of the group they are endeavoring to exploit.

A Communist attorney will frequently accept a case without any charge and will work tirelessly and effectively on behalf of his client in the courts of the land. To the individual and his friends, he appears a true angel of mercy. They know nothing of the deeper motives that lie behind his conduct.

An example of the effective and apparently sincere assistance Communism can render to oppressed minorities comes from Italy. A missionary representing an evangelistic Protestant denomination came into conflict with the local authorities and was prevented from conducting his Sunday evening services. He was approached by the Communist leader of that city who sympathized with him in his predicament and claimed that it was a violation of the Italian constitution that granted freedom of religion.

To prove his sincerity he invited the missionary to utilize the facilities of the Communist Party headquarters to conduct his evening service. Thus, the preacher stood on the platform provided by the Communist Party under the photograph of the benign and smiling Joseph Stalin and proclaimed the Christian gospel. It is easy to imagine how difficult it would be to convince such a man that Communism is incompatible with religious liberty. His own experience assures him that they are the great practical supporters of religious liberty. He is entirely oblivious to the fact that once Communism assumes power not only his liberty to preach but also his liberty to breathe would be in serious jeopardy.

In the second place, the local objective advanced by the Communists is frequently one which, taken in isolation, would merit support. They go to religious groups, for example, in the name of peace. They are ardent advocates of slum clearance and improved housing. Today they are the exponents of a puritanical morality in contrast to their position some time back.

In foreign countries, Christian missionaries teach the natives such Christian principles as "Thou shalt love thy neighbor as thyself," and "Love your enemies." The Communist then approaches the mission convert with a program that seems to do nothing but advance the immediate well being of his neighbor and therefore merits his support as a Christian. He teams up with the Communist for this one purpose and the first step is taken on the bitter pathway of deviation and doom that Communism has marked out for his unwary feet.

A knowledge of the true program of Communism and its strategy and tactics is the only protection good people of every sort have against the Communist snare.

The Communist at Work

FRONTS

In order to involve as many people as possible, the Communists organize large numbers of Fronts, each of them designed to exploit the self-interest of a given group. Some of these are local and temporary, simple in formation and outline, and designed to exploit some local situation to the full. Others are on a world-wide scale with vast, permanent apparatuses working year after year throughout the world. Whether large or small, the purpose of these Fronts is to recruit well-meaning people to unconsciously serve the Communist conspiracy.

The following experience illustrates rather well a simple Communist method of operation. After addressing a civic club one noon, I visited the Communist book store in Berkeley, California. It was called the Twentieth Century Bookstore and at that time was located outside the gate of the University of California. With me was a minister who was very well informed on the subject of Communist techniques.

One entire window of the store was given over to a display of booklets prepared by the Communists on behalf of a Negro called Wells. While serving a life sentence in San Quentin prison, Wells had thrown a cuspidor in the face of his guard and had smashed his face. Under California law, a prisoner serving a life sentence who uses violence against a guard is customarily condemned to death. The death sentence had been passed. Many people thought that the sentence was excessive.

The Communists saw in this situation a social force, an emotion common to a group of people that could be exploited for the Communist purpose. They set out to stir up agitation on behalf of Wells. After some months of agitation, they had prepared a book of some eighty or ninety pages showing what they had allegedly done on Wells' behalf. The book did not help Wells very much, but it presented the Communist Party in a very benign and humane light.

The minister who was with me took the book and started to browse through it. He had glanced through the Legal Committee for Justice for Wells, and was reading through the Religious Committee for Justice for Wells when he was startled to find there the name of a friend of his, the minister in whose church I was to speak that evening. He said, "Take this book out to him, tell him where you found it, and see what he has to say."

That evening we had a fine meeting. The minister was intelligent and patriotic. He was a fervent evangelical Christian and apparently an informed anti-Communist. Visiting after the meeting I produced the book, told him where I had found it, opened it, and showed him his name. His face fell. He said, "Fancy their doing that!"

"How did you come to get mixed up in this?" I asked.

"I didn't sign that his sentence be changed," he replied, "but only that it be reviewed."

"No, you didn't," I said, and I read him the letter to which his signature was attached. "How did you become involved in it?"

He said, "A man said to me that here we had an example of cruelty and barbarity, and that as the Christian ministry was the servant of the forgiving and loving Christ, and that surely it was their duty to protest against the cruel, barbarous treatment of this man. If they did not protest, who would? He gave me the names of other ministers who were associated with this protest, and I thought it would not do any harm if I let my name go in too."

"What was the man's name?" I asked.

"He didn't tell me his name," was the reply.

"What did he look like?"

"I didn't see him."

"How did he get in touch with you?"

"He called me on the phone."

The Communist at Work

"Do you mean to tell me," I asked, "that a man called you on the phone, and without knowing who he was or what he represented, you allowed your name to go into an organization of this nature? Do you know what will happen? The Attorney General's Department, the House Un-American Activities Committee, or some official investigative agency will classify this movement as a Communist Front. Somebody will then observe your name, and you will be classified as a supporter of Communist Fronts. What is more, the truth is that you are supporting a Communist Front. You did not do so willingly, but you have been outsmarted. They have exploited your basic Christian compassion for their purpose."

This is a regular Communist method of operating. Anybody not specifically informed about their methods could have been trapped in a similar fashion. It has happened to thousands. J.B. Matthews made the statement that seven thousand Protestant ministers in the United States have been involved in the Communist apparatus by allowing their names to be associated with some Communist Fronts.[2] His statement was met with indignant and angry protests and treated as an attack on the Protestant ministry. There were a few honest ministers such as Daniel Poling of New York who humbly and courageously acknowledged the truth. Daniel Poling said, "As one of the seven thousand, I think the figure is far too low."

The principles according to which a Communist Front is organized can best be understood in terms of a series of concentric circles. At the center is the Communist Party, a small group whose members are organized, disciplined, and dedicated, and which has a single mind, will, and purpose. This Party is composed of both open Communists such as William Z. Foster, National Chairman of the Communist Party USA and author of *Toward Soviet America*, and crypto or hidden Communists, people who deny their Communist association and affiliation, but who are nevertheless dedicated Communists. The Communist Party is never entirely above ground. Clear rules to this effect were laid down in the by-laws of the Comintern where it is stated that in countries where a Communist Party is allowed legal existence, the legal party must be associated with an illegal party, and that the legal party must be under the control of the illegal party. The controlling segment of the Party is always underground.

Surrounding this small party at the center there is the zone of "fellow travelers." A fellow traveler is one who approves of Communist philosophy, Communist objectives, Communist organization and tactics, but who, for some personal reason, has not submitted himself to total Party discipline. He has never been able to reach the point of complete personal surrender necessary for actual Party membership. Fellow travelers frequently have guilty consciences because they are not Party members. They are subject in large measure to Party discipline, and they will willingly and sacrificially work with the Communists, but they can go into any court in the land, and swear under oath that they are not Communists because they are not members of the Party. Some of the prominent and powerful Americans who have served Communism most faithfully have been fellow travelers. There is no evidence, for example, that Harry Dexter White, who betrayed American governmental secrets to the enemy and provided aid to the Communists in every possible way,[3] was a Communist. He was a fellow traveler.

Surrounding the zone of fellow travelers is the zone of "sympathizers." This zone contains different groups who are sympathetic to the Communist Party—various brands of Socialists, collaborators, and pacifists. Sympathizers are against certain features of Communism. They claim to be against the brutality of the Communists, as well as against their use of censorship and their denial of individual liberty. Nevertheless they believe that, on the whole, Communism

The Communist at Work

has achieved many good things. While they cannot approve of Communism altogether, they feel that there are many good features about it, and that it is progressive and in the interests of the working class, and that it is possible to associate with the Communists in a local worthy objective. They feel that if they work with the Communists, are tolerant of them, and love them a little, they will win them from their extreme practices and that the evil features of Communism will wither away, leaving only that which is worthwhile. In the group there are a number of religious men who are particularly prone to argue in this way.

Surrounding the zone of sympathizers is the zone of "pseudo-liberals." Most of these liberals are to be found in the ivory cloisters of colleges and universities, frequently occupying professorial chairs, and usually characterized by a pseudo-intellectual outlook. They take this attitude: "I am against Communism; I am against the Communist restraint of human liberty; I am against their censorship; I am against their dictatorship; I am against their brutality. Nevertheless, I refuse to become like my enemies in order to oppose them, and while I hate what the Communists say and do, I will fight for the rights of the Communists to speak and organize even as I will fight for my own rights." Thus, in effect, they become the protectors and the runners of interference for the Communist conspirators. They uphold the right of Communists to be professors in schools and universities.[4] They are the great defenders of the Fifth Amendment. They contend that no restraint or restriction of any kind should be applied to an individual because he has availed himself of the Fifth Amendment. Apparently their viewpoint is that nobody should suffer any social restraints or disadvantages unless there is evidence that is valid in a court of law.

Their argument is fallacious because they project certain conditions, that prevail in the realm of law into the realm of privilege and social activity where they do not apply. For example, a man seeking employment approaches the president of a bank. The president, however, has heard a rumor that he was dismissed from his last employment because he had embezzled funds and asks the man if this is true. The man refuses to answer on the grounds that he might incriminate himself. The man is quite within his rights in refusing to incriminate himself and certainly cannot be sent to prison because of his reply, but if the bank president were to employ that man, he would be foolish indeed. The Fifth Amendment refers merely to imprisonment and legal penalty. Any attempt to project it beyond that realm is not intellectualism or liberalism, but stupidity.

The following little fantasy which I have called "The Liberal's Dilemma" outlines the position reached when it is claimed that no restraints can be placed on anyone in any situation unless there is evidence that is valid in a court of law and that the Fifth Amendment carries no implication of guilt.

THE LIBERAL'S DILEMMA

Motherhood is gathered in its beauty and its purity, desperately concerned because of the increase in juvenile delinquency due to the prevalence of organized vice in the district. Juvenile delinquency is becoming so widespread that the very foundation of the family itself is in danger. The mothers are determined that something must be done to eliminate organized vice.

It is decided to form a Committee of Maternal Purity. The meeting is called, and a woman of great liberal outlook is installed as temporary chairman. She calls for nominations from the floor for the position of permanent chairman of the committee. To everybody's astonishment, the name of Madame Vice, the Madame of the local brothel, is nominated for the position. The chairman looks startled, then says, "I hear the name of Madame Vice nominated for the position of chairman of our Committee of Maternal Purity. Does anyone wish to speak on this motion?"

An indignant voice cries out, "But that's ridiculous! She's the cause of most of the trouble! She's a prostitute and a keeper of a house of prostitution."

"These are serious charges," the chairman says. "They must be supported by unimpeachable evidence. Anybody who can rise and say that they have first hand evidence that this woman has indulged in these alleged practices, please rise and speak."

Nobody moves.

The chairman says, "Since there is apparently no evidence to support these charges, I'll ask the woman herself. Madame, are you, as alleged, a prostitute and a keeper of a house of prostitution?"

The fur clad figure indignantly rises, "I ain't going to answer that question! You have no right to ask it! I ain't going to incriminate myself."

"Yes," says the chairman, "that is your privilege. Certainly no inference can be taken from that reply. There is no evidence to support these charges. From the woman's own words we can get no indication of their truth or falsehood. I have but one last recourse. Has this woman been indicted and convicted in a court of law?"

Silence again prevails, and the voice of liberal learning, rich and mellow, is heard. "I accept the nomination of Madame Vice as the Chairman of the Committee of Maternal Purity of this city."

By the same process, it is easy to conceive the election of Al Capone as Chairman of the Committee for Public Security. Such ridiculous situations become possible when a provision of the Constitution designed solely to grant immunity from legal punishment is projected into the realm of normal life that involves privilege and responsibility far removed from legal punishment. This is the error that is made by the pseudo-liberals who fail to see the basic malignancy of Communism and thus become a zone of protection behind which the Communist conspirators pursue their evil schemes.

Surrounding the zone of pseudo-liberals is the zone of "dupes." In this zone are to be found the genuinely patriotic American citizens from a great variety of walks of life. They have simply been deceived. Many solid citizens are astonished when they discover the trap into which they have fallen.

Consider the hypothetical case of a successful businessman whose name appears on the letterhead of a Communist Front. He is whole-heartedly against Communism but is also exceedingly busy. He wishes to help good causes and will support them financially and with the use of his name. However, it must be remembered that he has many pressing demands upon his time and he cannot attend meetings or participate in the day-to-day activities of the organization. That task he must leave to others. In this manner, the Communists have successfully utilized the money and the prestige of many of their most fervent opponents.

THE BIRTH OF A FRONT

The essential purpose of the Communist Front must be camouflaged with an alleged purpose of wide popular appeal. The Communists are very well aware of what the true objective is, while most of the Front members see only the camouflage. A permanent Communist objective is to shift the balance of world military power in favor of Communist military strength. Wherever they can weaken the military strength of any free country, they help to achieve this purpose. One basic objective, then, is to weaken militarily all those countries opposed to Communism. Obviously if that real objective were proclaimed, it would not recruit many people in those countries. An organization that had the announced purpose of weakening America militarily so that Communist conquest would be easier, would rally few supporters. Therefore, there must be an announced objective which will accomplish the same purpose, but which will present itself in a totally different guise. One announced purpose could be the preservation of peace in the face of the possible horrors of a thermonuclear war. This is the basis of the array of unholy peace movements spawned by Communism.

Communist personnel are allotted to set up the organization of the Front. They enlist a few fellow travelers and together they decide the precise nature of the organization to be formed. The purposes are clearly designated, the basic executive officers are selected, mostly from the ranks of Communists or fellow travelers, and the slogans, which are to recruit the people, are formulated. When these preparations have been made, the fellow traveler approaches the sympathizer. The Communist himself does not customarily approach the sympathizer, for the sympathizer has certain qualms about Communists. He knows that they cannot always be trusted. But the fellow traveler is able to assure him that he is not a Communist, and thus can make the approach with every hope of success.

He outlines to the sympathizer the objective, namely the preservation of peace in the face of the desperate threat of war and annihilation that hangs over us all. He describes the demands for disarmament which are to be made to Communist and non-Communist countries alike. He does not point out, of course, that these demands cannot possibly have any effect in Communist countries because there is no public opinion there that they can influence and that the people of the Communist countries cannot even find out about these demands unless the Communist Party decides to tell them. He does not indicate that the real purpose is to influence public opinion in free countries where the government is elected and controlled by the people. The sympathizer, satisfied when these demands are nominally extended to all countries, is sold on this magnificent idea and is enlisted in the cause.

The sympathizer then approaches the pseudo-liberal who thinks it a wonderful idea. He would not be happy to participate in a Communist plan, but he knows the sympathizer is not a Communist. He is aware, maybe, that the sympathizer has some radical ideas, but he, unlike most other people, is open-minded and does not hold that against him. Obviously the idea is an excellent one and merits his support. Thus, the pseudo-liberal becomes the spokesman who approaches the dupe, the patriotic businessman who will supply the finances and the respectability. Then at the periphery, the patriotic businessman is approached by an anti-Communist liberal for a worthy objective. The money is provided, names are written on the letterhead, a public relations department is established, the propaganda is proclaimed, and the organized Communist Front goes into operation. Superficially, it appears to be the work of patriotic businessmen, educators, scientists, and others of repute, but behind these dupes are the pseudo-liberals; behind them are the sympathizers; and behind the sympathizers, at the very center, are the unseen Communists and fellow travelers who are in control of policy and program.

Fronts such as this have been formed a thousand times and in a thousand ways. They have recruited many well-meaning anti-Communists into the service of Communism. Thus, is Communist science applied whereby the organized few multiply their effectiveness by organizing a mass movement that, on specific issues, can sometimes make and break democratic, anti-Communist governments. Again, the conclusion is clear that an understanding mind and an alert attitude are the only protection the individual has against involuntary involvement. Eternal vigilance is the price of liberty.

The Communist at Work

CAPTIVE ORGANIZATIONS

Communist Fronts have been organized to exploit labor, religion, art, civil liberties, culture, and nationalism. The Fronts that proclaim Peace and National Liberation have been particularly effective. In addition to these specially organized Fronts, the Communists make use of organizations that have been in existence for long periods. Frequently, these organizations were formed by non-Communists for non-Communist purposes, but nonetheless they become captives of Communism. This is made possible by the Communists' willingness to work hard at unpleasant tasks in the interests of such organizations. In every organization, there is a certain amount of routine work to be done, work that is not spectacular or interesting, and therefore not very appealing to most people. When the Communists join the organization, they work hard. They are available for dull and menial tasks. They write the letters, they wrap the packages, they prepare the mimeographed materials. Very often they are the finest workers the organization has. When election time comes around, nothing is more natural than elected them to executive office. Thus, the Communists, by reason of their clarity of purpose, their drive towards an objective, and their hard, dedicated work, take over institutions that have been created with the money of Capitalist enterprise and use them to destroy liberty.

The Communists are magnificently organized. They have dedicated personnel and they have acquired vast experience. Only on a basis of understanding, organization, and dedication can we hope to meet and defeat them. To hate them is futile. Some of their most effective servants have been their bitterest enemies. Eyes that see and minds that think must merge with hearts that love freedom, to meet this challenge.

FURTHER STUDY

Chambers, Whittaker. *Witness*. New York: Random House, 1952.

de Toledano, Ralph de and Victor Lasky. *Seeds of Treason: The True Story of the Hiss-Chambers Tragedy*. 4th ed. New York: Funk and Wagnalls, 1950.

Kimball, Linda. "The Materialist Faith of Communism, Socialism, and Liberalism." *American Thinker* (January 27, 2010), http://www.americanthinker.com/2008/02/the_materialist_faith_of_commu.html.

Kimball, Roger. *Tenured Radicals: How Politics Has Corrupted Our Higher Education*. New York: Harper and Row, 1990.

Klein, Aaron and Brenda J. Elliott. *The Manchurian President: Barack Obama's Ties to Communists, Socialists and Other Anti-American Extremists*. Washington DC, WND Books, 2010.

Kubek, Anthony. *How the Far East Was Lost: American Policy and the Creation of Communist China, 1941–1949*. Washington, DC: Regnery Publishing, 1963.

Penkovsky, Oleg. *The Penkovsky Papers*. New York: Collins, 1965.

Philbrick, Herbert A. *I Led Three Lives: Citizen, Communist, and Counterspy*. New York: Grosset & Dunlap, 1952.

Romerstein, Herbert and Eric Breindel. *The Venona Secrets: Exposing Soviet Espionage and America's Traitors*. Washington, DC: Regnery Publishing, 2000.

You Can Still Trust the Communists

CHAPTER FIVE

Techniques for Seizing Power
Philosophy of Violence

by
Fred C. Schwarz

The Communists have worked out both theoretical and practical techniques for the achievement of their goal of world conquest. One of their fundamental theoretical texts is Lenin's book *The State and Revolution*, which has now become the world's most translated book.

Lenin was in the process of writing this book when he left Switzerland to return to Russia in 1917 to organize the Communist seizure of power. The revolution that overthrew the Russian Czar in February 1917 was not a Communist revolution, but a spontaneous mass rising supported by many different groups of people. When this genuine revolution took place, most of the important Communist personalities were in exile either in Siberia or in countries outside Russia. Once the revolution was accomplished, a political amnesty was declared. Thereupon, Bolsheviks and revolutionaries who had been scattered throughout the world converged on Petrograd.

Stalin returned from exile in Siberia to assume editorship of the Communist Party newspaper, *Pravda*. Trotsky returned from Nova Scotia. Lenin returned from Geneva where his pen had been pouring forth a floodtide of literature urging civil war in Russia. Upon his arrival in Petrograd, he informed the revolutionary workers that he had returned to conquer and govern Russia. His claim caused considerable astonishment, particularly in the ranks of the orthodox Marxists. It must be remembered that the Bolsheviks of whom Lenin was leader were but a small party numbering some twenty thousand members. Lenin's Marxist critics, when they heard his claim, said, "Farewell, Lenin the Marxist; welcome, Lenin the anarchist!"

Nonetheless, Lenin achieved the impossible. Within six months, with a small band of faithful followers, he had stolen the legitimate fruits of the revolution, betrayed the working people of Russia, and established the greatest tyranny and dictatorship the world has ever known. *The State and Revolution* which he was writing at that time is still considered a fundamental theoretical textbook. In it Lenin sets forth how the Communists are to come to power within the State and what they must do once they are in power.

Lenin here concentrates upon the necessity of violence. He considers government the instrument by which the ruling class controls and exploits the subject class. All government is class government, and the institutions of a State, such as the legislature, the executive, the judiciary, the police power, the tax power, and the educational institutions, are the instruments of the ruling class for the exploitation of the subject class. According to Lenin's thesis, the governments of Europe and America were bourgeois governments which existed to exploit the people. These governments could be overthrown only through violence and bloodshed.

To Lenin, the use of force and violence was not to be merely a reaction to force and violence used by the Capitalists. To him, force was an instrument of positive purpose and he was totally devoid of any apologetic attitude towards its use. He states categorically that violence is essential to their purpose: "The supersession of the bourgeois state by the pro-letarian state is impossible without a violent revolution."[1]

In saying this, Lenin went further than his mentor, Karl Marx. Marx had allowed the possibility of bloodless revolutions in England and America. Marx claimed that since the bureaucracy was not developed to the same extent in these countries as in other European countries, and since the police and military power of these states were not so great, there existed the possibility of a peaceful transition to Socialism. Lenin said that these conditions no longer applied. In Europe, in England, and in America, the revolution to bring about the transition from the bourgeois State to the proletarian must be violent. There could be no possibility of successful nonviolent revolution.

One of the specific crimes for which Lenin mercilessly chastised Karl Kautsky, the leading Marxist theorist of the Second International, was his continued clinging to the possibility of a peaceful transition to Socialism in England and America as had been admitted by Marx. In his tirade, *The Proletarian Revolution and the Renegade Kautsky*, Lenin writes:

> Further, was there in the seventies anything which made England and America exceptional in regard to what we are now discussing? It will be obvious to anyone at all familiar with the requirements of science in regard to the problems of history that this question must be put. To fail to put it is tantamount to falsifying science, to engaging in sophistry. And, the question having been put, there can be no doubt as to the reply: the revolutionary dictatorship of the proletariat is violence against the bourgeoisie; and the necessity of such violence is particularly created, as Marx and Engels have repeatedly explained in detail [especially in "The Civil War in France" and in the preface to it], by the existence of a military clique and a bureaucracy. But it is precisely these institutions that were non-existent precisely in England and in America and precisely in the 1870's, when Marx made his observations [they do exist in England and in America now]![2]

The Communist attitude on violence is frequently misunderstood. Even the opponents of Communism think that the Communists do not necessarily want violence, that they use violence only because the exploiting class resists their assumption of power. This was never the viewpoint of the Communist leaders, particularly Lenin and Engels. Kautsky, who was reputed to have learned the entire works of Marx by heart, was viciously attacked by Lenin for his lukewarm attitude toward violence. Kautsky's attitude was that they might have to use violence, but that if they had to do so it would be regrettable, for violence was bad and corrupted those who used it. In reply Lenin quoted from Engels' book, *Anti-Dühring*:

> That force, however, plays also another role [other than that of a diabolical power] in history a revolutionary role; that, in the words of Marx, it is the midwife of every old society which is pregnant with a new one, that it is the instrument with the aid of which social movement forces its way through and shatters the dead, fossilized political forms—of this there is not a word in Herr Duhring. It is only with sighs and groans that he admits the possibility that force will perhaps be necessary for the overthrow of the economic system of exploitation—unfortunately, because all uses of force, forsooth, demoralizes the person who uses it. And this in spite of the immense moral and spiritual impetus which has been given by every victorious revolution! And this in Germany, where a violent collision—which indeed may be forced on the people—would at least have the advantage of wiping out the servility which has permeated the national consciousness as a result of the humiliation of the Thirty Years' War. And this parson's mode of thought—lifeless, insipid and impotent—claims the right to impose itself on the most revolutionary party that history has known.[3]

Lenin was an enthusiastic advocate of violence. His revolution was not a peaceful transition. It is possible to sense the delight with which he proclaimed Engels' teaching on this subject:

Techniques for Seizing Power

> Have these gentlemen [the anti-authoritarians] ever seen a revolution? A revolution is certainly the most authoritarian thing there is; it is the act whereby one part of the population imposes its will upon the other part by means of rifles, bayonets and cannon—authoritarian means, if such there be at all; and if the victorious party does not want to have fought in vain, it must maintain this rule by means of the terror which its arms inspire in the reactionaries. Would the Paris Commune have lasted a single day if it had not made use of this authority of the armed people against the bourgeois? Should we not, on the contrary, reproach it for not having used it freely enough?[4]

The second feature of the revolution described by Lenin in *The State and Revolution* was its purpose. The purpose of the revolution was not to seize control of the State, but to destroy it. Most of the book is given over to the thesis that the State must be destroyed. The State functions in many ways. It functions through the constitution; it functions through the executive authority—the President, the Cabinet, the Justice Department, the Police Department, the Defense Department; it functions through the legislature, through the judiciary, and through the civil service. The goal of Communism was not to secure a president exercising constitutional power. It was not to appoint the cabinet officers such as the Secretary of State or Defense. The appointment of the judges was not their avowed objective. The purpose was to utterly destroy the constitution, the legislative system, the judicial system, and the administrative system, to wipe out the State and build a new one in a totally different form.

Lenin's argument is based on Marx's analysis of what had happened to the French Commune in 1871 when the Communards tried to take over the Capitalist State and use it as an instrument of government. The Commune was soon overthrown. Lenin said that when a State is allowed to continue, it inevitably carries within itself the seeds of counter revolution. Its members have their vested interests in the old society. The State must be destroyed. This was expressed by William Z. Foster, Chairman of the Communist Party of America, in his statement:

> No Communist, no matter how many votes he should secure in a national election, could, even if he would, become President of the present government. When a Communist heads a government in the United States—and that day will come just as surely as the sun rises—that government will not be a capitalistic government but a Soviet government, and behind this government will stand the Red Army to enforce the Dictatorship of the Proletariat.

SEIZURE OF POWER

The assumption of power, then, is by violent revolution leading to the destruction of the State and the establishment of the dictatorship of the proletariat. The Communists worked out theoretical processes by which this seizure of power was to be realized. History now records the practical methods by which they have seized power in a number of countries, specifically Russia, China, and the misnamed People's Democracies of Eastern Europe.

The assumption of power may be by various methods of which three will be discussed. They are:

1. Internal revolt through control of the labor unions
2. Military conquest
3. Piecemeal surrender to military blackmail

REVOLT THROUGH LABOR UNION CONTROL

This traditional method which the Communists have advocated for many years has not as yet succeeded in the establishment of an effective Communist power in any country. Originally, they saw the labor unions as the instrument through which the Communist Party was to come to power. The program was as follows: The Communists were to infiltrate the labor unions and secure executive power within them. They were then to call an industrial strike. This industrial strike would become a political strike, then a general strike, and finally a revolutionary strike, leading to armed insurrection and the conquest of power.

The first necessity was to infiltrate the labor unions. Lenin specifically states this in his book, *Left-Wing Communism: an Infantile Disorder*. How they got into the labor unions did not matter. They were to work their way in, lie their way in, or buy their way in. The all important thing was that they get in.

> We must be able to withstand all this, [i.e. insults and persecution], to agree to all and every sacrifice, and even—if need be—to resort to various stratagems, artifices, illegal methods, to evasions and subterfuges, only so as to get into the trade unions, to remain in them, and to carry on Communist work within them at all costs.[5]

INDUSTRIAL STRIKE

Once in power, at the appropriate moment, they were to call an industrial strike. An industrial strike is defined as one directed at the achievement of an industrial goal such as higher wages or shorter working hours. Generally speaking, such a strike can always be called. There are always grievances and desires for improved conditions that any intelligent Communist leader can exploit. Moreover, an industrial strike is, generally speaking, the only type of strike that can be organized and maintained with the support of the workers. The industrial strike must then be transferred into a political strike.

POLITICAL STRIKE

A political strike is not designed to secure immediate, tangible, industrial benefits for the workers, but to destroy the Capitalist system. A political strike is designed to undermine the foundations of authority by creating chaos, unemployment, bitterness, hunger, and fear. Usually, a political strike, as such, cannot be called, but an industrial strike can be transformed into a political one. As the political strike extends and grows into a general strike, many situations will arise where the striking workers come into conflict with organized authority, usually with the police, but sometimes with the military forces.

REVOLUTIONARY STRIKE

As acts of violence come to be associated with it, the political strike transforms itself into a revolutionary strike. When the revolutionary strike has developed sufficiently and drawn into its orbit enough working people, a general insurrection can take place. Thus, if the insurrection is successful, the Communists, through their control of the labor unions, will be able to establish their dictatorship of the proletariat.

This method, their traditional method for the seizure of power, has not yet brought them success in any country. But it has been a most important adjunct to their seizure of power, and rehearsals of the process have taken place in many countries.

The last great strike wave organized by the Communists for this purpose was in 1949. During that year there were world-wide, coordinated, organized strikes. There was a dock workers' strike in England when the British authorities expelled from Britain as an international Communist agent Louis Goldblatt, secretary-treasurer of the International Longshore Workers and Warehousemen's Union. The islands of Hawaii approached economic strangulation during the dockworkers' strike that year. In Australia, there was a coal-miners' strike. These strikes were coordinated on a world-wide scale.

The coal-miners' strike in Australia is of special interest as it was a rehearsal of the Communist program for the assumption of total power. In Australia, the Communist

Techniques for Seizing Power

Party is an open political party and nominates candidates for political office in federal, state, and municipal government. These nominations are made in the name of the Communist Party. But the Communists in Australia have always been a small, politically insignificant minority, and their candidates invariably fail miserably. There is a system in Australia whereby a candidate, when he nominates for an elective office, must pay a deposit which is refunded if he secures a certain percentage of the votes of the leading candidate. This is designed to prevent frivolous candidates with no prospect of victory from swamping the candidate list. It is a great day for the Communist Party if one of their candidates saves his deposit. The Communists in Australia do not get elected to political office.

However, their industrial power is very strong indeed. By following Lenin's technique, this handful of Communists has come to power in a vast segment of Australia's labor unions. They are very hard workers, they are good organizers, and they are dedicated. Because of their organizing ability and dedication, they are frequently elected to executive union office.

When I was a resident medical officer in the General Hospital in Brisbane, Australia, the largest hospital in the Southern Hemisphere, the labor situation was most interesting. The official union of the non-medical workers at the Brisbane General Hospital was the Australian Workers' Union which, in its leadership, was fervently anti-Communist. The representative of the workers at the hospital was a man called King who was a fanatical Communist. King was elected by the workers as their representative in the hospital not because he was a Communist, but because he was prepared to work for them assiduously and courageously. Every day when they received their pay checks, King stood at the office and waited. If one of them had a grievance, he went to King, who immediately went to the management. There he yelled and shouted if necessary in order to have the supposed wrong righted. Those workers knew that if they had a grievance, King would be on their side, right or wrong, and that they could depend on him. Therefore, they made him their representative. The union itself was fanatically anti-Communist in its leadership and in its official publication. But local Communists such as King were able by sheer hard work to exercise considerable influence and authority. The workers served by such men saw only the dedication, not the ultimate purpose.

By this method, the Communists were able to come to power in a large number of Australian unions. These unions included the Seamen's Union of Australia, of which the secretary was a fervent, self-proclaimed Communist; the Waterside Workers' Federation, of which the secretary, Jim Healy, was a prominent Communist; and the Coal Miners' Federation, which was under effective Communist control. In 1949, the steelworkers' union of Australia, known as the Federated Ironworkers' Union, was directed by Communist officials, though these have since been expelled. Thus, the Communists were in considerable power in a very significant section of organized labor in Australia.

In the winter of 1949, a strike was called in the coal mining industry. Coal is the life blood of Australia. The country has no natural petroleum and no natural gas. Coal is the source of gas, electricity, and basically, the source of transportation. It is the economic life blood of the country. This was particularly true in 1949. There had been a severe coal shortage since the end of the war. There were no coal stocks anywhere in Australia. Coal that was mined one day was transported for use the following day. The coal that is used to provide gas for heating and cooking in Sydney comes from Newcastle, one hundred miles to the north. If a storm was raging and a coal ship was held up, it was quite common for gas rationing to be imposed until the coal arrived. Public utilities generally operated under the constant threat of coal starvation.

In this situation, a coal strike was called. It was called in defiance of the established lawful processes for settling disputes, while the dispute was still before the arbitration authorities. It was called as an industrial strike demanding increased wages and fringe benefits.

When the strike began, chaos became the order of the day. There was immediate rationing of gas and electricity. Industries that depended upon electricity had to close down. Hundreds of thousands of men were thrown out of work. It was illegal to burn more than one electric light bulb in a home at any one time. Gas was allowed for an hour in the morning, and an hour in the evening for cooking purposes only. It was mid-winter. Gas fires and electric radiators, which provide the only heat in most Australian homes, were prohibited without a medical prescription. There were a number of tragedies. Old age pensioners, living in rooms by themselves and feeling desperately cold, would illegally light their gas fires and go to sleep. As they slept, the gas would be turned off at the main. Later the gas would be turned on again and flood their rooms with deadly fumes while they slept on. Many did not awaken.

The government in power at that time was the Australian Labour Party, an avowed, self-proclaimed Socialist Party. They declared that this was a revolutionary assault upon the authority and economy of the country and introduced drastic legislation. They sent the armed forces into the strip coal mines to mine coal for the people. They froze labor union funds retrospectively. The Waterside Workers' Federation, the Miners' Federation, and the Steel Workers' Union under Communist leadership had withdrawn large sums of money from the bank to use as strike pay. The executive officers of these unions were taken before the courts and ordered to produce these sums of money which they had withdrawn before the law freezing their funds was introduced. When they refused, they were sentenced to imprisonment for contempt of court.

Chaos developed. Everywhere there was strife and bitterness. The unemployed and the cold were ripe for Communist agitation. The Communist agitators placed the whole blame on the Capitalist system, urging its overthrow.

There was a rehearsal for the armed insurrection. When Jim Healy, the secretary of the Waterside Workers' Federation, was sent to prison for refusal to obey the court's order to produce the money which had been withdrawn from the bank, the Communists agitated on the waterfront. They gathered the longshoremen together and told them that this was an assault on them. This man was their representative. They had elected him. It was their duty to stand by him. If they let this go without protest, soon more serious measures would be taken against them such as reductions in wages. The men were stirred up, and thousands strong, they marched through the streets. It did not break out into open violence, but all the potentials were there. If the moment had been considered ripe, an incident could have been started, leading to fighting. In this way a political strike becomes a revolutionary strike, and a revolutionary strike becomes armed insurrection.

The most revealing aspect of the whole situation was the helplessness of the workers and the power of the leaders in the crisis hours. Every labor union in Australia lined up, not in terms of the patriotism of its membership, but in terms of the Communist affiliation of its leaders. The membership of the unions was helpless while the leadership was all-powerful. This was very well illustrated by the different behavior of the railway men in the states of Victoria and New South Wales. Victoria and New South Wales, the two most populous Australian states, are contiguous to each other. There is no possible way by which you could differentiate the

Victorian workers from those in New South Wales. They are similar in every respect. Nevertheless, the Victorian railway men were part of the Communist revolutionary front. They sided with the strikers and refused to move the coal mined by the army, declaring it hot. The railway men of New South Wales, on the other hand, handled the coal, transported it, and delivered it to public utilities, thus playing a large part in the maintenance of essential services. The railway men of New South Wales effectively thwarted the Communist objective of a transport strike to advance the revolution.

There was one all-important difference between the railway men of the two states. In Victoria, the secretary of the railway men was Jack Brown, a Communist, while the secretary in New South Wales was Jack Ferguson, an anti-Communist. That was the sole difference, but in the crisis hour, these men had legal authority to make decisions which were binding on thousands of other men. The executives had the power to make the decisions unless a mass meeting was called to overthrow them. This was well nigh impossible since mass meetings may require up to fourteen days' notice. Multitudes may starve in fourteen days.

Frequently the argument is made that, provided that workers are patriotic, a few extreme union leaders do not matter very much. History has proven this to be nonsense. The International Longshore and Warehouse Workers' Union of the West Coast of the United States was expelled from the CIO because it was a consistent instrument of the international Communist conspiracy. The Longshore workers of California are no less patriotic than the Longshore workers of the East Coast, but on the West Coast they are controlled by a handful of Communist officials.

That the ILWU is slavishly devoted to Communist purposes is revealed in the published report of the Subcommittee to Investigate the Administration of the Internal Security Act and Other Internal Security Laws to the Committee on the

Judiciary, United States Senate. This report reveals that during the collective or popular front period of the Communist Party, the ILWU supported Roosevelt's anti-aggression program. With the signing of the Stalin-Hitler pact, however, the ILWU suddenly discovered that the war in Europe was of no concern to it. It attacked President Roosevelt and his policy of giving aid to the allies. Following the opening of hostilities between Germany and Russia in June 1941, the ILWU leadership reversed its policy and declared that the war in Europe was, after all, of vital concern to the labor movement. In the summer of 1944, Bridges and the ILWU executive board urged that the no strike pledge be extended into peacetime. With the end of the war in Europe and the collapse of the wartime collaboration between the Soviet Union and the Democratic Nations, the position of the ILWU, like that of the Communist Party, underwent another change, and the no strike pledge was forgotten.

When the Truman Plan for Greece and Turkey was announced in the spring of 1947, it was bitterly attacked in the newspaper of the ILWU, *The Dispatcher*. In a front page editorial, it was compared with the international gangsterism of Hitler. When the Marshall Plan was enunciated, it too was condemned by the ILWU The ILWU has demanded that the United States cease testing and producing the atomic bomb without calling for international inspection of the Soviet's production of atomic weapons. The ILWU has opposed the North Atlantic Alliance. In June 1949, *The Dispatcher* hailed the liberation of China, comparing it with the American and French Revolutions. Thus, thousands of men follow in minute detail every twist in the Communist Party line, because they are helpless in the hands of a few Communist leaders who control and direct their assets and utilize them for the Communist purpose.

A sample of this Communist process for the seizure of power has occurred here in America. It took place in San

Techniques for Seizing Power

Francisco in 1934. Sam Darcy, former district organizer of the Communist Party of California, outlined the Party's plan of operation in his article on the San Francisco Bay area general strike in *The Communist* for October 1934. The substance of the article was later presented in a report by Darcy to the seventh congress of the Communist International meeting in Moscow in August 1935. The report reads as follows:

> Let me state here that there would have been no maritime or general strike except for the work of our party. The very fact that it was a sympathy strike gives it its political character. The fight began in the decisive sector of San Francisco's economy, namely, the maritime industry. It is apparent from the stated facts that the strike had a definite political character. "About a week previous (to June 18), in anticipation of the possible needs for a general strike, we had succeeded in convincing the Painters Local 1158 to sign a circular letter addressed to all other locals of the A.F. of L., declaring their own support for a general strike, and asking their vote for it, so that, should a general strike become necessary, it would be possible to call it at the critical moment without any harmful delay.
>
> The very next day the Machinists Local 68, the oldest and very influential A.F. of L. local in San Francisco voted to join the general strike movement.
>
> Of course, the general strike movement was in no sense a spontaneous movement. It took long and careful preparations. At first the militants [i.e., the Communists] sent small committees, chiefly from the longshoremen's local, to other A.F. of L. locals, appealing for support by a vote for a general strike. First we tackled only those locals that we knew were most militant. As we began to tackle the larger locals and those in the key industries which would be critical for the outcome of the general strike, we sent, not small delegations, but delegations ranging from fifty to as much as four hundred. The general strike movement was actually advancing very rapidly, by the votes which were daily taking place in the local unions stimulated largely by the delegations of militants.
>
> Yet the workers in the Longshoremen's local, an A.F. of L. affiliate and a craft union, were able under the pressure of circumstances, quickly to break down their own routine work inside their own local, and reach out to other locals as far removed from longshore work as bakers and cleaners and dyers, and help organize them for the

general strike. Our strategy was to use the Joint Maritime Strike Committee as a base.

On July 5 the National Guard took control of the waterfront. On that day finally the Joint Maritime Strike Committee issued a leaflet openly calling for the general strike.

Getting the Teamsters to join the strike was at this time the main force needed to make certain the eventuality of the general strike. This was due to the prestige and strategic post which the Teamsters had. On the night of the 11th the Teamsters met. This was, in a sense, a point which was decisive for the general strike. The Teamsters demanded to hear Bridges, who was given a tremendous ovation, and they finally voted to go out the next morning.

By the next morning, July 12, 60 local unions had voted for the general strike and about 10 locals were already out.

Saturday and Sunday were used by the militants for two activities, first, to pull the remaining locals out and, secondly, to mobilize for organizational contact. We had to develop a movement within all the local unions, for special membership meetings to elect the five to the General Strike Committee instead of appointing them. The militants also tried through agitation, such as a leaflet issued by the Longshoremen's local, a statement by Harry Bridges, an appeal by the party and the Western Worker, etc., to stimulate the workers to force the election of the delegations of five to the General Strike Committee in their locals. We tried to get an appeal from the San Francisco General Strike Committee to the Portland workers.

On Monday morning the general strike was effective beyond all expectations. Nothing moved in or out of the city. For practical utility there are six ways of entrance to the city. These are: (1) Bay Shore Highway; (2) US 101 road; (3) Skyline Boulevard; (4) the ferries; (5) by sea; (6) the railroads. Every one of these ways, excepting the ferries and railroads, was patrolled by our picketing squads of workers. Nothing moved without permission of the strike committee. Within the city, transportation was tied up; production stood at a standstill. It was obvious that the military forces were helpless against such a strike movement.

In a widely popularized radio address by Governor Merriam that very day, he said: "By its very nature the general strike challenges the authority and ability of the Government to maintain itself."[6]

A similar situation is potentially possible again. The formation of all transport unions into one association such as that being considered at present under the leadership of Hoffa and Bridges carries potentials of great danger. A mass transport strike could so paralyze this country that starvation and death would be rampant in every part. The danger is not limited to America. An international transportation tie up could be fearful in its outreach through all the world.

The mechanism outlined by the Communists is still in operation. It is not completely out of date. Though it has not as yet fully succeeded in taking over a country, any person of intelligence has great reason for concern when workers can be compelled to join organizations, contribute their money, and obey the leadership imposed by a small group. When that money can be used for political purposes by a constant propaganda campaign by press, radio and television so that the public may be influenced to elect legislators under obligation to the union leadership, the very foundation of republican, democratic government, is in danger. When government becomes irreversible, dictatorship is at the door.

FURTHER STUDY

Conquest, Robert. *The Great Terror: A Reassessment.* 40th
    Anniversary ed. Oxford: Oxford University press, 2007.

————. *The Harvest of Sorrows: Soviet Collectivization
    and the Terror-Famine.* Oxford: Oxford University
    Press, 1987.

Courtois, Stephane, ed. *The Black Book of Communism:
    Crimes, Terror, Repression.* Cambridge, MA: Harvard
    University, 1999.

Pidhainy, S.O. *Black Deeds of the Kremlin: A White Book.*
    2 vols. New York: Ukrainian Victims of Communist
    Terror Press, 1953.

Pipes, Richard. *Communism: A History.* New York: The
    Modern Library, 2001.

————. *The Russian Revolution.* New York: Vintage, 1991.

Rummel, R.J. *Death by Government.* New Brunswick, NJ:
    Transaction Publishers, 1994.

CHAPTER SIX

Successful Techniques for Seizing Power

by
Fred C. Schwarz

The Communist attempt to seize power through labor union control has not yet achieved complete victory for the Communists in any country. In those countries where they have established their rule, the means employed have been quite different. The methods by which they achieved power in Russia, China, and Czechoslovakia merit special study. In each case they seized power utilizing deception, established themselves by violence, and maintained their dictatorship by totally enslaving helpless people.

Russia

Revolution broke out in Russia in February 1917. The Czar was overthrown, and a republican order was established. The declaration of a political amnesty brought into the open the various Russian revolutionary parties. These parties were numerous, and the degree of their revolutionary fervor and devotion to violence varied considerably.

The most moderate of these parties was the Constitutional Democratic Party known as the Cadets. They favored the establishment of a Parliamentary Republic and change via the ballot box.

A second was the historic Russian revolutionary party, the Social Revolutionaries, whose program was agrarian reform rather than industrial development. The Social Revolutionaries were also called the populists because of their slogan, "to the people." Desiring to improve the lot of the peasants, young Russian intellectuals went out to the people with their revolutionary message. They advocated land ownership by the peasants themselves. They were not a Marxist Party but did not believe that Russia should follow the pathway of Capitalist development. As their name indicates, they favored radical action and were addicted to violence. Lenin attacked them frequently during his career.

The anarchists were another significant group. They were addicted to violence, assassination, and sabotage; they had a long revolutionary tradition and a total contempt for governmental authority of every form.

The Marxists were divided primarily into the Bolsheviks and the Mensheviks, the former being under the leadership of Lenin. As has been related, the Bolsheviks became the Communists.

Finally, there were various independent revolutionary groups, as well as individuals who owed allegiance to no party but were devotees of violent revolutionary action.

These various parties set to work, organized, and published their newspapers. They participated in common organizations known as the soviets. The soviets were born in the 1905 Russian revolution when the historic technique of the mass strike had been tried and failed. The soviets were committees formed in strategic areas to direct the strike and the revolution. There were soviets of workers, soldiers, and peasants' deputies. Their delegates were elected from the proletariat working in the factories, from the peasantry, and from the ranks of the common soldiers and sailors. They began as completely unofficial bodies.

The soviets were reformed in the days of the Russian Republic after the overthrow of the Czar. The Mensheviks and the Social Revolutionaries were well represented in these soviets. The latter were divided into two groups, Left and Right. The Bolsheviks were in a small minority in the first half of 1917. The slogan at this time was, "All power to the soviets." But Lenin, filled with a desire to seize complete power in Russia and aware that the soviets were far from being under Bolshevik control, was only half-hearted in his support of this slogan.

Meanwhile, Russia was staggering under the blows of the 1914–1918 war. Enormous losses had been suffered on their western front. The soldiers, short of necessary weapons, were in a mutinous mood, while at home, the people were consumed by a desire for peace and for land. Lenin, the dynamic Marxist who seized every opportunity to advance his cause, developed a program that promised peace and land. Everywhere he agitated for the end of the war. He urged the peasants to throw down their arms, return to their homes, and seize the fields of their landlords, which he said, were rightfully theirs. The slogan "Peace and land" was very popular.

In adopting such a program, Lenin had contravened all the accepted standards of Marxist doctrine. Classical Marxist doctrine had been that private ownership of land was to be replaced by collective ownership. Lenin utterly reversed this policy by promising land to everybody. The other Marxist parties indignantly accused him of stealing the program of the Social Revolutionaries. This is exactly what he had done, brazenly and shamelessly. Lenin was a dynamic Marxist, a believer in the dialectic, which allowed him complete freedom of action and policy. If his goal of power could be achieved by doing the exact opposite of what he had long advocated, then that is what he should do. The basic doctrine of Marxism-Leninism is, "Come to power." The Marxist-Leninist will promise whatever is necessary in order to achieve that end. Lenin, therefore, promised peace and land. But the gift of land was merely the bait that covered the barbed hook of Communist dictatorship.

It is interesting to notice in passing how Communist policy with regard to the ownership of land varied in the years that followed. In 1917, Lenin gave the land to the peasants, but confiscated the crops when they were harvested. The disgruntled farmers lost their enthusiasm and the harvest diminished. The grain shortage became serious and a desperate famine arose. In 1921, after four years of power, the Communists were on the verge of being overthrown. To avert this, Lenin made a dramatic reversal in policy. He reestablished Capitalism. He introduced the New Economic Policy which allowed private trading in grain. Many of the Communists regarded this as a confession of utter defeat, and some ideological extremists committed suicide on the streets. But Lenin, regarding the situation in the light of the dialectic, saw it as a temporary withdrawal for future advance.

During the period of the New Economic Policy, the farm produce of Russia increased, and the food situation improved greatly. Meanwhile, the Communists were establishing their power in the cities. By 1928, Stalin, who had succeeded Lenin, felt that they were strong enough to put their real program into operation. He therefore reversed the New Economic Policy and declared war on the peasants. The most prosperous of the peasants, who were known as "kulaks," were arrested, herded together, and deported to Siberia. The slogan was, "Liquidation of the kulaks as a class." The kulaks were not landlords. The landlords had been annihilated in 1917–1918. The kulaks were peasants who had farmed efficiently and employed labor on their farms.

The kulak's land was made the basis of the collective farms to which the middle and poor peasants were urged to contribute their land and livestock. These peasants, however, resisted attempts to make them join the collectives, preferring to work their own land. When they were forced to join, many of them slaughtered their animals and a great famine arose in the land.

In 1931, Stalin decided to teach the peasants a final lesson. He took all the wheat from the Ukraine and dumped it down in Western Europe, leaving the Ukrainians to starve. During that fearful winter of 1931, it is reported seven million starved to death. Speaking at a meeting in California, I was informed by a young woman who had been a school child in Kiev in the Ukraine at that time that the game they had played on the way to school was counting the dead bodies in the streets. In this manner, Stalin fulfilled Lenin's policy of giving the land to the peasants long enough to consolidate Communist power as a prelude to taking it from them to establish collective ownership, which had remained the real objective even while land was being distributed.

However, in mid-1917, all this was in the womb of the future. The war against Germany dragged on, and the situation in Russia became worse. The Bolsheviks gained in popularity through their "peace and land" program, and they increased their representation in the soviets by means of their magnificent organization. In July 1917, they organized a revolt, but it was ill-timed and unsuccessful. Lenin was forced into hiding. In October of that year, however, the Bolsheviks secured a small majority in the Petrograd Soviet. Lenin decided that the hour of revolution had come, for they could now speak, not only in the name of the Communist Party, but also in the name of the soviet, which represented the entire working class. The revolution was opposed by some of Lenin's co-workers, particularly Zinoviev and Kamenev, but Lenin's desires dominated, and the revolution was called by the soviet. The Bolshevik-led revolutionaries marched on the Czar's winter palace and arrested the provisional government, which was in power until the election of a constituent assembly and which included many Mensheviks and Social Revolutionaries in its ranks.

The Bolsheviks did not have wide popular support. The only group in the soviet to stand by them at that time was the left-wing of the Social Revolutionary Party. Bolshevism thus came to power with a tiny minority of the people, but they established their reign of terror, and Lenin became the ruthless lord and master of Russia.

In all rural areas, peasants' committees were formed. These were composed largely of poor peasants and criminal elements. Some were motivated by idealism, while others were motivated by hatred. These aggressive peasant bodies became a key tool of Lenin's reign of terror. He encouraged them to seize the land, kill the landlords, and divide the estates among themselves. Frequently the letters ended thusly: "Anyone who opposes this is to be shot without mercy."

Resistance to the Communist regime developed in every area of life. The first group to revolt openly were the anarchists, who were shot down mercilessly in the streets. Following the anarchists, the Left-Wing Social Revolutionaries revolted and met a similar fate.

Confronted with such problems at home, the new regime was faced with the necessity of ending the war against Germany. When the Commander-in-Chief refused to obey the Communist order to lay down arms, Lenin and Stalin telephoned his dismissal and appointed a private as general of the army to conclude the surrender.

Lenin realized that to remain in power he needed a fearful instrument of terror. The Czar had always had a secret police force called the Okrana. The Communists took it over, renamed it the Cheka, and refined and sharpened it into the most fearful instrument of terror the world has ever known. Seeking for a man to head up this organization, Lenin found a remarkable young Polish Bolshevik named Dzerinski. Born of wealthy, aristocratic parents, as a child Dzerinski had forsaken the comforts of his home to dedicate himself to the poor of the earth as a revolutionary organizer. His teenage years were largely spent in Polish prisons where his rule of conduct was that he, as the most enlightened and advanced, was duty bound to perform the most menial tasks. He therefore insisted on cleaning the latrines of the other prisoners as an example of enlightenment and dedication. What better man could Lenin have found to serve as a selfless instrument of murder and extermination? Motivated by his idealistic dedication, Dzerinski became the organizer of the red terror and the master murderer of modern times.

The story is told that one day as the Bolshevik leaders sat in conference, Lenin asked Dzerinski how many traitorous Social Revolutionaries they held in prison at that time. Dzerinski replied that there were about fifteen hundred, whereupon Lenin asked for the list so that he might see which were old friends and supporters. Having read the list, Lenin marked the corner of the sheet with a tiny cross. Dzerinski took the sheet, noted the cross, looked at Lenin, and quietly left the room. The following day he informed Lenin that the fifteen hundred had been executed. The cross that Lenin had made to show that he had read the paper had been interpreted as an order for the execution of fifteen hundred people. Lenin had merely intended to indicate that he had read the document. On the misinterpretation of a doodle of Lenin's pencil, fifteen hundred people went to their deaths.

Communist power in Russia was consolidated by limitless, pitiless violence. Lenin had said, "What does it matter if three quarters of the world perish providing the remaining quarter is Communist!" Any act of terror was justified if it assured continuing Communist control. Group by group, the opposing forces were liquidated until at last the impossible was achieved and the Communist Party held Russia in total enslavement. When the Communist monster had devoured all other revolutionary groups, it turned and destroyed most of its own creators.

CHINA

The Communist conquest of China is a classical manifestation of the five steps of Communist conquest:

1. The conquest of the student mind
2. The organization of the students into the Communist Party
3. The scientific exploitation of group self-interest to bring that party to popularity and power
4. Revolutionary conquest of power
5. Communist dictatorship and universal slavery

1. THE CONQUEST OF THE STUDENT MIND

The students in China were a very special class. The scholar was always an object of veneration to the Chinese, so the influence of the students was very considerable. The Communists were highly successful in recruiting students into the ranks of the Communist Party. Almost the entire leadership of the Chinese Communist Party had joined as students. The arguments used to recruit the student-intellectual have already been discussed.

2. ORGANIZATION OF STUDENTS INTO THE COMMUNIST PARTY

The Communist Party of China was formed on typical Leninist lines. The inner core came from the ranks of the intellectuals. The bulk of the general membership came from the peasants. The members derived from the working class were few indeed. This is a peculiar structure for a party claiming to be proletarian. The Party was formed with a single leader, Mao Tse-tung. With complete discipline, the entire Party membership absorbed the thought and obeyed the orders of Mao Tse-tung.

3. SCIENTIFIC EXPLOITATION OF GROUP SELF-INTEREST

The disciplined, fanatical Communist cadres worked feverishly among the masses of the people. Their objective was not to convert them to the theories of Communism, but to exploit their desires and grievances. Many of the Chinese people were landless, tenant farmers. A great burden of debt hung round their shoulders. Their burning desires were centered around the ownership of the land on which they labored and freedom from their burden of debt.

The Communist approach was therefore very simple. They promised the people the ownership of the land on which they worked and the abolition of all debt. In addition, China had known the oppression of foreign power, so the Communists exploited Chinese nationalism with a program to exclude the white man from Asia. With such a program so closely tuned to the deep-seated desires of the masses, it is easy to understand why the Communists achieved certain popularity. From the peasants attracted by the Communist promises, Mao Tse-tung gathered the youth, trained them with great efficiency, and built the Chinese Communist Army.

4. REVOLUTIONARY CONQUEST OF POWER

The conquest of China was successfully accomplished through the strategy of the brilliant Chinese Communist leader Mao Tse-tung. He developed two new techniques that were in large measure responsible for Communist success in the face of great odds. The first of these was the principle of political warfare in association with military conflict. The war was waged not only by the armed forces, but also by political agents who always preceded the Communist soldiers into any given area. Their task was to infiltrate and to undermine the will of the people to resist. They spread rumor and utilized blackmail and terror. They took advantage of civil liberty to destroy civil liberty. They combined assassination with sabotage so effectively that many communities were neutralized and fell easy prey to the Communist military advance. No advance was made by Communist troops until the way had been prepared by the Communist political agents.

The second technique developed by Mao Tse-tung was that of guerilla warfare. By means of this art, he was able to transform strategic inferiority into tactical superiority. Although his army was outnumbered for many years, he was able to manipulate his troops with such skill that he never engaged in pitched battle unless he outnumbered the enemy by three to one. He was able to achieve this because of the superior mobility of his troops and by the technique of guerilla warfare that he perfected. He would gather together a considerable number of his soldiers in a given area, launch a lightning offensive against the enemy at a point where they were gathered in smaller number, and disappear with his troops before the enemy could rally. His soldiers would hide their uniforms, adopt the character of the surrounding peasantry, and mingle with the people. By the time the superior forces of the enemy had gathered, the Communist army was nowhere to be found. By this dual offensive of political warfare and guerilla mobility, the Chinese Communist forces advanced to victory, conquering the vast land mass of China.

In addition to the internal forces operating within China, the international Communist machine worked ceaselessly on their behalf. Russia provided military instructors and weapons. Throughout the world the Chinese Communists were pictured as benign agrarian reformers and the Chiang Kai-shek government as the epitome of corruption. The American government endeavored to achieve the impossible—establish a permanent, peaceful coexistence between Communism and the Chinese government. This played right into Communist hands and after the defeat of Japan, Russia delivered the vast weapon hoard of the Japanese Manchurian Army to the Chinese Communists, and their successful southward march began.

5. COMMUNIST DICTATORSHIP AND UNIVERSAL SLAVERY

Once in power, the Communist Party systematically set about the process of securing a monopoly over the lives of all Chinese citizens so that the Party could remain permanently all-powerful while the people were reduced to the impotence of isolated slaves. Every vestige of alternative authority was smashed. The Communist Party secured a monopoly of all police power, all economic power, all military, and all educational power. It became the universal policeman, employer, administrator, judge, newsman, entertainer, and teacher. It imposed the "Dictatorship of the Proletariat."

CZECHOSLOVAKIA

The means adopted by the Communists for the conquest of Czechoslovakia differ somewhat from those used in Russia and China. Since it is closer to the method which they probably envisage for the conquest of America, it merits some attention. They came to power in Czechoslovakia by utilizing an internal Communist minority that operated in the blackmailing shadow of massive external Russian military power. Hanging like a threatening cloud over Czechoslovakia was the Red Army.

At the conclusion of the Second World War, Czechoslovakia was the most industrialized, the most prosperous, and the most democratic of the Eastern European states. Communism was an insignificant force. Three years later, Czechoslovakia was bound hand and foot as a Communist slave. This was brought to pass by a series of small concessions to Communism, each relatively insignificant in itself, each presented as an alternative to attack by the Red Army, and obviously to be preferred to such an attack. The cumulative effect, however, was the surrender of Czechoslovakia to Communism. This is the program for America. The concessions are to be obtained because they are preferable to an atomic war. Each in itself may appear indecisive, but each will be a step to surrender. Every time the Communists can persuade Americans the false alternative exists, that is, to make this concession as the only alternative to atomic or thermonuclear war, they win a great victory.

Within Czechoslovakia, government was administered by various departments of executive authority, each department being headed by a cabinet minister. Authority in each department of the government was thus largely centralized in the hands of one man. Police power, for example, was in the hands of the Minister of Internal Security. The same applied in education, communications, transportation, agriculture, justice, and defense.

The first step taken by the Communist minority was to establish themselves in a coalition government with democratic and socialist parties. They then proceeded to infiltrate Communists into the top positions in all branches of government. Once the top position in each department of government was filled by a Communist, non-Communists and anti-Communists within the organization were powerless to withstand his total authority and power. When, for example, the Communists took over the police force, they used the power to arrest and destroy all those who differed from them politically, including those to whom they had temporarily showed friendship. Thus, Communism took over the most democratic nation in Eastern Europe. It is to be noted that it was not done by the use of the Red Army, but simply by the threat of its use.

It is a program of this nature that the Communists probably envisage for America. When America is encircled economically, and militarily, when foreign markets are disrupted and foreign trade destroyed, when America is an island in a Communist sea, and lies under the shadow of military annihilation, the Communists believe that America will make concessions as did Czechoslovakia. Authority will be centralized and a few Communists will wield great power. At the chosen moment, the final Communist assault will take place and resistance will be token and half-hearted.

FURTHER STUDY

Chang, Jung and Jon Halliday. *Mao: The Unknown Story*. New York: Anchor Books, 2006.

Courtois, Stephane, ed. *The Black Book of Communism: Crimes, Terror, Repression*. Cambridge, MA: Harvard University Press, 1999.

Klein, Aaron and Brenda J. Elliott. *The Manchurian President: Barack Obama's Ties to Communists, Socialists and Other Anti-American Extremists*. Washington DC, WND Books, 2010.

Pipes, Richard. *Communism: A History*. New York: The Modern Library, 2001.

———. *The Russian Revolution*. New York: Vintage, 1991.

CHAPTER SEVEN

Consolidation of Power
The Dictatorship of the Proletariat

by
Fred C. Schwarz

Once the Communists have come to power, whether it is in Russia, China,[1] Czechoslovakia, or America,[2] the next step is to establish the dictatorship of the proletariat. Lenin defined this as "the rule—unrestricted by law and based on force—of the proletariat over the bourgeoisie, a rule enjoying the sympathy and support of the laboring and exploited masses."[3] This rule is theoretically exercised by the proletariat, or in other words, by the toiling masses of the people. But since the Communist Party considers itself the executive of the proletariat, this rule is exercised in practice by the Communist Party. The definition of the dictatorship of the proletariat is then, "the rule, based on force and unrestricted by law, of the Communist Party over everybody else."

Since this rule is based on force, the first act of Communist power is invariably to disarm the people as was done in China. Since this rule is based on force, and since force inevitably generates revolt, a second precaution taken by the Communists is to destroy the potential leadership of a counter revolution before such a revolution can occur. Any individual with qualities of leadership who is not subject to

Communist discipline is arrested and executed. Whether he is pro-Communist or anti-Communist is immaterial. If he has qualities of leadership that may be used when the people awaken and desire to end Communist rule, he is a danger and must be destroyed.

The dictatorship of the proletariat is accompanied by a monopoly of the means of communication. Every medium of mass communication is taken over. Every newspaper is a Communist newspaper. Every radio station, every television channel, every publishing house, every book, every magazine, every school class is completely controlled by the Communist Party.

Under the dictatorship of the proletariat, an economic monopoly is gradually established whereby the Communist Party becomes the sole employer. A man then has but one choice—he works for the Communist Party where he is told to work, or he starves to death. He may not leave his job and go to another, for there is only one employer—the Communist Party.

Yet another feature of the dictatorship of the proletariat is the establishment of a vast internal espionage network. This espionage system is patterned on the human body. The body is made up of billions of cells. The body preserves itself against the external forces that threaten it by a vast grouping of espionage agents. Certain cells become informers. Physiologically, they are called sensory receptors and are to be found in the skin, muscles, and various organs. These sensory receptors perceive heat, cold, pain, and contact with other objects. In other words, they collect information from their environment and send it to the brain. The brain assembles this information and sends orders down another nerve pathway to the executive authority, the muscles, whereupon muscular reaction is taken in relation to the information collected by those sensory nerve cells in the environment. The simple act of blinking, which closes the eyelids to protect the sensitive eye against an advancing foreign body, is a good example of such a mechanism.

The Communists see the State, not as a mass of individuals, but as an organic unity, a higher form of being. Just as the body has sensory receptors, throughout the State there are informers who collect information in their environment and send it back to the central nervous system—the secret police. Children are set to spy on their parents, wives on their husbands, employees on employers, pastors on their congregations, parishioners on their pastors. Every group, large or small, would have in its midst a number of informers. None of these informers would know who the others were. If one informed and the others did not, those failing to report would automatically be discovered. Thus, a stream of information from every segment of the community flows back to the central authority.

With such a system in existence, it is inevitable that a revolt with any organization whatsoever will be discovered at birth and strangled in infancy.

In the days of the Czar, a thousand men armed with sticks and stones were quite a formidable force. If revolution broke out somewhere in Siberia, it took three months for the news to reach Moscow and six months for troops to get there and quell the uprising. With modern means of communication, however, the news is back in seconds, and an air force detachment is there in minutes to deal with the trouble. The people are helpless against machine guns and bombs. The question is frequently asked, "Is it likely that the people of Russia will revolt?" Of course they will. They have already revolted a thousand times! But the revolts are spasmodic and unorganized, and they are wiped out almost casually. Ten miles away it is not even known that the revolt has taken place because of the power of the Communist dictatorship.

The steps by which the dictatorship of the proletariat was established in China show the situation very clearly. The

Communists came to power in China behind the seductive promises of land ownership and debt abolition. Immediately after seizing power, they kept these promises. The landlords were wiped out and their land was divided and given to the peasants whose debts were simultaneously cancelled. For a brief period, happiness flooded the land. The peasants set to work to till the land that was now theirs.

Meanwhile, the Communists consolidated their power in anticipation of the day when they could take the land away from the peasants. They knew that when they did this, resistance would develop, and that such resistance would require leadership. They surveyed the community to discover those with potentials of leadership. If these people were not subject to Communist discipline, they were arrested on some pretext or another and destroyed.

The Communists set about to disarm the people completely. Great rewards were given to those who could tell them where weapons were hidden, and the rush to deliver concealed weapons began. They introduced a system of universal espionage in which everyone spied on everyone else. This had special reference to the children who were encouraged to spy on and report their own parents.

They stopped freedom of movement and introduced internal passports. No one could travel from village to village without official permission. Upon arriving at the village, the visitor was not free to go and stay with friends, but had to stay at an inn set aside by the Communists and closely scrutinized. They stopped freedom of association. No group could gather except under official Communist sponsorship and control.

Every individual was compelled to write or give a life confession detailing all the crimes committed throughout his entire life and naming all other persons implicated in these crimes. This provided the Communist government with a vast hoard of information to be used against any individual as they desired.

A major assault was made on the child's mind. They were filled with pride. Their affections were turned from their parents towards the State. They were given guns and appointed sentries with orders to challenge, and if necessary, to shoot adults. The school children would be marched out and given the task of searching all shops in an area for weapons and currency, and of accosting and searching all adults in the area.

Finally, there came the day of the mass trials and executions. A band would march through the streets of the city. Behind the band a group of prisoners would march with hands bound behind their backs. Into the bonds of each prisoner a stick would be stuck with a placard on top telling the crimes of which he was allegedly guilty. Behind the prisoners the school children would march to observe the execution. Then came the general populace. Mothers were compelled to take their babies in arms to observe the hideous spectacle. Eye witness reports abound concerning these things. Multitudes of missionaries of impeccable character testify that these things really happened.

Harvest day arrived and the peasants who had been so thrilled to become owners of their land were now forbidden to thresh their own grain except in the presence of an armed soldier. When the harvest was reaped, the government took far more than the landlords had ever taken.

At this point, hatred of Communism was the dominant emotion amongst the people, but they were so leaderless, so weaponless, so immobilized, so disassociated, so spied upon, and so cowed that organized revolt appeared unattainable. The Communists had imposed their total tyranny.

The period of peasant land ownership was brief indeed. Soon came the period of collective farms and then the great communes, which have attacked the very fabric of the

Chinese nation, the Chinese family, and the character of the Chinese people. Today, no Chinese individual owns even one acre of ground. He has been betrayed to a new serfdom more terrible than that of the past, a serfdom in which he is the helpless slave of the gargantuan Communist State.

The dictatorship becomes ever more intense. The powers in the hands of the top few become greater and greater until finally there emerges the man of all power, the Joseph Stalin, who sits in the seat of the mighty while millions of slaves rush to and fro to do his bidding. Such is the reign of brutality, violence, and tyranny that inevitably comes behind the beautiful promise with which Communism deceives its way to power. Only knowledge can enable us to stand against the intermediate seductive phase of limitless deception practiced by those whom J. Edgar Hoover defined as Masters of Deceit.

FURTHER STUDY

Chang, Jung and Jon Halliday. *Mao: The Unknown Story*. New York: Anchor Books, 2006.

Conquest, Robert. *The Great Terror: A Reassessment*. 40th Anniversary ed. Oxford: Oxford University Press, 2007.

Courtois, Stephane, ed. *The Black Book of Communism: Crimes, Terror, Repression*. Cambridge, MA: Harvard University Press, 1999.

Klein, Aaron and Brenda J. Elliott. *The Manchurian President: Barack Obama's Ties to Communists, Socialists and Other Anti-American Extremists*. Washington DC, WND Books, 2010.

Rummel, R.J. *Death by Government*. New Brunswick, NJ: Transaction Publishers, 1994.

CHAPTER EIGHT

Allies of Communism

by
Fred C. Schwarz

The significance of Communism can never be measured by the number of Communists. Lenin's slogan was "fewer but better." It has been a long-established slogan that "the Party grows strong through purging itself." The theory of Communism is that of the chosen few who are organized, disciplined, dedicated, and equipped with superior intelligence and understanding of the laws of history. By this chosen few, the conquest of the world and the regeneration of mankind will be accomplished. The number of actual Communists has never been great.

Even acute observers, noting the numerical weakness of the Communists, have taken false hope from this fact. Such people fail to understand that the Communists are able to rally into their service multitudes who are completely unaware that they are serving the Communist cause. Our purpose here is to study those attitudes that transform well-meaning, patriotic, Christian people into the allies of Communism.[1]

INTELLECTUAL DISHONESTY

Outstanding among these attitudes is intellectual dishonesty. When the truth is too unpleasant, a natural tendency is to refuse to believe it. As a medical man, I have seen this often. A man of character and intelligence is afflicted with cancer. He knows the symptoms perfectly well, and if he saw them in another, he would never have a moment's doubt about the final outcome. When he observes these symptoms in himself, however, a strange thing happens. His characteristic honesty and clarity of judgment disappear. He ignores the central, symptomatic stream, and seizing on peripheral symptoms, builds them into a dream world in which to take refuge while doom advances.

The situation confronting us is dark and fearful. To face the true situation requires courage and honesty. The vast majority of people are quite unwilling to acknowledge the truth, preferring to ignore the evidence, or to select only those facts that will support their preconceived ideas and will not threaten the fulfillment of their desires.

Some time ago I met a man I had long admired. As a journalist sympathetic to the Soviet government, he had been sent to Russia in the 1930s. There he discovered what was really taking place and set out to inform the world of the truth about Communism.[2] He wrote splendid books that influenced me profoundly when I read them some years ago. When I met him, I thanked him for what he had done and told him how greatly his books had influenced me. He looked at me with a gloomy expression and said, "It didn't do much good, did it? When I wrote those books, the Communists had a hundred and sixty million. Now they have a billion. Western civilization is doomed. We are as certain to become extinct as the Indian civilization was before the advance of the white man."

You may dismiss this man as an abject pessimist if you will, but you cannot so easily dispose of the facts. If we weigh the evidence of impending Communist conquest by any of the standard methods of judging human knowledge, it is very difficult to escape the conclusion that he reached. This evidence may be considered under five headings:

1. The numerical evidence
2. The military evidence
3. The educational evidence
4. The economic evidence
5. The communications evidence

1. THE NUMERICAL EVIDENCE

In the year 1903, Lenin established the movement called Bolshevism with seventeen supporters. In the year 1917, Lenin conquered Russia with a Party of approximately forty thousand members. By 1959, the party of Lenin had conquered one billion people. In one generation, the godless Communists have brought under their control twelve times as many as Hitler ruled at the beginning of World War II, twelve times as many as Japan ruled, and six times the population of the United States. In less than half a century, they have conquered far more than the total number of the world's population who have heard the minimum story of Christ from any source after nearly two thousand years. [As of 1960, those] who have heard of Christ from any source—Protestant, Catholic, Jehovah's Witness, Mormon, or Christian Scientist—add up to approximately seven hundred and fifty million. In one generation the Communists have conquered a billion. There are, in the world today, five children in school learning in detail the godless doctrines of Communism for every one child in any school anywhere learning anything about Christ. These facts are fearful to contemplate, but they are inescapably true.

These figures are all the more frightening when they are examined as any honest businessman would examine them.

I spoke in St. Louis, Missouri, to the management club of a small but very prosperous firm. The president of the firm told me that he wanted to show me the secret of their success. Taking me into a room, he showed me an electronic computer. He said, "We are not satisfied to know the past and the present. We need to know the future. At last we have found how to discover the future. This machine is the answer. We feed into it the figures of the past and we get from it the predictions of the future. Those predictions are so accurate that upon them we base our production and marketing schedules." The machine was so valuable that they were paying over $2,000 a month rental for it though they were a small company employing only about three hundred people.

I said to him, "Here is a set of figures to feed into the machine. Lenin established Bolshevism with seventeen supporters in 1903. He conquered Russia with forty thousand in 1917. Today, the party of Lenin has conquered one billion. The population of the world is two and three quarter billion. By what year will that figure be reached?"

He replied, "I'm frightened to try it."

2. THE MILITARY EVIDENCE

The oceans that surround America, traditionally the barrier of protection against the enemy, have become the source of an infinite danger. The Communists have at their disposal some five hundred submarines. Many of these are long range, and many can fire missiles which have a radius of several hundred miles. They can carry an atomic or thermonuclear warhead. At any time the Communist leader so chooses, submarines can emerge from the waters of the Pacific, the Atlantic, and the Gulf of Mexico, discharge their guided missiles, and submerge. Simultaneously, Washington, DC, Baltimore, Philadelphia, Boston, Miami, New Orleans, Houston, San Diego, Los Angeles, San Francisco, Portland, and Seattle could be wiped from the face of the earth. The power to do this

[136]

exists right now. There is no effective defense against it. It is true that the United States could retaliate through her Strategic Air Command and by means of her missiles located in Europe. Should she do so, devastation in Russia would be terrible indeed. But this would not bring back to life one destroyed American citizen or rebuild from the vapors one shattered city.

Richard Arens, director of the House Un-American Activities Committee, tells how they called before their committee the military man they considered best equipped to deal with the subject of Communism—General Wedemeyer, aide to General MacArthur in the Far East. Arens asked him, "General Wedemeyer, how late do you consider it to be on the Communist timetable for world conquest?"

General Wedemeyer thought for a few moments and then replied, "Too late. If I were advising the Communist leaders, I would say, 'Don't change one thing you are doing. You are winning as certainly as any group ever won any battle in the history of mankind.'" At the conclusion of the general's testimony, Richard Arens asked, "General, in light of these frightening things that you have told us, what do you advise that we should do?"

General Wedemeyer replied, "Had you asked me that question fifteen years ago, I could have answered it with ease. Had you asked it ten years ago, I could have answered it with difficulty. When you ask it today, the only honest reply that I can make is that I do not know."

Big business in America takes considerable trouble to make long range future predictions. In one city they have established what is known as a "think center." Here they have gathered together the finest electronic equipment and skilled personnel to make these predictions. Into the equipment they fed all the data they were able to collect related to the relative war-making capacities of America and Russia to determine by what year the balance of power would be favorable to Russia in a future war. The date delivered by the machine was the year 1965.

3. THE EDUCATIONAL EVIDENCE

By a tremendous concentration on education, the Communists are today graduating in Russia alone three times as many engineers and scientists as the United States. When their China program matures, they will graduate ten times as many. They are graduating, at a rough estimate, one hundred times as many language specialists. When their China program matures, their linguistic superiority will be astronomical.

A common reaction to this information is to draw comfort from the fact that in Communist countries there is no academic freedom. One of the great delusions of American educators has been that academic freedom is necessary for the achievement of material results. If a child is trained in habits of study, and then forced to study mathematics, science, and foreign languages, he will learn a lot whether the system is free or not. Regimentation and tyranny have always been able to achieve great things. The pharaohs built the pyramids; the Chinese built the Great Wall; Hitler achieved miracles in Germany, and there is no evidence whatsoever that he had any trouble controlling his educated classes. Under an authoritarian system of regimented education, the Germans made tremendous progress in the science of rocketry and electronics and in the development of the jet aircraft. In a similar way, the Communists with their emphasis on science, foreign languages, and mathematics, are making tremendous progress. It is not a question of which system of education develops better balanced personalities. The question is which system will win this universal war.

I was visiting an American college. Before I had been there ten minutes, the president told me with great pride of a young man who had brought glory and honor to their school. Wherever I went on the campus, I heard his praises sung. At last I met him, and a fine young man he was. His body was lithe and slender, and he stood some six feet two inches tall. He was their leading basketball player. His skill at the game was so great that he had been chosen to go to Melbourne, Australia, to represent the United States in the Olympic Games in 1956. What an honor for the school!

Frequently I asked, "Who is your leading science student?" He looked at me in wonder and amazement. He could not answer the question. To find out information like that a careful study of the records would be required.

I want to make it quite clear that I have nothing against basketball. I think it is a splendid sport. The ability to project accurately an inflated spherical ball through an iron hoop is a remarkable gift indeed. However, it is difficult to envisage how ballistic missiles can be effectively stopped with basketballs. Faced as we are with a struggle for survival against an enemy who spares no effort to educate the young in those fields that will help to secure victory, it would seem that the scale of values in the American educational system might well be revised.

4. THE ECONOMIC EVIDENCE

If we were to plot on a graph the total economic product of Russia and America and their rates of growth, the lines would cross within a measurable period ahead. The exact length of that period of time has been variously estimated. A few years ago it was said that they would cross within fifteen years. Khrushchev has claimed that they will overtake America within seven years. All authorities agree that the gap between Russian and American production is closing.

The problem, however, is not merely that the Russian total economic product may soon equal that of America. The great problem lies in the percentage of the Russian economic product that is available to the Communists for class warfare. Because the Communist Party has a monopoly ownership of the entire Russian economic product, it can use the economic product as it will. Because of their monopoly ownership, the Communists can decide how much the individual Russian may have, and how much of the total product will be retained for use in economic warfare against the United States. By keeping the people at a very low standard of living, they are able to use a large proportion of their economic product to destroy American foreign markets by underselling the American product.

Monopoly has a tremendous advantage in competition with small industry. Unprotected by law, no small concern with only a few employees could stand against any of the great national corporations. Were it not for the protection afforded by antitrust laws, a big chain store could very easily put out of operation the little grocer on the corner. All the chain store would need to do would be to open up a market nearby. Since this market would be only one of hundreds owned by them, they would not need to make a profit. They could undersell on every line. Their little competitor, however, has limited financial resources. He has to make a profit to pay his debts and to carry on his business. The time he can compete is limited. In time his resources are exhausted and he is forced to close down.

The Communists are doing a similar thing on a world scale. They can move into any American foreign market they consider desirable. They do not need to make a profit; their profit is in the chaos they create in the American economy and in the agents they infiltrate into the country through their trade.

An example of Communist techniques of economic warfare may be seen in their activities in Iraq. Iraq had vast sums secured from oil royalties to be invested in developmental projects. A large number of the contracts for these projects went to Russia. To secure a contract, the Communists followed this simple procedure: they found out from pro-Communist elements in the Iraqi government the lowest bid made by any Western firm and tendered a bid twenty percent below it. They did not need to make a profit directly, for their profit was in the Communist agents they infiltrated and the subversive literature they distributed, as well as in the weakening of the American economy. It is difficult to see how any concern that must make a profit to survive can compete against them.

The advancing Communist economic penetration is causing grave concern among business leaders and the governmental authorities. The situation grows more serious year by year.

5. THE EVIDENCE IN THE FIELD OF COMMUNICATIONS

The world is divided into three major areas: there is the Communist area, a great prison containing a billion slaves; there is what is known as the Free World consisting of America and her allies; and between these two, there is the vast, uncommitted area of the world that numbers one billion people. This uncommitted area is composed primarily of the new nations of Asia and Africa. With them should be included the nations of Central and South America. These countries are the great battle ground between East and West. If the Communists secure them, they will have two billion and their superiority will be absolute. If the Free World can keep them outside the Communist fold, there may be some hope of maintaining the present unstable balance of power.

The peoples of these countries are being wooed and won by the Communists, not with bombs and bullets, but with words and books. One hundred people are being reached with Communist lies for every one being reached with the Christian or the democratic truth. The Communists are engaged in the greatest literature crusade mankind has ever known. They are producing beautiful literature in almost every language and distributing it in every corner of the earth. In many countries this literature costs practically nothing. An example of this is *Problems of Leninism* by Joseph Stalin. This book of more than eight hundred pages may be purchased in a Communist bookstore in America for four dollars; in Canada it costs a dollar and fifty cents; in Australia, it costs seventy cents; in India or Japan it may be purchased for ten cents. The price charged has no relationship to the cost of production; it is related merely to the economic capacity of the purchasers.

An example of their beautiful color magazines is *China Pictorial* which is printed in Peking every two weeks in Chinese, Mongolian, Tibetan, Uighur, Korean, English, Russian, German, French, Japanese, Vietnamese, Indonesian, Hindi, Spanish, Arabic, and Burmese. Every face wears a radiant smile. The color photography is beautiful. The moral tone is excellent: there is no violence, no crime, no nudity, no sex, and no alcohol. Every page portrays abundance, beauty, prosperity, liberty, and peace. You cannot look through such a magazine without being impressed.

How thoroughly the Communists are carrying out this literary crusade is indicated by the children's books they are producing in practically every language. Visit any Communist bookstore in the United States and you will find English translation of books printed in Moscow and Peking for one, two, and three-year-old babies.

These have titles such as *The Rose and the Earthworm, The Golden Ass, The Little Bird Who Hurt His Wing, The Caterpillar, Punchy the Elephant, Chickens and Ears, The Lamb and the Wolf, The Ant and the Grasshopper, The Adventures of the Little Swallow, How the Monkeys Reached for the Moon, Beautiful Leaves, Wow-wow's House,* and *Tolstoy's Short Stories.* The Communists want the children. They do not care so much about the adults whom they consider contaminated with the disease of Capitalism and consequently of little use to them. When the Communists rule the world, the diseased social classes will have to be eliminated. But the children are different. They can do something with them. This children's literature is a preliminary step towards winning the children of the world.

An examination of some of the children's literature produced by the Communists induces bewilderment in most loyal Americans, for they can discover nothing wrong with these books. The stories are well told, beautifully illustrated, and do not teach Communism in any way. The trouble with these books is that there is nothing wrong with them.

If a kidnapper wishes to gain the confidence of a child to entice her into an automobile for dreadful purposes, he does not give a long lecture about what will happen after she gets into the automobile. He gives her candy to win her confidence. The candy he gives is not bitter or poisoned candy, for the sweeter and better the candy, the greater the likelihood that the child will get into the automobile. These children's books are the Communist literary candy with which the Communists are endeavoring to entice the children of the world into the Communist automobile for their journey into slavery and death.

The Communists divide their literature into two categories: Propaganda and Agitation. Propaganda they define as that which conveys many ideas to a few people. Propaganda teaches Communist theory, philosophy, organization, and doctrine. It is designed primarily for the thinking student mind.

For the many, they publish Agitation. Agitation they define as that which conveys one idea to many people. The Communists' great literary crusade is designed to convey to the people of the world the simple idea that wherever Communism comes to power, the people immediately become happy, healthy, prosperous, and free, whereas America is evil and degenerate and a threat to the peace of the entire world. The Communists are reaching one hundred people with these blatant lies for every one being reached with the Christian or democratic truth.

The truth is very simple. No matter what promises Communism makes, this fact stands out with crystal clarity: wherever people can escape from Communist rule, they do it by the millions. Try to imagine what it would take to cause parents to gather together their children and what few articles they could carry in their arms and go on foot into the night, not to a bright future, but to the bleak unknown. How bad would things have to be to cause people to do that? Millions are doing this wherever Communism comes to power. When faced with these unanswerable facts, the Communist spokesmen are helpless.

During his visit to the United States, Nikita Khrushchev was asked the following question by Karl Feller, president of the International Union of United Brewery, Flour, Cereal, Soft Drink, and Distillery Workers of America: "Mr. Chairman, I cannot understand, since the Communist Party proclaims itself to be the liberator of the working class, yet we see a mass exodus of workers in other countries following the Communist seizure of power. You have the example of three million workers fleeing from East Germany to West Berlin, and about three million fleeing from North Korea to South Korea, and as mentioned a moment ago, three hundred or so thousands of Hungarians braved arrest and death in escaping to freedom. Mr. Khrushchev, can you tell us of a single instance where, following Communist seizure of power, there has been a mass influx of workers from surrounding non-Communist countries into the Communist country? If the Communist Party is the liberator of the working class, why don't we see this phenomenon?"

Mr. Khrushchev: "Is that all? Think it over. Drink your beer. Perhaps that will help you to find the answer to your question."

Allies of Communism

Mr. Feller: "That certainly is no answer, and apparently nothing will make you understand why millions want to escape from Communism—."

Mr. Khrushchev: "I've told you, I'm not even afraid of the devil."[3]

There are many things that may be said by way of criticism of America, but when all has been said, the fact remains that America is the magnet that draws to its shores people from all over the world.[4] It is still the land of hope and promise, a vision living in the hearts and minds of millions. The unfortunate thing is that these facts do not speak for themselves. They must be made known by the means of communications. By an extensive and effective use of the means of communication, the Communists have convinced two thirds of the people of the world that the exact opposite of these facts is true. A lie that is believed has great power for evil.

An honest consideration of the evidence—numerical, military, economic, educational, and communicational—is frightening indeed. The most comforting thing to do is to put it out of the mind or to refuse to believe it. This is the attitude adopted by a large number of people.

While visiting Philadelphia, I went to a radio station at eleven o'clock one night to be interviewed. A psychiatrist was to be interviewed at the same radio station on the subject of mental health. His interview was to follow mine. He arrived early, and we talked for some minutes before I went on the air. During that time, I gathered that he was quite unsympathetic towards my position and viewpoint.

When I went on the air, I explained, as I frequently do, that my greatest problem is to persuade people that Communists are Communists. Just as the Catholics are Catholics and have certain beliefs and programs, the Communists are Communists and have clear beliefs and a very well developed program. The aim of their program is to conquer the world. The realization of the plan necessitates the encirclement and demoralization of the United States, leading finally to surrender. I pointed out that many intelligent people are unwilling to acknowledge that these things are so, even though all the facts point in this direction.

I went on to describe how the program of the Communists is being fulfilled. While America is being lulled to sleep with a false picture of friendship and talk about coexistence, the Communists are making devastating progress in many parts of the world. They are operating in all the Asian countries, in Africa and the Near East, and are looking forward to the time when Western Europe will be economically strangulated and defenseless; they are invading South and Central America by their infiltration of the colleges and universities. When these countries have been taken, America, isolated, confused, and demoralized, economically and militarily encircled, will be offered the choice of surrender or annihilation. The Communists are certain that she will choose surrender.

As I was speaking, the psychiatrist seethed. At last he could stand no more and spontaneously came onto the program to try and counteract the damage I was doing. When a man's evidence cannot be discredited, the simplest alternative is to discredit the man himself. This he proceeded to do. He told the listening audience that I was apparently the victim of certain deep-seated, inner emotional conflicts which I was projecting into my external environment. Out of this inner conflict sprang this vision of a great encircling force. The inference was clearly my need of psychiatric treatment.

When he had finished speaking, I thanked him very much for giving me the perfect example of what I had been talking about. Here was an apparently intelligent man who was quite unwilling to face the truth. I had with me the book *How to Be a Good Communist*. I showed him that the author was Liu Shao-chi, President of Communist China. I opened the book and asked him to read: "What is the most fundamental and common duty of us Communist Party members?

As everybody knows, it is to establish Communism, to transform the present world into a Communist world."[5] On another page I showed him the following passage:

> ...the cause of Communism has become a powerful, invincible force throughout the world. There is not the slightest doubt that this force will continue to develop and advance and will win final and complete victory. Despite this, however, the strength of the international reactionary forces and of the exploiting classes are still more powerful than ours, and for the time being are still predominant in many respects. Consequently, we shall have to go through a long, bitter, circuitous and arduous process of struggle before we defeat them.[6]

When he had finished reading, the psychiatrist indicated that I was putting my own interpretation on these passages and giving my own opinion as fact.

"In the name of all that's honest," I replied, "please tell me what other interpretation these words can have, 'the fundamental duty of Communist Party members is to transform the present world into a Communist world'?"

We have always had people in our midst who thought that fire would not burn, that if you jump out of a tenth story window, you may go down, but then again, you may go up. We used to call it insanity. Only recently has it taken to itself the name of mental health. The malady of intellectual dishonesty has afflicted large segments of the educated and the religious groups, leaving them quite unable to face the unpleasant truth. Intellectual dishonesty is one of the greatest allies of Communism. Like cancer, it cannot be treated adequately until its malignancy is recognized.

CULTURAL INTERCHANGE

A second ally of Communism is the naïve belief that the truth about Communism can be learned by superficial observation. An idea which has currently gained wide acceptance is that legitimate information about Communism may be secured by a brief visit to a Communist country.

As I travel throughout America lecturing on Communism, I am frequently asked if I have visited Russia. The inference is that if I have not, I cannot possibly understand very much about Communism. To audiences that pose this question, I reply that I have not been to Russia and that I realize that this is a serious disadvantage. I then express the hope that after I have outlined my qualifications, they will all feel moved to contribute generously in order to send me. To prove my qualifications for such a visit, I proceed to give them the fruit of my acute observations concerning America. I have been in America, on and off, for about nine years. I have traveled in forty-six states; I have addressed hundreds of thousands of people, and have enjoyed complete freedom of movement and freedom of speech. As far as I know, I have never been followed by an agent of any investigative group, or by the police. As an Australian, I speak the English language exceedingly well, though I have great difficulty persuading Americans that this is so. During this time, therefore, I have had ample opportunity to observe America and Americans.

The first thing that astonished me when I arrived was that apparently nobody approved of the character or record of President Roosevelt. In Australia we had thought him to be a universal American hero. When the first fifty people to whom I spoke unanimously castigated him, I received the shock of my life. During my nine years in this country, I have never heard an African American complain of discrimination though I have addressed thousands and conversed with hundreds. I have never seen a violent crime; I have never witnessed a major automobile accident; I have never seen a basketball game; and, as far as I know, I have never seen a professional gambler or a prostitute. After ten years of personal, first hand observation, I make my report: "Inside America" by Fred C. Schwarz. "Nobody in America voted for President Roosevelt; no African American is concerned with discrimination; there is no violent crime; there are no automobile accidents; nobody plays basketball; there is no gambling and there is no prostitution." This is the truth because I have been there and I have seen it for myself.

If someone would just send me to Russia for three weeks or so, I could bring back the truth about what is happening over there. Admittedly I would be slightly handicapped because I cannot speak the language. However, this is not really important because the Communist government thought of it long in advance and has made adequate provision for it. They have trained as interpreters some of their finest young Communists who are totally dedicated to the Party and very quick of mind and tongue. These interpreters have a three-fold task. In the first place, they are to take me around and supervise what I see and whom I meet. Secondly, they are to keep an eye on the contacts I do make so that if any of them get out of line they can be dealt with later. Thirdly, they are to misrepresent my questions and misinterpret the answers. I approach a group of people and ask the interpreter to ask them if they love the Communist government. He turns to them and utters a stream, of what to me, is unintelligible gibberish. They answer in a similar vein. He turns to me and says, "They love Communism with all their hearts." The only difficulty is that I have no way of knowing what he asked them or what they said in reply. He may have said, "He wants to know what you had for breakfast." They may have said, "You know very well that we didn't have any breakfast." Since he is a devoted Communist, utterly dedicated to the interests of the Party, it is highly improbable that he will repeat anything that reflects badly upon it.

Ninety-nine out of a hundred people who visit Russia and come back to tell their friends and acquaintances all about it are in exactly the same position I would be in if I went. They have no way of knowing how much of what they have been told is really true. The tragic part is that most of them do not realize this. They quote authoritatively what they have been told by the Communist interpreter as the objective truth.

A well known businessman, a prominent clergyman, or a politician goes to Russia for a brief tour. On his return he is met by representatives of the press at the airport where he gives his impressions of the present mood of the Russian masses. He is whisked off to a radio station where he discusses the changes that have occurred in the personal relationships of the Presidium of the Communist Party. He may even appear on television where he talks at some length about the present attitude of the Red Army towards their Communist masters. The only people who are bigger idiots than he are those who take any notice of what he says. By the very nature of things, he can be nothing but an unconscious agent of Communist propaganda. He can report only what he saw and heard. What he saw was limited and superficial, and what he heard was channeled to him through the Communist Party.

It has been well said, "A fool learns by his own experience; a wise man learns by the experience of others." The major portion of our knowledge is gained through the means of communication. In Russia these are completely controlled by the Communist Party. Every newspaper is a Communist propaganda sheet. All radio and television programs are designed to convey messages selected by the Communist Party. Every textbook, every novel, every play and movie is designed to advance the ideas approved by the Party. Thus, information which is the raw material of thought is fed to the Russian people by the Communists. Public opinion in Russia is carefully molded by the Communist Party.

If a tourist realizes the serious limitations of his situation, in certain specialized fields, he can obtain valid information from his trip. For example, he can secure clear information about the Russian boast that they have equalized the status of women. Their boast is quite justified. Americans do not really treat their women with equality. They do not allow them, for example, to mine coal or to perform heavy manual work on the roads. Such tasks are kept solely for men. There is no such bourgeois discrimination in Russia, and tourists to Russia may observe that this is so. One tourist told me that when he came out of a theatre at eleven o'clock at night that he saw a group of old grandmothers working in the rain laying blacktop on the roads. As he travels on the train, the tourist may see women swinging their picks in the railway gangs, usually under the supervision of a male foreman. Such things a tourist may see, but to secure a genuine insight into the minds and feelings of the people is an impossibility in the situation existing in Russia.

Discussing this with some wide-eyed innocents recently returned from Russia, I made the statement that tourists returning from behind the Iron Curtain are very frequently instruments of Communist propaganda. They were horrified at the suggestion. As we continued in conversation, one of the women commented on the encouraging progress being made by Russian Baptists. She said, "They now have seven thousand churches."

"Here is the very kind of thing to which I was referring," I replied. "You are unconsciously giving Communist propaganda."

"I resent that very much," she said.

"Let's consider your statement," I said. "You tell me that there are seven thousand Baptist churches. How do you know?"

She mentioned the name of a friend of hers as the source of her information.

"And how does he know?"

"He knows the Baptist preacher in Moscow and has known him for years," was the reply.

"I know one of the Baptist preachers here in Los Angeles and have known him for years. Were I to go to him and ask how many Baptist churches there are in California, what would he do? He'd pull down a Baptist yearbook, seek the information, and give me the answer for the different Baptist segments. Somebody has to take the statistics. Who do you suppose took these statistics that you are giving me?"

She said, "I don't know."

"The Communists took them, of course. Whether they are true or false, we have not the faintest idea."

No tourist of Russia can get any idea whatsoever of the strength of Baptist work in Russia. All he can do is to go and see one or two Baptist churches, usually those in Moscow or Leningrad. When Bob Pierce, President of World Vision, was in Kiev, he asked the guide to show him the Baptist church there. The guide was at a loss. Tourists do not ask to visit the Baptist church in Kiev. They go only in Moscow and Leningrad. In the city of Kiev, which has a population of a million people, she did not know where a Baptist church was to be found. By the following day, however, they had discovered one. It consisted of a mere handful of people meeting in a house. When we consider that the Protestants of Russia are all in these Baptist churches, the complacency of Christians is appalling.

The statistics regarding the strength of Baptist work in Russia vary greatly from time to time. When the leaders from the Russian Baptists toured America in 1955, they quoted the number of Baptists then in Russia as being three million. In 1959, the number was given as five hundred thousand. Either the Baptists in Russia backslid greatly in those few years, or someone manipulated the statistics.

In Indianapolis, I spoke to the farm editor of the television station who was about to visit Russia. I told him that he would come back a propagandist for the Communists. He replied, "I know I will. How can I help it?"

"Oh, that's easy," I said. "As soon as you get there, overthrow the Communist government and re-establish freedom of speech, freedom of movement, freedom of the press, and freedom of communication. Abolish all the psychological inhibitions Communism has produced in the people during their rule of forty years. Then go around and dig under every child's playground and see what you find."

In the Ukraine, the Germans were welcomed by the Ukrainians as liberators. In the city of Vinnitza there were discovered mass graves of ten thousand bodies. Over some of these graves the Communists had built Parks of Culture and Rest including a child's playground and a sporting arena. A tourist going there at normal times would see nothing except excellent recreational facilities for the citizens and particularly for the children.

Delegations are the source of dangerous delusions indeed. What we see with our eyes is limited. Observation is no substitute for understanding. A man can learn more about Communism in an hour by reading a book like *How to Be a Good Communist* by Liu Shao-chi or *Problems of Leninism* by Stalin than he can in a year as a tourist who sees nothing but what the Communists show him. Observation may be minutely accurate and interpretation completely erroneous.

A visitor went on a tour of a tuberculosis sanitarium. He walked through the grounds, first of all, and there he was greatly impressed by the well kept lawns and the beautiful landscaped gardens. Upon entering the building, he was met by a charming receptionist who smiled at him warmly and took him on a tour of the sanitarium. In the spotless kitchen, he found the finest cooking equipment he had ever seen. He examined the plumbing and found it exceptional in quality and efficiency.

After duly admiring the facilities of the institution, he was escorted into the wards. In preparation for his coming, the patients had all been given a dose of anti-percussive mixture, otherwise known as cough syrup. The peaceful atmosphere was not disturbed by undue coughing. The patients were propped up neatly on snowy white pillows. Many of them had flushed cheeks. Hovering around were nurses who were giving them personal attention far better than any service available in the best hotel. When mealtime arrived, each patient was served with tasty food which had been carefully prepared and attractively served on individual trays.

When his tour was ended, the visitor was duly impressed by all he had seen. He said, "There are many good features about tuberculosis, features which are at least equal, if not superior to the features of a healthy life. The patient lives in an environment of cleanliness and beauty. He has economic security. He does not need to rise at six o'clock each morning to battle his way through the teeming traffic and compete in the struggle to earn a living. Food, clothing, and shelter are all provided. Every need is supplied by attentive young female nurses. He has reached the goal of economic security for which we all strive. I think that the dangers of tuberculosis are grossly exaggerated. We can at least coexist with it."

Hearing this, some puzzled person might turn to him and say, "But what about the tuberculosis germ?"

"I didn't see one."

"Did you look?"

"Of course I looked. I looked everywhere—in the drawers, under the beds, behind the doors, everywhere—and I swear I did not see a single tuberculosis germ. I don't believe they exist."

Suppose that such a report was made by a medical man who had been trained to know that what he saw was merely superficial, and that out of human sight was an evil, pathological organism doing its fearful work; who should have known that behind the apparent calm, there was a world of agony and racking coughs which would cause the patients to spit up their lungs in pus and blood and would send them to their deaths. A medical man who made a report like that would be judged criminally insane.

Allies of Communism

Preachers should be physicians in the realm of the spirit as medical men are in the realm of the body. When preachers report only the superficial things they see, and by inference, minimize the gravity of the germ of godlessness, they betray their responsibility as Christian leaders. The tragedy is that they do it all unwittingly.

A preacher visited Russia in 1938. He saw some splendid new buildings going up, and he reported that Russia was fulfilling the kingdom of God on earth. What was going on at that time was horrible to imagine. It was the period of the great Stalinist purges, when Stalin was watering the soil of Russia with the blood of the Communist elite. As a visitor, the clergyman did not see one execution or one trial. He saw only magnificent new buildings and on the basis of this he made his report. Seeing without understanding is the certain pathway of delusion.

Seeing is not necessarily believing. If seeing is believing, you cannot tell me anything about American football because I have seen it with my own eyes. I want to describe to you what I saw. If you do not believe me, I am prepared to go into any court in the land and swear under oath that this is what I saw.

It was in Los Angeles at the Coliseum. The University of Southern California was playing the University of California in a homecoming match. It was a magnificent spectacle. A hundred thousand people were gathered together. A hundred thousand people is a huge crowd. They must be entertained because the devil finds work for idle hands to do. Clowns have always been found to be very entertaining, so with typical American genius the organizers hit upon a remarkable scheme. They dressed all the football players up like clowns. They put them in the most ridiculous and grotesque garments I have ever seen. They were padded and patted in every direction like an Eskimo bride at a winter wedding breakfast. They had baggy pants. They protruded at the rear and at the knees. They wore enormous helmets with protruding jaws. It was the funniest looking sight I had ever seen.

About fifty of these clowns ran on to the playing field and a strange thing happened. Instead of bursting out laughing as would have been quite natural, everybody began clapping and cheering. I admit bewilderment at this incomprehensible manifestation of American psychology. After these clowns had run around throwing the ball to one another for ten or fifteen minutes, most of them became weary or bored and went to sit down on some benches at the side of the field. Eleven clowns remained on each side of the line running across the middle of the playing field, and seven of them knelt down opposite one another and started to pray. When they had said their prayers, one of them flicked the ball back to a guy standing behind. He apparently took a liking to it and thought he would take it home, so he cut across that field like a streak of lighting. The others saw what he was doing and rushed after him. He swerved and he weaved. He approached the sideline. It looked as though he was going to get away. But suddenly, hurtling through the air came a massive body which crashed into him and knocked him right over. This was rather cruel, but maybe it was fair enough since he was trying to steal the ball like that.

At this point nobody seemed to know quite what to do. A clown in a costume all of his own, with up and down stripes that made him look like a convict, blew a whistle and the game stopped. One side called a committee meeting. What took place at this committee meeting, I do not know exactly. One thing they did was to interchange a few of the clowns who had apparently grown tired in the struggle.

They resumed with another session of prayer. I feel that this recurrent prayer in American football is one of the hopeful signs of the day. When the center man flicked the ball back to the one standing behind him, he played them a dirty trick. In all my living days, I have never seen a dirtier deed.

How he had the gall to do it before two hundred thousand staring eyes, I will never know. Right in the middle of the game, he changed his side. Instead of running forward, he turned and ran round backwards. When he had gone back about ten yards, however, someone caught him and knocked him over. Wasn't that a dirty trick to change his side in the middle of the game like that? I know he did. I saw him with my own eyes.

You say to me, "Oh, you're crazy! That man hadn't changed his side at all. He'd gone back to get into a good position to make a forward pass and they trapped him." You know this because you know the rules of the game. You know its purposes and you know its motives. You are in tune with its spirit. But if you knew none of these things, if you came as I do, from another land where the rules for football are quite different, where the game has no forward pass, and if you took the rules which were familiar to you and interpreted what you saw in those terms, you would be apt to make conclusions very similar to those which I reached.

When we observe what the Communists do without knowing the rules of their game, without knowing Communist doctrine, morality, objectives, and methods, when we project upon them our own basic Christian standards, our conclusions are as ridiculous as my interpretation of American football game. They are far more dangerous. There must be assiduous study of the doctrines of Communism if the necessary understanding of their psychology, morality, and program is to be achieved. There is no substitute for knowledge. Ignorance is evil and paralytic. The greatest ally Communism has is the existing ignorance concerning its true nature. War must be declared on this ignorance.

FURTHER STUDY

Coulter, Ann. *Godless: The Church of Liberalism*. New York: Crown Forum, 2006.

————. *Treason: Liberal Treachery from the Cold War to the War on Terrorism*. New York: Crown Forum, 2003.

Dobbs, Zygmund, ed. *The Great Deceit: Social Pseudo-Sciences*. West Sayville, NY: Veritas Foundation, 1964.

————. *Keynes at Harvard: Economic Deception as a Political Credo*. Revised ed. West Sayville, NY: Veritas Foundation 1962.

Foster, William Z. *Toward Soviet America*. New York: International Publishers, 1932.

Goldberg, Jonah. *Liberal Fascism: The Secret History of the American Left, from Mussolini to the Politics of Change*. New York: Doubleday, 2007.

Howse, Brannon. *Grave Influence: 21 Radicals and Their Worldviews that Rule America from the Grave*. Collierville, TN: Worldview Weekend Publishing, 2009.

Klein, Aaron and Brenda J. Elliott. *The Manchurian President: Barack Obama's Ties to Communists, Socialists and Other Anti-American Extremists*. Washington DC, WND Books, 2010.

Strachey, John. *The Theory and Practice of Socialism*. New York: Random House, 1936.

CHAPTER NINE

Brainwashing

by
Fred C. Schwarz

The word "brainwashing" is a very recent addition to the English language. A new word was necessary because it signified an experience that was previously unknown. Since its introduction it has passed into common speech and is used routinely by large numbers of people, many of whom have only the vaguest idea of its meaning. In many cases it is used to describe processes that have existed for centuries and its specific meaning has, to a large degree, been lost. But the phenomenon of brainwashing is one of the more frightening developments of the twentieth century. It is an accurate and destructive science. It is an assault upon the human mind itself. The Communists have proved they can distort the human mind as the torturers of history distorted the body.

An American girl went to China as a Fulbright scholar. She was not a Communist, but neither was she an active anti-Communist. After studying for a year or so in Communist China, she was arrested and underwent various mysterious treatments. At the end of this treatment, she confessed that she had gone to China as an imperialist spy and professed profound repentance for her treachery. She was then allowed to go free.

As she crossed into Hong Kong, she was met by newspaper reporters, and a remarkable story unfolded. She told the reporters she had been a vicious spy on behalf of the American imperialists. Her attitude was a composite of guilt and self-loathing, mingled with hatred of her own country and a passionate love for the Chinese Communists. She was almost lyrical in her gratitude and devotion to her captors. She described how wonderful they were. She had deserved to die, but they had spared her life. In their hands she had been born again. To them she owed an eternal debt of gratitude for the new life she now lived.

The reporters questioned her about her treatment in prison. Had not her feet been in chains? Oh yes, her feet had been in chains, but what loving, kind, wonderful people the Communists were. Was it not true that her hands had been handcuffed behind her back? Yes, her hands had been handcuffed behind her back, but they had treated her with absolute kindness and wonderful love.

What were the experiences that had brought about this remarkable situation where she believed she had done things she had not done, felt guilt for crimes she had not committed, and loved with a passionate intensity those who had tortured and tormented her? We see in this young woman an end product of the phenomenon known as brainwashing.

A young man joined the armed forces of his country and crossed the sea to fight in Korea. Early in the Korean War he was taken prisoner by the Communists. He soon confessed that he had engaged in germ warfare. While in the hands of the Communists, he fell ill and was transferred back to America at operation "Little Switch"—the interchange of sick prisoners. Upon his return, he needed to be institutionalized. In the institution he sat squat-legged in his cell in the grip of a profound, irreducible melancholy, with a tendency

Brainwashing

towards self-destruction. He was in love with his mistress, Death. This young soldier is a second example of the results of brainwashing.

The word is sometimes used to describe the experience, on a mass scale, of American prisoners in the hands of the Chinese Communists. America has fought in a number of wars in which prisoners have been taken. Such prisoners always proved a thorn in the side of their captors. They were very difficult to control; they were courageous; they were subject to the discipline of their officers in the prison; they were gripped with a comradely devotion to their fellow prisoners,; and they made numerous attempts at escape. When American prisoners of war fell into the hands of the Communists, however, a disturbing transformation occurred. They were reduced to a selfish, uncoordinated rabble without discipline or unity. Informing on one another was the order of the day. A handful of Communist Chinese kept large groups of American prisoners under control without brutal bashings, without barbed wire entanglements, and with little apparent difficulty. Of many thousands of prisoners, not one made any attempt to escape during the entire period of the imprisonment. Only a small segment were able to completely withstand the attempts of the Communists to indoctrinate them. Another small group became openly pro-Communist. The remainder were demoralized. Forty percent of them died. The Turkish prisoners, on the other hand, maintained an excellent record. Their discipline was held completely from top to bottom. Not one Turkish prisoner died and not one collaborated.

The American authorities were so concerned that they instituted an inquiry to seek out the causes of this revolutionary conduct in the American prisoners. A team of trained medical officers examined the prisoners, collected details of the treatment they had received, and probed for the causes of this debacle. This evidence was published in the book *In*

You Can Still Trust the Communists

Every War but One.[1] Their findings were alarming indeed. In an effort to prevent similar occurrences in the future, the army sought to establish a code of conduct for any future soldier unfortunate enough to fall into the hands of the Communists. The Communist assault on the human mind is historically unique and alarming in its effectiveness.

To understand the rationale of this attack we need to understand the Communist concept of the mind itself. The Communists are complete materialists. They believe that matter in motion is the sum total of all being, that there is nothing in the universe but matter in motion. Man is a material machine. Within his body a stomach secretes gastric juice, a liver secretes bile, a brain secretes emotion and thought.

A materialist scientist built a mechanical dog which he kept in a room in his home. When he opened the door and allowed the light to shine on the eyes of the dog, it moved forward and growled. When he shut the door, it moved back into position. If he stroked the dog along the back, it wagged its tail. If he tickled it underneath, it lay down. Said the scientist, "The only difference between this dog and my pet dog that runs, jumps, barks, and comes with me when I take a walk is one of degree. There is no difference in kind."

The Communists go further. The only difference between the mechanical dog, the living dog, and the human being is one of degree. There is no difference in kind. The human body is simply a material machine. It is as automatic as an automobile. Man is a complex of conditioned behavior. The machinery is very complex, particularly the brain, which is so complex that it gives the impression of freedom, choice, and volition. But thought is merely a reflection of certain electronic impulses within the brain. The Communists, therefore, believe that if they can understand brain structure, the building up of brain patterns and brain circuits, they will be able to understand the formation of human thought, as well as control and direct it.

The functional unit within the brain is the conditioned reflex. The Communists have studied the formation, control, and elimination of conditioned reflexes. A reflex is an unlearned muscular response to a natural or unconditioned stimulus. At birth, a baby has certain remarkable skills. For example, it can cry, and crying is a complex mechanical process requiring the coordination of a number of groups of muscles. Again, a baby can suck. These muscular skills are the external manifestations of certain inborn brain patterns. They are unconditioned reflex actions.

At birth, the process of development and learning begins. Learning is the accumulation of new brain patterns leading to muscular coordination of a more complex nature. The baby is laid in a bassinet over which is suspended a little colored ball. The little hands strike at the ball. At first the movements are uncoordinated and multi-directional, but gradually skill is acquired until at length the little hand can hit the ball at will. The skill is revealed in coordinated muscular activity, but the controlling mechanism is the pattern that has been developed within the brain. The skill is a conditioned reflex.

As experience continues, the baby learns to sit up, to walk, to talk, to write, to ride a bicycle, to play the piano, to use a typewriter, and to drive an automobile. All these skills are conditioned reflexes. Experience shows itself in intricate patterns of muscular activity, but the real pattern is established within the brain.

The Communists believe that the mind is simply a complex of conditioned reflexes, and that if they can understand the techniques by which these conditioned reflexes are built up and how they can be broken down, they have acquired mastery over the mind itself.

The great scientist who studied the conditioned reflex thoroughly and systematically was the Russian, Ivan

Pavlov. He began his scientific experiments under the rule of the Czar. Early on, Lenin realized the vast significance of Pavlov's studies for the Communist program of changing the entire mental outlook of the Russian people. Pavlov was therefore given favored treatment by the Communist regime.

The experimental animal that he used was the dog. The basic reflex that he studied was the salivary reflex. When a dog is hungry and is shown some meat, his mouth waters. The sight or the smell of the meat is the normal stimulus for the flow of saliva. In preparation for this experiment, Pavlov operated on these dogs and introduced a tube into the salivary duct to divert the saliva from the intestinal tract into a bottle so that its flow could be measured. When the dogs were hungry, he showed them meat and the saliva flowed. The next step was to associate the ringing of a bell with the viewing of the meat and the flowing of the saliva. At first he rang a bell at the same time as he showed them the meat. Then he rang the bell a few seconds before he showed them the meat. In this way, the ringing of the bell was associated with the normal stimulus in such a way that the ringing of the bell itself was sufficient to start the salivary flow. Gradually the time interval was extended until finally the dogs were so conditioned that whenever the bell rang, the saliva flowed. The flowing of the saliva in this situation was a conditioned reflex. The ringing bell was the artificial stimulus that produced the reflex response.

Pavlov experimented with a large range of stimuli to reflex action. He took colored lights that moved in a circular pattern, lights that moved in an elliptical pattern, and after due training and conditioning, was able to obtain specific responses for each of the lights that he showed. He subjected the dogs to contradictory stimuli and studied their behavior to see which reflexes were more powerful. He had a whole kennel of dogs, each of which was conditioned to react to a given stimulus in a fixed manner.

Brainwashing

In 1924, Leningrad experienced a major flood. Pavlov's dogs were trapped, and for several days cut off from human help. When finally they were rescued, their muzzles were just sticking out of the water. For several days they had been cold, frightened, hungry, and exhausted. After their rescue, the acute observer Pavlov, noticed a strange thing. Some of his dogs went into a state of profound depression. They lost interest in food and in the normal activities of a dog's life. There was no barking and no rushing about. Their movements were slow and infrequent. To them life seemed to have lost its luster. Most interesting of all was the fact that in this state their conditioned reflexes were abolished. Pavlov found that he could then condition them according to an entirely different pattern.

Pavlov applied the information thus accidentally discovered to experiments to destroy conditioned reflex patterns. At first he continued to experiment with dogs, but during the last ten years of his life, man became his experimental animal. He developed techniques which could shatter the established pattern of human personality so that the fragments could be integrated into a new structure of memory, judgment, and emotion in line with the desires of the Communist craftsmen.

The first step in the process was to bring about a state of breakdown similar to that experienced by the dogs. Pavlov called it cortical inhibition of the higher cerebral function. This is the state commonly known as a mental breakdown, which has occurred naturally in humans for many years. Pavlov established techniques whereby he could cause an artificial mental breakdown. The four things necessary to bring about this state were present in the breakdown of the trapped dogs. They are exhaustion, confusion, chronic physical pain, and emotional tension or fear.

EXHAUSTION

To parody a statement of Tolstoy: "When the Communists wish to brainwash, they first exhaust." The first step, then, is to exhaust the individual. He is subjected to long periods of wakefulness. Various tactics are adopted to make sure that he cannot rest. He may have to snatch brief periods of sleep with a light shining in his face. If he turns over, the attendant comes along and awakens him with a command to get back into position. Sleep is short and sporadic. The techniques to induce prolonged wakefulness may vary from pleasurable, continuous excitement, to physical pain. The essential feature is to rob the body of sleep so that utter exhaustion prevails.

CONFUSION

With exhaustion, there is the concurrent development of confusion. While the defenses of his mind are weakened and undermined by his extreme weariness, the patient is subjected to lengthy periods of questioning. He sits facing his interrogator. A bright light shines relentlessly into his eyes. Questions are asked one after the other. There is no attorney present to warn him against loaded questions. There is no privilege of refraining from answering for fear of possible self-incrimination. Every question must be answered. At first the questions are simple. They often concern social origin, early childhood, and family. The questioner often shows a conciliatory attitude. Gradually the questions pry deeper and deeper into the hidden recesses of his mind. Questions are framed in such a way that any simple answer contains a damaging admission. Questions relative to imaginary crimes he is alleged to have committed are subtly introduced.

One of the most frequent accusations made against missionaries in China was that they operated secret radio transmitters to broadcast the fruits of their espionage to Chiang

Kai-shek or to America. The questioner might suddenly ask, "Are you sorry now that you transmitted this information?" If he answers simply "Yes," or "No," he is admitting association with a "transmitter." If the mind is alert, the trap is seen and avoided, but this requires clear insight and lucid expression. As exhaustion develops, the defenses of the mind break down. A question containing a trap is asked; a simple answer is given; and the subject is caught. After a few more questions, they confront him with the hidden admission contained in the simple answer he gave. He denies it. They take him back to his original answer and ask, "Isn't this what you said?" He replies that this is so.

"Well, does this not acknowledge so and so?" He has to admit that it does.

Relentlessly they continue. "Previously you acknowledged this; now you deny it. When were you lying, then or now?" He insists that he is speaking the truth now.

"If you were a liar then, how can we believe you now?" they demand. He becomes so confused that the borderline of truth and falsehood becomes blurred. The connection between reality and fantasy is lost, and he is no longer sure what is true and what is false. In such a condition, he becomes an easy prey for the suggestions of the Communist brainwashing therapist.

CHRONIC PHYSICAL PAIN

Along with exhaustion and confusion, the "brainwashed" is subject to chronic physical pain. This is applied with great care for their goal is always clearly before them. They are not aiming at torturing their victim until he confesses to something he knows to be untrue. They desire to reduce him to a state where he believes the untruth to be true. They do not want a physical breakdown before they get a mental one. Physical damage should not be permanent or leave clearly visible scars. The physical pain, therefore, is chronic in nature and not acute torture. If the weather is cold, the victim may be left without adequate covering so that his hands and feet become frostbitten. He may be made to endure hunger and thirst. Chronic sores may break out. He may be left in a position of extreme discomfort, unable to stand up and unable to sit or lie down. Physical movement may be restricted by handcuffs or chains. He longs and prays for an end to his apparently endless ordeal.

FEAR

In addition to exhaustion, confusion, and chronic physical pain, there is the constant application of emotional tension or fear. The emotional personality is analyzed to determine the weakest point. If there is intense devotion to wife or family, threats to them may be held constantly before the victim's eyes. A group may inhabit a cell. One by one they are called out at intervals of a few days. The sound of a shot is heard. The man taken out does not return. Anxiety and fear are experienced by those who remain. Each lives in constant inner emotional torment. By such processes as these, a mental breakdown is induced. The old personality pattern is shattered and the victim is ready to be molded according to the desires of the Communist Party.

Exhaustion, confusion, chronic physical pain, and emotional tension, employed in scientific balance, finally achieve the first goal. A breakdown occurs. The mind fragments. In Pavlovian language, cortical inhibition of the higher cerebral function occurs.

The characteristics of this breakdown are as follows.

1. *Physical retardation.* The victim tends to remain almost motionless in the same position for long periods of time. Movements, when they do take place, are slow and ponderous. There is a total lack of vitality, interest, and enthusiasm.

2. *Memory fragmentation.* The integrated pattern of past experience embracing memory, interpretation, and judgment is shattered. Fragments of past experience are remembered dimly but without relation to other memories of events. The time sequence of events is lost. The borderline between fact and fancy, between memory and dream, is blurred.

3. *Melancholy.* The typical pattern is one of deep melancholia. The mind is gripped by a nameless woe. There is deep and enduring depression. Frequently suicidal tendencies develop as the misery appears too heavy to be borne. If the physical means are available, the sufferer will readily end his own life.

4. *Increased suggestibility.* The barriers of the mind are down. Memory is faded. Logic is impaired. Judgment is impossible. In the absence of the restraints of the healthy mind, the power of suggestion is enhanced.

The Communists take advantage of this weak and unresisting state, and by suggestion, link the shattered fragments of memory into the new pattern. They suggest the new ideas which they want believed. To these ideas they attach the sense of guilt which the victim is already feeling. They remove the excess emotional depression and then identify themselves with measures to alleviate his suffering, but they are careful to leave the delusional beliefs unaltered. They now have their end product—a person with memories of things he has not done, with a sense of guilt for crimes he did not commit, and with a passionate love for those who have persecuted and tormented him.

Suggestion is a powerful force even under normal conditions. This has been discovered by advertisers and used to considerable advantage. I myself have frequently carried out an interesting little experiment on the power of suggestion. One of the problems confronting me in my itinerant life is that perfectly well-meaning, hospitable Americans try to persuade me to drink that dark, viscous, bitter beverage called coffee. Sometimes I drink it, but sometimes I say, "I used to drink it, but I carried out some research and discovered what coffee really is. Do you know what it really is? They take the castor oil bean, soak it in shellac until it is thoroughly impregnated. They put on a great advertising racket and pretend that it comes from Brazil so that they can triple the price. They grind it up and they brew it. The castor oil gives it the flavor, the shellac gives it the color, and the idiots drink it." It is amazing how many people have looked at me with wide open eyes and said, "Is that true?" No matter how stupid the statement, if it is made with an attitude of apparent sincerity and conviction, there are always those who will be convinced of its truth.

Once people are conditioned so that a certain word is associated with emotions of repulsion or anger, that word becomes a trigger by which those emotions may be discharged. Reason and logic are quite unnecessary. That word is used; the trigger is pulled, and out come the emotions. This was brought home to me very powerfully one evening when I was speaking upon the subject of brainwashing at a church. I used my illustration about coffee to indicate how suggestible people are. I reached the climax: the castor oil gives it the flavor, the shellac gives it the color, and the idiots drink it. To my great surprise, the whole audience broke out into loud, sustained applause. I was startled. I had thought I was telling a joke. Suddenly the truth dawned on me. The audience consisted of a group of coffee haters. This was a group to whom drinking coffee was a sin. They did not examine my argument critically; they responded to the trigger. The word became a stimulus to a reflex response. Once people are conditioned like that, there is no need for logic, reason, or truth. All that is needed is for the word to be said and out will come the emotions.

The Communists have taken the words "Capitalism," "American imperialism," and even the word "peace" and made them trigger words and used them in slogans. "Capitalism" immediately conjures up a picture of greed and exploitation, and releases emotions of scorn and anger. "American imperialism," attached to the most altruistic American action, makes them appear shabby and shameful. The word "peace"—associated with Communist treachery, brutality and tyranny—clothes Communism in garments of hope and beauty. To these trigger words, young people throughout the world are being conditioned to respond.

This campaign of the Communists has been so successful that even the most ardent supporters of Capitalism hesitate to use the word and search for some less offensive synonym. It needs to be constantly taught that Capitalism has produced a standard of economic well-being, and simultaneously sustained individual liberty, to a degree unapproached by any other system. Capitalism is a dynamic system that can adjust to changing conditions, and it is infinitely preferable to the tyranny of regimentation under the dictatorship of a self-proclaimed elite, whether this latter system calls itself "Communism" or some more euphemistic name.

Let us return to our victim undergoing brainwashing. He has reached the point of mental breakdown with fragmentation of mind and memory. By a process of suggestion, the Communists link together the shattered fragments of their victim's mind. Certain memories they carefully retain. Others they deliberately confuse and eliminate. A missionary serving with the China Inland Mission when the Communists took over China underwent the experience of brainwashing. He tells how they convinced him that under every church that he had built, he constructed a storeroom for ammunition for Chiang Kai-shek's soldiers. It was true that he had built a room under each church where he had been. This room was the baptistery for the baptism of adults by immersion. When the Communists had him thoroughly exhausted, depressed, and confused, they filled these rooms with weapons and showed them to him. They had him handle the weapons and ammunition. Later on, they took his finger prints from the ammunition that he had handled in these rooms and used them to convince him that he had built the rooms and filled them with weapons for the use of the forces of Chiang Kai-shek. He remembered building the rooms, and he remembered handling the weapons. By clever suggestion, the Communists were able to weave these scraps of memory together and to convince him of the truth of their accusations. He was then overwhelmed with guilt for his treacherous acts.

After the experience of brainwashing, the victim suffers from severe emotional depression. The excessive elements of this depression are removed in various ways. They allow time to do its healing work. It is possible that they use electric shock treatment. The advantage of shock treatment is that it can remove emotional depression without affecting the ideas associated with the depression. If an individual is convinced that his grandmother left him a million dollars and that his wicked step-sister stole it from him, he is likely to be exceedingly miserable in his delusional state. After shock treatment, he remains convinced that his grandmother left him the million dollars and that his wicked step-sister stole it from him, but can now face this fact with a measure of equanimity. Moreover, shock treatment is followed by amnesia, and there is no memory of the treatment's being received. It could be given privately and the individual would never remember that he had received it.

In time, the victim of brainwashing is brought out and presented in court. He makes his confession. He is observed and interviewed by the reporters. No apparent physical damage is noted, and his confession goes out to the entire world.

It is possible to recover from brainwashing just as recovery is possible in cases of mental collapse induced by the pressures of society. For a cure to be affected, the victim must be removed from the environment containing the pressures that produced the collapse. The missionary who believed himself guilty of building ammunition storerooms in the churches was kept quiet in a dark room, after his release from China, and allowed to talk. As he released his tensions, the real became disassociated from the false, and he returned to a normal mental and spiritual state. Most people do recover, but not all. In any case, the scars of their ordeal remain.

INDOCTRINATION

The term "brainwashing" is not always used to indicate the process described. The word has captured public imagination and is used very loosely. The process of indoctrination by repetition rather than reason is frequently termed brainwashing. The Communists are adept at this also. They tell a lie, make it big, repeat it often, and the majority of people believe them.

This, of course, is a principle which has long been practiced by advertisers. There are some particularly remarkable examples in the field of tobacco advertising. There is little attempt at a reasoned, logical argument. They seek a catchy slogan to repeat over and over again. Some years ago when a certain company was promoting an especially long cigarette, the slogan adopted was, "Screens out irritants but never screens out flavor." The idea apparently was that the length of the cigarette acted as a filter. The question which should arise at once is what happens when the cigarette burns down to the normal size. Yet this obvious lack of logic and common sense apparently made no difference to the effectiveness of the advertising campaign. The slogan was repeated so many times that large numbers of people unquestionably assumed its truth.

Driving back one night from Milwaukee to Chicago, I listened to a remarkable interview on the radio. The man being interviewed was a prosecuting attorney. He was discussing drinking drivers. He was devastating. He said, "Anyone who drinks and drives an automobile is a potential murderer. Anyone who drinks, drives an automobile, and kills is an actual murderer. There is no difference between killing as a result of drunken driving and killing with a gun. Since everybody drives, nobody should drink. One drink lowers your efficiency and increases your reaction time. There is only one place for drinking drivers and that is prison. By God's grace, that's where I intend to put them!"

No sooner had he finished than the announcer's voice was heard: "The foregoing interview was sponsored by a well-known brand of beer." There followed a specious statement that since this beer was the best of all beers, you owed it to yourself and your friends to pick up some of it on the way home and to keep it in the refrigerator as you never know when your friends might drive by and call on you. If you did not have a drink there to welcome them, you were certainly a poor host and no gentleman.

The sponsors of this program were not trying to ruin their business. They doubtless knew very well that the program would do them no harm, for they were well aware that repetition would conquer reason. The listening audience would hear the prosecuting attorney once, and perhaps they would agree with him; but they would hear the beer announcement a hundred times. Reason may reach the conscious mind, while repetition influences the unconscious mind, which is the source of so much human conduct.

The Communists know that if they want something accepted without question, they must say it, say it, and say it again. Therefore, they are repeating day and night by radio, by television, by literature of every type, two simple lies: one is that wherever Communism is in power, the people are prosperous, healthy, happy, and free; the other is that America is vile and evil beyond measure, a land of hunger, malnutrition, depression, exploitation, poverty, and fear, and a desperate threat to the peace of the world. An evidence of this Communist technique is a book which they have published in Australia called *This Is America*. There is not one word in this book that is not quoted directly from the non-Communist American press. Out of the tremendous quantity of material published, the Communists have taken any statement that can help build a picture of a poverty-ridden, oppressed America. All the articles and statements that suggest otherwise, they have ignored completely. The following are some quotations from the book.

> One third of the city's babies, born and unborn, suffer from malnutrition as a result of high prices, the Right Rev. Charles K. Gilbert, Bishop of the Episcopal Diocese of New York, told the Congressional Committee. —New York *World Telegram*, September 25, 1947.

> We feed our hogs better than our children. —Heading on an article in the *American Magazine*, October 1947, by Fred Bailey, Executive Director of National Agricultural Research, Inc.

> Approximately 2,500,000 residents of New York face undernourishment and deficiency diets due to the inflated costs of food. This is the grim, outstanding evidence produced by a four-day hearing on food prices by the eastern sub-committee of a joint Congressional Committee. —Quoted in the *Christian Science Monitor*, September 26, 1947.

> Three fourths of the nation's children suffer from undernourishment, a study of Pennsylvania State College established. —Quoted by *Associated Press*, December 20, 1950.

The Communists do not need to tell lies in order to create the picture they desire. All they need to do is to select from the total picture those things that fit into their pre-conceived pattern. As Alfred Lord Tennyson said:

A lie which is half a truth is ever the blackest of lies,
For a lie that's all a lie can be met with and fought outright,
But a lie that is half a truth is a harder matter to fight.

The Communists are creating a picture of America that is completely false and are projecting this picture into the minds of the people of the world. What America does or does not do makes little difference to this picture. It is easy to say, "Let the facts speak for themselves." Unfortunately facts have a very soft voice, and their message is not heard by those who are not in the immediate environment. The United States-Canadian border is a fact. The absence of military establishments, the frequency and ease of two-way transportation are indisputable facts. They have not been able to contradict for millions of people the constantly reiterated Communist lie that the United States is viciously imperialistic, threatening the peace and integrity of all the people of the world.[2]

In the formation of public opinion, it is not what you do that counts, but what people believe you do. Opinions vary concerning the wisdom of the action of President Eisenhower in sending troops into Little Rock, Arkansas, in September 1958. The fact is indisputable that they were sent to enable African American children to attend school. However, competent observers report that the majority of people in Africa believe that they were sent in to prevent Negro children from attending school. The attitude of these people towards America is formed from their erroneous beliefs, not from the facts. The Communists spare no expenses and make prodigious efforts to print and distribute literature giving a completely false picture of life and character in the United States. The falsity of this picture of America is only surpassed by the picture they present of alleged universal happiness and contentment under Communism.

The difference between life under Communist rule and life in America is well illustrated by the fact that whenever Communism comes to power, in spite of the glory of their promises, the fearful reality proves the magnitude of their deception and people flee by the millions. At every Communist border in the world where there is any possibility of escape, this exodus continues. The United States, on the other hand, is a magnet to her neighbors. Millions of people a year risk their lives not trying to get out, but trying to get in, not to live at the highest standard, but at the lowest standard. Great numbers cross the Rio Grande River and enter illegally from Mexico. Conditions in Mexico are certainly very poor, but this alone would not account for the influx. Conditions in Turkey are far from ideal. Poverty there is rife also. Yet there is no stream of refugees from Turkey into Russia. These facts must be told until they are known in every nook and cranny of the earth. America should mobilize her remarkable skill with the means of communication to achieve this end. The alternative is to become an island of unease in a surrounding sea of hatred.

The phenomenon of brainwashing is one of the manifestations of the true nature of Communism. It is rebellion against God; it is rebellion against the human mind; it is rebellion against the purpose, significance, and value of the individual. The way to defeat it is to defeat the program of Communist expansion. When the door closes behind you in the brainwashing chamber, it will be too late.

FURTHER STUDY

Crichton, Michael. *State of Fear*. New York: HarperCollins Publishers, 2004.

Eakman, Beverly K. *Cloning of the American Mind: Eradicating Morality through Education*. Lafayette, LA: Huntington House Publishers, 1998.

Grabar, Mary. *Indoctrination without Apology: Social Studies Teachers Share Strategies on How to Mold Students*. Owings, MD: America's Survival, 2010.

Hunter, Edward. *Brainwashing: From Pavlov to Powers*. New York: Bookmailer, 1960.

————. *Brainwashing in Red China: The Calculated Destruction of Men's Minds*. New York: Vanguard Press, 1951.

Klein, Aaron and Brenda J. Elliott. *The Manchurian President: Barack Obama's Ties to Communists, Socialists and Other Anti-American Extremists*. Washington DC, WND Books, 2010.

Kupelian, David. *How Evil Works: Understanding and Overcoming the Destructive Forces That Are Transforming America*. New York: Threshold Editions, 2010.

Schwarz, Fred C. *Beating the Unbeatable Foe: One Man's Victory over Communism, Leviathan, and the Last Enemy*. Washington, DC: Regnery Publishing, 1996.

CHAPTER TEN

The Difficult, Devious, and Dangerous Dialectic

by
Fred C. Schwarz

The dialectical philosophy is the most difficult, the least understood, and possibly the most important aspect of Communism. It is this philosophy that directs the apparently unpredictable and constantly changing Communist course.

Most people are very practical. They believe the evidence of their senses. They look for an enemy that is obvious and tangible. They say, "I am interested in the Communists, and concerned by their actions. Tell me who they are and show me where they are and I will know how to act." Or they may say, "I am interested in Communist economic theory, in their military power, and in their subversive organization, but don't talk to me about philosophy. That is too deep for me. Talking about their philosophy only confuses me." Such people are interested in the superficial manifestations of Communist organization, but they are not interested in the philosophic credo from which they draw their motivating forces, their basic strategy, and their confidence in the future. They are reminiscent of dairy farmers who are interested in milk, but not in cows, orchardists who are interested in fruit, but not in trees, or apiarists who are interested in honey, but not in bees. The superficial manifestations of Communism are inseparably related to its underlying philosophic concept.

As I have travelled throughout this country addressing civic clubs, patriotic groups, churches, and schools, I have frequently asked three simple questions. The first is that all those present who have heard of Communism and who know that it exists should raise their hands. All hands are immediately raised. The second request is that all those present who are opposed to Communism and not ashamed to say so should raise their hands. Again all the hands shoot into the air. The vast majority of people readily affirm their opposition to Communism.

The third question I preface by the following remarks:

"Be careful how you answer this question, for if you answer it in the affirmative, I will test you by asking one further question. It will not be a difficult question, but if you cannot answer it, you have no right to answer this question in the affirmative. The third question is: Will those who know what Communism is please raise their hands?" One or two hands creep hesitantly and tentatively into the air. I then say, "Communism has a system of philosophic thought, an interpretation of being, and a book of fundamental rules known as its philosophy. To the founders of Communism, this was the most important feature of their entire program. It underlies, unifies, integrates, and directs the apparently contradictory phenomena of Communist conduct and unites them into a purposeful whole. It is the major subject in every Communist school in the world. From it they derive their definitions of such terms as peace, truth, righteousness, justice, and democracy. If you do not understand something about the philosophy of Communism, you understand little about Communism itself. What is the name of the philosophy of Communism?"

This question elicits a considerable range of answers but seldom the right one. The answer is, of course, Dialectical

The Difficult, Devious, and Dangerous Dialectic

Materialism. The Communists have made no secret of this. They have written it down, they have announced it to the entire world, they teach it in every school that they control. Yet it is a somber fact that many anti-Communists have never even heard the name. Until recently, it was most unusual to find individuals in most groups who could so much as name their philosophy. Even today, the number of those who have any understanding of Dialectical Materialism is very small indeed.

One Sunday afternoon, by a peculiar accumulation of circumstances, I found myself speaking from the Communist platform in the Domain in Sydney, Australia. The Sydney Domain, a lovely park adjacent to the Sydney harbor, is possibly the world's greatest open forum. To this park each Sunday afternoon come all those with a message, real or imaginary, and there they harangue the passing throng. People gather in the thousands. The Communists always have a large, well organized meeting. As I spoke from the Communist platform, I mentioned Dialectical Materialism, whereupon the Communist leader challenged me. "What is Dialectical Materialism?" he asked. I replied, "Dialectical Materialism is the philosophy of Karl Marx that he formulated by taking the dialectic of Hegel, marrying it to the materialism of Feuerbach, abstracting from it the concept of progress in terms of the conflict of contradictory, interacting forces called the Thesis and the Antithesis culminating at a critical nodal point where one overthrows the other, giving rise to the Synthesis, applying it to the history of social development, and deriving therefrom an essentially revolutionary concept of social change." The questioner looked at me with wide-open eyes. I added, "Don't blame me. It is your philosophy, not mine. You are the one who believes it."

If we examine the philosophy of Dialectical Materialism in more detail, we see that there are two elements in it. There is the dialectical portion, and there is the materialist portion.

Let us first consider briefly the materialism. The Communists are materialists. They affirm confidently, arrogantly, and repeatedly that there is nothing in the world except matter in motion. The precise form of their materialism was taken from the German philosopher, Ludwig Feuerbach, a renegade theologian who forsook theism in his book *The Essence of Christianity* and embraced materialism. His basic slogans are "Man is what he eats" and "The world and everything in it is at bottom matter in motion."

The argument between the materialist and the idealist is as old as the history of human thought. Into the two categories, realists and idealists, the philosophers of the world have been divided. The realists or materialists contend that matter is the ultimate reality and that thought is a secondary manifestation of matter. On the other hand, the idealists contend that matter is known only through thought. Take away thought and matter would be non-existent. The basic reality therefore is thought or mind.

The following simple question is quite an effective instrument for distinguishing realists from idealists. The question is: Do the wild waves beating on the shore make a noise when no one is there to hear them? Those who believe that the wild waves do make a noise whether anyone is there or not are realists; those who believe that the wild waves make no noise unless someone is there to hear them are idealists. The realists believe that the noise is in the movement of the water itself; the idealists believe that it is a concept in some mind following the sensory mechanisms of perception. To the idealist, the noise is actually a manifestation of the mind. It is interesting to note that when this question is put to audiences, the realists or materialists usually outnumber the idealists by three to one.

It is to be noted that the word "idealism" bears no moral connotation. Since this word is associated in many minds with moral issues, it is difficult for those minds to divest the term of its moral attributes. In this sense the terms "idealist" and "materialist" refer merely to concepts of ultimate reality.[1]

The Communists have no doubt as to where they stand. They are materialists. As far as Karl Marx was concerned, the idealist philosophers were simply the instruments of clerical reaction, servants of the clergy in their basic purpose of oppressing the working class in the interests of the Capitalist reactionaries. That disciple of Marx, Mao Tsetung, expresses it thusly: "There is nothing in the world except matter in motion."[2]

Most of the materialistic philosophers of Marx's day were mechanists. They believed that materialism allowed no room for individual, volitional action. Their view was that all of nature is automatic, that all actions were compulsory because of the forces that operated on the individual. Every man's destiny was beyond his control. Materialist philosophy thus resulted in nihilism in action and conduct. This philosophy is very well expressed by James Thomson in his poem, "The City of Dreadful Night," where he portrays a man as the helpless plaything of the forces of nature.

If one is born a certain day on earth,
All times and forces tended to that birth,
Not all the world could change or hinder it.

In marrying materialism to the Hegelian dialectic, Marx performed a remarkable operation. He brought into materialism an element of devotion, sacrifice, initiative, and purpose. He enunciated a deterministic, materialistic philosophy, and at the same time, brought into being intense, passionate dedication to make the inevitable come to pass. This is a truly remarkable Marxist achievement. If a group of people are utterly convinced that the sun is going to rise at 5:30 AM, it should be a very difficult task to persuade these same people to awaken an hour early and work like slaves to make the sun do what they know it is going to do. Marx's achievement was somewhat similar to this. He took materialistic philosophy, which taught that the force of history had decreed that certain things must inevitably happen, and married this philosophy to an intense, personal, sacrificial dedication to make these things come to pass. He did this by introducing a mystical element from the Hegelian dialectical.

The German philosopher Georg Wilhelm Friedrich Hegel, was the great philosopher of the early nineteenth century. His were the works and ideas that were discussed by the young intellectuals in the universities of that day. Hegel was an idealist, believing in the primacy of thought or mind rather than of matter. Within the framework of his idealistic philosophy, he developed the dialectic. Hegel's philosophic thought is very difficult to understand. According to Heine, Hegel himself on his deathbed is reported to have said, "Only one man has understood me, and even he has not!" Marx contended that *he* was the one man who understood Hegel and claimed that Hegel did not understand himself. Marx took the dialectical portion of Hegelian philosophy, married it to the materialism of Feuerbach, and produced Dialectical Materialism. Closely associated with him in his work was Frederick Engels, who became his lifelong collaborator, co-worker, supporter, and interpreter. Together Marx and Engels built the philosophic basis of Communist practice.

FEATURES OF THE DIALECTIC

1. PROGRESS
The first feature of the dialectic is the axiom or dogma that progress is inherent in change. The dialectic is a dynamic philosophy. It says that nothing is, that everything is in a state of flux or development. The dialectic would teach, for example, that no man can stand twice on the bank of the

same river, for the second time it is a totally different river. In a similar way, everything is in the process of development and change. Around us is a vast panorama of changing circumstances and conditions. Within the vastness of this change, there is a principle of developing organization; there is movement from lower to higher. Hidden within the diversity and apparent purposelessness of change there is a principle of progress.

The Communists make no attempt to prove that progress is at the heart of change. It is one of their axioms. They accept it by faith. In this sense, it is a pseudo-religious belief.

The word "progressive" has become one of their basic words. The Communist bookstore in Los Angeles is called the "Progressive" Bookstore. The last major political assault the Communists made on the presidency of the United States was through the "Progressive" Party. The Communists in labor unions always refer to themselves either as the "Militants" or the "Progressives."[3]

The Communists apply this principle of progress in change to their own status within society. Liu Shao-chi writes:

>...the question arises: Can Communist society be brought about? Our answer is "yes." About this the whole theory of Marxism-Leninism offers a scientific explanation that leaves no room for doubt. It further explains that as the ultimate result of the class struggle of mankind, such a society will inevitably be brought about.[4]

They are the wave of the future. Their victory is as certain as the rising of the sun because the same material law that causes the sun to rise in the morning has ordained that they shall conquer and rule the world. Of this they have no vestige of doubt.

Since they believe this completely, their convictions are undisturbed by any evidence to the contrary that may appear day by day. They stand above the changing scene of the daily ebb and flow and see the currents and tides of history. The idea that their faith can be shattered by anything they see at present is naïve to the point of imbalance. Just how widespread the ignorance of this is was revealed by many of the reasons advanced in support of Khrushchev's visit to the United States in September, 1959.

An argument frequently put forward was, let us show Khrushchev how the people of America live; let him see their fine homes, their modem automobiles, their open churches. When he sees all this he will be impressed and will realize the error of his previous viewpoint. Such an argument as this displays gross ignorance of Khrushchev's dialectical faith. In the first place, Khrushchev's espionage system is such that he was able to discover the most intimate secrets of American atomic science. To imagine that he needed to come to America to discover how the American people lived, in what kind of houses they lived, and how many cars they had, is utterly infantile. He was equally well aware of the power and preparedness of America's military might. But even if this were not so, even if Khrushchev's tour of America had revealed to him many unsuspected facts about the American way of life, none of these could have changed him fundamentally. For present conditions and circumstances have little authority to him. Khrushchev is a Communist, not because of the present, but because of the future. His life is governed by a vision of the future. The future belongs to the Communists. They will inevitably conquer the world. You do not judge a building by the temporary scaffolding on which its builders walk. You see the vision in the mind of the architect.

An analogy may be drawn from the production of steel. The manufacturer promises a beautiful burnished steel. In order to obtain this end product, the metal must go through certain dirty, unattractive stages. At one stage it is treated in the searing, flaming heat of the furnace. Were you to go to the manufacturer at this particular stage and say, "You have not kept your word. This is not steel. It's merely flame and heat. I can't use this," he would look at you in utter amazement.

When the Communists listen to our arguments based on present circumstances and conditions, they must certainly be amazed, for their whole program rests on the future. Khrushchev was well aware of America's present wealth and power. He is reported as having said, "Anyone who does not know that America is rich and strong is unbelievably stupid." This realization merely confirms his faith in the greater glory of the future Communist State.

It is this future in which he is interested and in which he firmly believes. In the last analysis, he believes in the inevitable triumph of Communism, not because of the evidence, but because of his faith in the dialectic. As a true believer, he has lived and labored during forty years of sacrifice, danger, and brutality.

2. THE DIALECTICAL NATURE OF PROGRESS

The second feature of the dialectic is the nature of progress. Dialectical progress takes place in a certain pattern. The Communist slogan is, "Nature acts dialectically." Wishing to advance dialectically in a room full of people, I do not walk through the aisle and straight toward my goal. Nor do I move slowly through the crowd shaking hands with friends and acquaintances, discussing points of interest, gradually nearing the objective. The dialectical pathway is different. It consists of a resolute forward advance followed by an abrupt turn and retreat. Having retreated a distance, there is another turn and advance. Through a series of forward-backward steps, the goal is approached. To advance thus is to advance dialectically.

The Communist goal is fixed and changeless, but their direction of advance reverses itself from time to time. They approach their goal by going directly away from it a considerable portion of the time. Lenin wrote the textbook, *One Step Forward, Two Steps Back.* Chinese Communist schoolchildren are taught to do the dialectical march, taking three steps forward and two steps back. If we judge where the Communists are going by the direction in which they are moving, we will obviously be deceived.

The Communist method of advance may be likened to the hammering of a nail. It is a very foolish person who brings the hammer down with a crashing, resounding blow and then keeps pushing. When the first blow has spent itself, back must go the hammer in preparation for the next blow. A person seeing the reverse movement of the hammer as an isolated act in time, and not understanding the process of which this was a part, might find it difficult to believe that this hammer was driving in the nail. When he sees the backward swing as a portion of a complete process, he realizes that the withdrawal is as important as the downward thrust to the realization of the objective.

For those not trained in dialectical thinking, it is very difficult to understand that the Communists have a fixed and changeless goal, but that their method of approach reverses itself all the time. The tendency is to judge where they are going by the direction in which they are moving. Many colleges taught, for example, that Communism as practiced in Russia by Lenin and Stalin was a departure from Marx. They claimed that Marx's teaching had many good features about it, but that Lenin and Stalin put into practice something entirely different. Superficially the argument is reasonable. Take, for example, Marx's teaching concerning marriage and what is practiced in Russia with regard to marriage. Marx taught the abolition of marriage. *The Communist Manifesto* says:

> On what foundation is the present family, the bourgeois family, based? On capital, on private gain. In its completely developed form this family exists only among the bourgeoisie. But this state of things finds its complement in the practical absence of the family

among the proletarians, and in public prostitution. The bourgeois family will vanish as a matter of course when its complement vanishes, and both will vanish with the vanishing of capital.[5]

In the light of this teaching, it might be expected that in Russia they would be weakening the family prior to its abolition. The truth is that they are presently strengthening the family. Divorce is discouraged; puritanical morals are encouraged; rewards are offered to those who have large families. They are strengthening the family in every way. Logically it would seem that since they are strengthening the family in Russia, they must have forsaken Marxism. The Communists, however, think and act dialectically. They realize that it is dialectical to approach their goal by going directly away from it. Their ultimate goal is to abolish the family. But they cannot abolish the family until they have changed human nature; they cannot change human nature until they completely control the environment that generates human nature; they cannot totally control the environment until they have conquered the world and destroyed the present environment; and they cannot conquer the world unless they develop a more courageous, more patriotic, more nationalistic people than their enemy. They have found by experience that they cannot develop a strong, nationalistic, patriotic people without encouraging a firm family base. They must therefore strengthen the family to develop the patriotism and courage of the people to increase the power of the Communist State so that they may conquer the world, establish a Communist dictatorship, and regenerate mankind. They will then abolish the family. By strengthening the family, they are dialectically abolishing it. There is no inconsistency here. They are applying dynamic Marxism.

The same thing applies in the realm of religion. The ultimate goal of Communism is the abolition of all religion. Lenin says, "Atheism is a natural and inseparable portion of

Marxism, of the theory and practice of scientific socialism. Our propaganda necessarily includes propaganda for atheism." It would be logical, therefore, to expect the persecution of religion wherever Communism is in power. In many places this is happening, but not in all. In some states under Communist rule, religion is being patronized and encouraged.

Religion constitutes a force that moves to action a certain segment of the community. Communism utilizes existing forces. Religion, therefore, must be utilized to advance the final goal of Communism, which is world conquest, and thus contribute to its own destruction.

There are various ways in which religion may be used. They may instruct various members of the Party to join various religious faiths; for while it is quite impossible for a Christian to be a Communist, there is no inconsistency whatever in a Communist's professing Christianity to aid the triumph of Communism. As Khrushchev said to the French Socialists, "Some of our comrades are atheists in the Party and believers at home." One Communist, then, may be instructed to join the Catholic Church. He is told to be baptized, to believe everything he has to believe to be the very finest Catholic imaginable and to secure influence in Catholic organizations. He will then have opportunity to influence Catholic organizations in a program which may appear to be completely unrelated to Communism but which may be important to their dialectical advance. Similarly, Communists are told to join various Protestant churches. Again they are to be fervently Protestant, orthodox to the core, ardent in spirit, and industrious in the program of that church. At the appropriate time, they too will be able to influence various church members and organizations for the Communist cause. Since to the Communists none of these religious systems has any ultimate validity, but all of them constitute social forces which exist at present, there is nothing inconsistent in an atheistic Communist being an apparently fervent religious believer in the interests of the final Communist objective.

An Australian Episcopal delegation to Communist China found well-filled churches and heard good sermons from apparently well-paid and contented preachers. Many reported that Christianity was flourishing in China. This report given by anti-Communists who were unaware of the Communist dialectic greatly helped the Communist cause. The Communist program for the church is threefold: to enslave, to utilize, and finally to destroy. The members of the delegation observed the phase of utilization. The initial stage of enslavement was brought about by extreme persecution. Genuine church leaders who were devoted to Christ were arrested, brainwashed, tried, and destroyed. The church buildings became halls in which accusation meetings were held rather than houses for the worship of God. When the church was thoroughly cowed and leaderless, a dialectical reverse took place and the persecution suddenly ceased.

The Communists united all the non-Catholic churches into one organization which they called the Three Self Movement.[6] They appointed a pro-Communist leader to formulate the policy of this organization; they appointed a Communist Commissar of Religion; and they paid the salaries of the preachers. Communist pressure was exerted to force everyone registered as a Christian to attend church. The preachers were obliged to meet twice a week with the godless Commissar of Religion to get the political line that they must proclaim on the following Sunday.

One of the goals of the Three Self Movement is the liberation of Formosa [i.e., Taiwan]. A certain Sunday could be designated "Liberate Formosa Sunday." The preachers, meeting with the political commissar, would be given stories of the dreadful American persecution of their Chinese brethren in Formosa. They hear the tear-drenched pleas of the Formosan people for their Chinese Communist brethren to come and liberate them. They are instructed to pass on this information to their congregations and to offer prayers for the liberation of Formosa. The preachers have no way of knowing that these stories are not true. They live in a closed environment. All media of information are controlled by the Communist Party. Provided they obey instructions and follow the right political line, they may preach what they like. Visitors to China, therefore, see filled churches and hear good sermons by preachers who are well-paid and who are certainly not going to tell them anything that might bring back the previous period of persecution. If they are uninformed and unaware of the subtleties of the Communist dialectic, they will report that Christianity is flourishing in China.

The dialectic gives the Communists complete moral maneuverability. They may wear any garments. They may accept any faith. They may work to advance the self-interest of any nationalist or economic grouping. Their strategic mobility is effective indeed. Christians are prevented from following many courses of action by certain absolute standards. A Christian may not, for example, accept the Muslim faith, rise in the Muslim ranks, and then use his position to subvert Muslim customs and introduce Christianity. The Communists, however, have no absolutes. Their dialectical relativity gives them a total strategic mobility. They may adopt the coloring, the shape, the ideology, the morality, or the religious faith of any group. They become all things to all men that by all means they may enslave all.

3. CONFLICT

The third feature of the dialectic is the role of conflict in the process of change. According to the dialectic, the driving force in any situation is the conflict of two opposing forces. There is the established force called the thesis and there is the conflicting force called the antithesis. The conflict between these two forces is the dynamic of progress.

In dialectical language, everything is interpenetrated by its opposite. Nothing exists in isolation. You cannot have up without down; you cannot have plus without minus; you cannot have beauty without ugliness; you cannot have life without death. To every action there is an equal but opposite reaction. Everything exists in a state of conflict with its opposite. This conflict is the dynamic of being.

Initially this conflict gives a period of slow, relatively stable progress, a period of gradual change. This slow change never continues indefinitely. As change continues, a critical point is reached. At this point, certain things happen. Slow, gradual change gives way to rapid, fundamental change. In dialectical terminology, the antithesis negates the thesis; there is a transformation of quantity into quality and the emergence of a totally new direction of progress known as the synthesis. The synthesis now becomes the new thesis. The new thesis generates a new antithesis, and the new conflict between thesis and antithesis becomes the dynamic of the next stage of progress. Again a critical nodal point is reached. The new antithesis negates the new thesis and there is another transformation of quantity into quality. This is termed the Negation of the Negation and results in the emergence of a direction of progress parallel to the original one, but different in quantity and quality.

The Communists believe that this dialectical conflict or contradiction is universal in being. Mao Tse-tung writes in the introduction to his textbook on dialectics entitled *On Contradiction*, "The law of contradiction in things, that is, the law of the unity of opposites, is the most basic law in materialist dialectics."[7] Lenin said, "In its proper meaning, dialectics is the study of the contradiction within the very essence of things."[8]

The dialectic is very valuable to the Communists. It can be used to express, in pseudo-logical form, a conclusion empirically reached. It is a very valuable tool for deceiving the intellectuals, and clothing with pseudo-logic, the edicts of the top Communist authority.

It was from the dialectic that Marx derived the doctrine of the inevitability of revolution as the climax of the class war. Surveying Capitalist society he said that the dynamic of Capitalism was a perfect illustration of the dialectic. Within Capitalism there are two conflicting forces: the bourgeoisie, consisting of the Capitalists who own the means of production and the proletariat consisting of the workers in industry who labor for wages. Between these two forces there is a state of absolute, truce-less conflict. The owners of the means of production want profit, while those who work for them want higher wages. If wages go up, profits go down. If profits go up, wages go down. Thus, there is a fundamental conflict between these two groups, which Marx called "class war." According to the dialectic, this state of conflict between Capital and Labor gives a period of slow, gradual change, but inevitably, a critical point is reached. At this point, the slow, gradual nature of change disappears. It becomes rapid and violent. Revolution breaks out. Capitalist society is negated. There is a transformation of quantity into quality and the emergence of a new synthesis called Socialism.

The Communists are proudly revolutionary in theory and practice. The term "reformist" is to them a synonym for one who is ignorant of, and treacherous to, historic reality. A reformist is so ignorant that he believes that fundamental changes in society can come about by slow, gradual means. The Communists are convinced that this cannot be, for they believe that history and nature declare that change must be wrought by revolution. To the Communist, the revolution is the golden experience of the future towards which they look with longing. As the bride looks forward to the day of her adorning, as the expectant mother looks forward to the day of her deliverance, so, with flashing eye and bated breath,

The Difficult, Devious, and Dangerous Dialectic

with leaping pulse and exultant heart, the true Communist looks forward to the coming, glorious day of the revolution.

Communist belief in the inevitability of revolution is derived from the dialectic. Unless we understand the dialectic, we will be deceived on every hand. Unless we understand the dialectic, we cannot intelligently counteract Communism. When we do understand it, we are in a position to anticipate their actions and to take defense against them.

The most serious accusation that can be made against a Communist theorist is that he does not understand dialectics. With this accusation, Stalin helped to destroy Bukharin. In Russia in 1928–1929, there developed what Stalin termed the "Right Deviation" led by Bukharin. Bukharin was a brilliant Communist intellectual. Before the revolution, he had been a theorist comparable with Lenin himself. After the revolution, he occupied many important posts culminating in the leadership of the Communist International known as the Comintern. He was the author of *The ABC of Communism*, and most authorities agree that he was the principal framer of "The Stalinist Constitution." His prestige and popularity among Communists were tremendous. It was thought by most people that he would emerge supreme in the struggle for power in 1928–1929. When the climax of the struggle was reached, however, it was Stalin who had the votes. Finally Bukharin received the reward Stalin gave to most of his old comrades—a bullet in the back of the head.

Stalin had to find some justification for the ideological destruction of Bukharin. In the peculiar fashion of Communist theoretical debate, some quotation had to be found in the works of Marx, Engels, or Lenin that could be used against Bukharin. Stalin found his justification in a statement by Lenin. Stalin writes:

Reference is made to a letter in which Comrade Lenin speaks of Bukharin as a theoretician. Let us read the letter:

"Of the younger members of the Central Committee," says Lenin, "I should like to say a few words about Bukharin and Pyatakov. In my opinion, they are the most outstanding people (of the youngest forces), and regarding them the following should be borne in mind: Bukharin is not only a very valuable and important theoretician in our Party, he is also legitimately regarded as the favorite of the whole Party; *but it is very doubtful whether his theoretical views can be classed as fully Marxian, for there is something scholastic in him (he has never studied, and, I think he has never fully understood dialectics).*"[9]

Thus, he is a theoretician without dialectics. A scholastic theoretician. A theoretician about whom it was said: "It is very doubtful whether his theoretical views can be classed as fully Marxian." This is how Lenin characterized Bukharin's theoretical complexion.

You can well understand, comrades that such a theoretician has still much to learn. And, if Bukharin understood that he is not yet a full-fledged theoretician, that he still has much to learn, that he is a theoretician who has not yet assimilated dialectics—and dialectics is the soul of Marxism.[10]

Upon this statement of Lenin, Stalin based his condemnation of Bukharin. Since Bukharin did not understand dialectics, he was second rate and could safely be destroyed.

The proof that Bukharin was not dialectical was to be found, according to Stalin, in his attitude towards the State. Communist theory taught that in the establishment of Communism, certain steps were necessary. A revolutionary situation had to be created, a violent revolution had to take place, and the bourgeois State had to be destroyed. The Communists had then to establish the dictatorship of the proletariat and to eliminate the residue of the bourgeoisie. When they had eliminated all possible counter-revolutionary elements of the old regime, the dictatorship could become less rigid and more benign and begin to wither away. With the change of human nature, the dictatorship would become unnecessary and Socialism would turn into Communism.

The Difficult, Devious, and Dangerous Dialectic

Bukharin wanted to know why events in Russia were not following this pattern. He contended that in the eleven years since the revolution, they had consolidated their power, that they had liquidated all remaining members of the bourgeoisie,[11] and that it was time that the powers of the dictatorship became a little less centralized and showed some signs of beginning to wither.

Stalin seized upon these views of Bukharin's as proof that Lenin had been right, that Bukharin was a scholastic who did not understand dialectics. Bukharin thought that the State was not withering away because it was growing stronger whereas, according to Stalin, the fact that the State was growing stronger was the dialectical proof that it was withering away. Contradiction is the core of dialectics, and dialectics is the heart of Marxism. When a baby is born, it immediately begins to wither, but the process of withering demands growth to maximum strength. The growth in strength of the Communist dictatorship was dialectical proof that it was "withering away."

Communist theory contains some strange dialectical anomalies. It teaches that Capitalism must change into Socialism by a "revolutionary" or dialectical process. Socialism will then evolve into Communism by a slow, non-violent, non-dialectical development. I have asked numerous Communist theorists the following question: "If Capitalism MUST change into Socialism by a dialectical process, why MUST Socialism change into Communism by a non-dialectical process?" I have always been referred to some comrade of higher theoretical statue. I am still seeking the Communist theorist who can provide the answer.

The difficult, devious, and dangerous dialectic became the tool with which Stalin justified the murder of millions. Unless we understand it, it is probable that it may be used historically to justify the demise of all free peoples.

FURTHER STUDY

Noebel, David A. *Understanding the Times: The Collision of Today's Competing Worldviews*. Revised 2nd Ed. Manitou Springs, CO: Summit Press, 2006.

Wetter, Gustav A. *Dialectical Materialism: A Historical and Systematic Survey of Philosophy in the Soviet Union*. Westport, CT: Greenwood Press, 1977.

CHAPTER ELEVEN

Program for Survival

by
Fred C. Schwarz

It is apparent that on the record to date [1960], anti-Communist programs have completely failed to halt Communism. The Communists are riding high. Their program is in top gear. They are going from strength to strength.

Many groups think that they are successfully fighting Communism, but the record does not support their opinion. When giving evidence before the House Un-American Activities Committee in 1956, I was asked if I could name any unified, world-wide organization which was successfully fighting Communism. I replied that I could not do so. The reply has drawn more criticism than any other statement I made in that testimony. A number of groups have written in to rectify my ignorance on that point and to tell me about their own organization that is successfully combating Communism. No matter what the group, the measure of their success is limited indeed. The Communist program for world conquest continues to make phenomenal gains.

The fact is that progress is a relative thing. Many anti-Communist groups are moving in the right direction, but their progress up to the present time has been rather insubstantial.

The degree of their success is somewhat similar to that of the missionary priest who had been working on a cannibal island. When asked what sort of success he was having, he replied, "Well, we are certainly making progress! Now the natives will eat only fishermen on Fridays." He was, perhaps, making progress, but it must be admitted that he had a long way to go.

For any program to be effective, there are three essential elements: motivation, knowledge, and organization. Without adequate motivation, knowledge, and organization, any program must fail.

MOTIVATION

If people are to perform unpleasant tasks sacrificially and on a continuing basis, they must have a reason for doing so. An effective program against Communism demands time, money, energy, and sacrifice. The first question to be considered is what motivating forces are available. What are the things which move people to action?

It is regrettably true that most people are moved most effectively by immediate selfish interest. In most cases, self-interest dominates all other considerations. If a patriot wishes to arrange for an anti-Communist speaker to address a civic club or some corresponding group, there are two approaches he may use. He may approach the program chairman with arguments such as these: "This man has a message your club should hear, a message that is vital to their businesses, to their homes, to their families, and to their very lives. It is your duty to have him bring them this message." Such an approach is likely to meet with little success. On the other hand, he may approach the program chairman and say, "Here is a good, entertaining, stirring speaker. Wherever he has spoken before, he has had a wonderful reception. He will really give you a good program." An approach like this is nearly always successful because it appeals to the self-interest of the program chairman. He wants to have people come up and pat him on the back for securing a good speaker.

This is true not only of civic clubs, but of all groups. Churches, for example, have their own program, and they are mainly concerned with the success of that program. You may approach a pastor with the argument that here is a message that is absolutely vital to his people. You may point out to him that Communism has conquered one billion people, far more than the Christian church has reached after its entire history; that Communism is rapidly closing the mission fields of the world; that Communism is the enemy of God, and that these things should be told to the people. Such an approach is not usually successful. You may, on the other hand, point out to the pastor that here is a man whom people like to hear and that if he holds a meeting in this church, he will attract into the church many people who do not normally attend. This is a very powerful argument and one which is apt to be successful.

Motivating forces must be found that are so powerful that they can overwhelm the lethargy, the immediate self-interest, the greed, and the routine that dominate so many lives. Life is a daily competition between conflicting interests for most intelligent and effective individuals. They must select from a host of matters clamoring for their attention: those that appear to be the most urgent, the most entertaining, or offer the greatest prospect of reward. The struggle against Communism must successfully compete with other matters clamoring for attention.

It would seem that a sufficient motivation would be found in the fact that a billion people under Communist control are being prepared to encompass the conquest and destruction of the Free World. The truth is, however, that generally speaking, an immediate motive of appetite or personal advantage will triumph over the long-range, distant motivation of danger. To most people, Communism is still a long way off. It is causing a lot of trouble in many parts of the world, but it does not present, as far as they can see, a real, immediate threat to themselves or to their families.

A primary necessity, then, is an honest acknowledgment of the gravity of the danger. There must be a willingness to face the truth, avoiding the temptation to gloss over the dangers, or to take refuge in vain imaginations and pious phraseologies. The Communist enemy must not be sold short. Nothing is to be gained by a denial of his material assets, his strategic mobility, and his inflexible determination to conquer.

There is certainly the danger that a true understanding of the perilous situation may lead some to the abyss of despair. The temptation is to shrug the shoulders and to declare that the task is hopeless. An alternative attitude is to search for some vast organization that can meet the danger. Responsibility is laid at the door of the government, the State Department, the military forces, or the churches. It is a rare individual who asks, "What can I do to avert disaster?"

Two students came up to me after I had spoken at a college in the Midwest. One of them was burning with anger. "How is it possible that our elected officials can be so ignorant?" he wanted to know. "It's their necks that are at stake! Why don't they do something?" I endeavored to redirect his attention from what the government should be doing to what he should be doing, but in vain. He was too filled with concern and anger against the government for its failure.

The second student reacted very differently. He said, "Let's forget about the government and look at ourselves! I feel ashamed to think of the little I have done. I don't know just what I can do, but I am going to try to find out. I want to read and study and discover what I can do before I start worrying too much about somebody else." This is the kind of attitude that is needed. Each person must face his personal responsibility before he starts to criticize others.

Program for Survival

When faced with this challenge, the average person raises the objection that the power of the individual is very limited. From one point of view, that is true; but from another point of view, what can be accomplished by individuals is unbelievable. Most of my time is spent trying to inform people and to arouse them to the Communist threat. However, even if I were to speak to a thousand people every night and could convince the thousand, it would take me five hundred years to speak to everybody now living in the United States, and I would go behind at the rate of two and a half million a year due to the continuing population increase. If, on the other hand, I were to speak to one person a week and could convince, inform, and instruct that person, and if we each convinced, informed, and instructed another person the following week, and the four of us enlisted another the following week, by this process everyone in the world could be reached in less than twelve months.

The power of individuals is limitless. The time has come for people to cease looking for great organizations afar off and to begin looking for things that can be done close at home. Every man who invites a friend into his home, gives him literature to read, and informs him of the danger is helping to thwart the Communist program. The powers of multiplication are limitless. The principle on which to work is the recruitment of individuals one by one on a basis of knowledge, understanding, and motivated service.

A stirring address at a mass meeting may stimulate the emotions and provoke great enthusiasm. Such a response is like a tropical thunderstorm that creates a flash flood rather than consistently soaking the thirsty soil needs. The problem is to convert temporary emotional enthusiasm into sacrificial study and dedicated work. This is a difficult task and one that cannot be done on a mass basis.

A short time ago, I spoke to the legislature of one of the New England states. It was a magnificent meeting. My coming had been well prepared. The governor escorted me into the chamber. The chamber was packed and the galleries were filled. As I spoke, the legislators listened most attentively. When I had finished, they arose as one man in ecstatic, tumultuous, prolonged applause. The governor shook my hand. The legislators crowded around. One of them said, with the sparkle of a tear in his eye, "That was an emotional experience. I suffered with you." It was truly a great meeting.

That same evening, after a mass rally in a nearby city where I had spoken, the Attorney-General of the state came up to me and said, "I was dying to have you tell the people that this morning the legislature was shattered to its foundations, and that this afternoon, they went back to the real business of their existence: whether to have greyhound or horse racing in this state."

Many find it appalling that a situation of such gravity should be treated so casually. And yet this happens with ninety-nine out of every hundred who hear the message. This is the reality within which we must work. People will never be enlisted on a mass basis. They must be enlisted and trained one by one. If that is done, the powers of multiplication are miraculous.

The question of motivation is of basic importance in the struggle against Communism. It is not only a questioning of the forces that will motivate people in the United States, but a question of the forces that will move people in South America, Japan, Arabia, and India. What motives are adequate to make the people in these areas stand firm against the deceptive allurements of Communism? Despite its vital importance, this question of motivation has received very little attention.

I had occasion to address the Texas Legislature and received the warm response so characteristic of the generous people of that state. After the address, one of the legislators came up to me and said, "India's the trouble! We must stop them from getting India!" He thought for a moment, and suddenly the answer came. It was the legislator's answer to all problems. He said, "I've got it! We must spend a lot more money!"

"Let's think about that a moment," I replied. "You spent a lot of money in Iraq and Bolivia, didn't you? What did your money achieve in these countries? In Iraq, it provided the weapons with which the pro-Communists destroyed their enemies. In Bolivia, the American embassy personnel had to flee in shame from raging, Communist-led mobs. Your money does not seem to have done much good there, does it?"

All the money in the world is useless without dedicated personnel through whom it can be channeled. The great need is for dedicated, motivated personnel.

There are various motivations effective within a free society. A primary one is the profit motive. In its proper environment, this has been very effective. It has produced abundance and has improved the material wellbeing of millions of people. There are certain spheres, however, in which it is quite inadequate as a motivating force. It certainly will not stir to selfless devotion the student-intellectuals who are attracted to Communism. The appeal to them must be much more idealistic.

The problem of the Communist appeal to the student-intellectual is one that money alone cannot solve. It is quite obvious that should a student rise in a university in Central or South America and say, "I'm opposed to Communism because it is against the interests of American big business," or even, "I'm against Communism because it will prevent my making a personal fortune," he would be scorned by a majority of his fellows. Reasons given for opposing Communism must be meaningful to the people concerned. People are needed who will oppose Communism in terms of an ideology that will command respect from the other students to whom they are speaking.

Such ideological forces are numerous. Forces that operate widely are religion, nationalism, morality, and love of family, as well as the desire to improve general economic well-being.

The great paradox is that people with a rich spiritual culture appear unaware of the motivating strength of spiritual forces and overwhelmingly convinced of the dominant power of the materialist motivation of improvement in economic conditions. On the other hand, the Communists boast of being complete materialists. They affirm there is nothing in the entire world but matter in motion. Nevertheless, they have shown a deep appreciation of the multiplicity of forces that lead groups of people to action and have used these forces with great skill. The appeal of economic betterment has been by no means the only motive utilized by Communism. In actuality, they have made far more effective use of the appeal of nationalism.

The strange situation has developed in which the materialistic Communists are conquering the world with idealistic promises, while the professedly idealistic Free World is endeavoring to combat them with material gifts. An idea widely accepted by leading Americans is that Communism will not appeal to people with a degree of economic security. The policy adopted to combat Communism, therefore, is to improve the economic conditions of those who are still outside the Communist fold.

A program to combat Communism that rests upon such an economic foundation is doomed. To feed the hungry and the poor is a Christian act. To assume that as a result of being fed, clothed, and housed they will automatically think the right thoughts and feel the right emotions is Marxism, not Christianity. A well-fed Communist is just as dangerous as a hungry one. In fact, he is likely to be more efficient.

There are things more important to many people even than life itself. The devout Hindu will feed his sacred cow while he starves to death. The devout Muslim will willingly die for Islam. There was a day when it was considered the normal thing for Christians to die for their faith. Powerful motivations indeed reside in religious faith.

Communism is the mortal enemy of these idealistic forces. It is the enemy of all religion. It will destroy the national integrity of every country. It will finally abolish home, family, and all moral codes. Here is a great unexplored pool of motivating forces for the struggle against Communism.

What must be realized is that government as practiced in America has little access to these deep motivating forces. Constitutional government is limited government. There is strict separation of church and state. The government cannot directly mobilize a specific religious group in any land and utilize its motivating religious self-interest to thwart Communism. They would appear to be favoring one religious group as against another. Thus, the role of the government in the struggle against Communism is limited. Individuals and groups of individuals can and must do what the government cannot do. The urgent need is to discover individuals and groups in all countries with motives that will lead them to effective service against Communism and to provide them with the knowledge and the tools of communication to make their work effective.

Students educated in the universities of the free countries have been among the most effective agents of Communism. The Communists have always realized the potential of such students and have concentrated upon recruiting them, training them, and providing them with what they needed to serve Communism effectively in their own lands. For a number of years, it was almost routine for Australian Rhodes scholars who went to study in England, to return to Australia as dedicated Communists. Fortunately this tendency has eased off in recent years, but the Communist attempt to recruit the lonely foreign student continues and is all too frequently crowned with success.

After I had spoken at a Midwestern university, I was somewhat startled when an exchange student from Afghanistan publicly and unashamedly extolled the virtues of Communism. His mentor was an American girl who sat by his side. He finished with the ringing assertion, "Communism is science. You said so yourself. The Communists say that any advance in science helps them. You must therefore acknowledge Communism or repudiate science."

I replied, "Arson is fire. I acknowledge it. Everyone knows it. I must therefore acknowledge arson and become an arsonist or repudiate fire to cook my meals and heat my home. Is that what you are trying to say?"

It is not enough to train students in technical science in American universities. They must be transformed into devotees of freedom. This can be done as they are the recipients, not only of knowledge, but of friendship and love. The student in a foreign land is often homesick and heart sore. The Communists provide not merely Marxist-Leninist ideology but also hospitality, companionship, and social life. They make this lonely student feel they are interested in him as an individual, that he is important. When they have won him to Communism, they equip him with organizing skills and the necessary tools to serve Communism in his homeland.

We can and we must do likewise, not for Communist slavery, but for Christian liberty. This can be done. An illustration is found in the story of an exchange student from India whom I met in Seattle. He had just completed his degree as Doctor of Philosophy at the University of Washington. He was a handsome young Indian, a splendid student, and devoted to the principles of individual liberty. He was an evangelical Christian. Upon completing his degree, he was offered a job with the United Nations. He could have lived like an American gentleman, but he chose to return to his home in Kerala, India.

Shortly before his return, Kerala had become the first Indian state to elect a Communist government. It might have been expected that Kerala, the best educated and the most Christian of the Indian states, would have been the last state to elect a Communist government to power. The fact is, however, that the majority of the Christians voted Communist because of their ignorance of the true nature of Communism and the deceptive but glowing Communist promises.

He understood the nature and program of Communism. He determined to do what he could to inform his countrymen. Since the Communist government in Kerala was merely a state government that had to operate under the eye of the federal government and within the framework of the Indian constitution, the Christians still had their basic liberties. The Christian group to which he belonged began to publish a Christian magazine called *The Light of the World*. He and his helpers took the finest anti-Communist literature, translated it into the language of the people, and circulated it in the very face of Communist terror. Their basic motivation was their informed Christian faith.

Some months later, I received a letter saying, "Do we really mean business? You and I know that the conquest of India is a step in the encirclement and surrender of America. The Communists are not conquering India with guns, bombs, and missiles, but with promises, photographs, magazines, and newspapers. In Kerala we have a unique opportunity. The Communists will have to run for re-election. When this time comes, they can be expelled without violence if the people can be told the truth. The tragedy is that we do not have the means to tell the people the truth. The Communists have many daily newspapers and large numbers of magazines. Can you help us to get a daily newspaper dedicated to truth, democracy, and freedom and resting on a Christian foundation?" In reply to my question about costs, he said that it would take $50,000.

Raising such a sum of money posed something of a problem. I sought help from one of the very large foundations in New York. I had been told that the members of this foundation were interested in India. The officials were courteous and friendly. They listened with great interest to the program and commended it highly. Then they said, "Magnificent as the project is, much as we commend it, we cannot help you because you are Christian. We cannot get mixed up in religion in India."

I tried to argue with them. "Can't you see what you are doing? You have told me yourselves that you have difficulty securing anyone to go to India representing your group unless you increase his salary by twenty-five percent. When that individual with his increased salary gets to India, what does he do? Does he go out into the villages where the temperature may be 120 degrees in the summer, where the drinking water may be filled with dysentery, bacilli, and amoebae? Or does he sit in an air-conditioned room at some hotel and write reports?

Each year the Communists appoint thousands of full-time agents, primarily recruited from students who are motivated, dedicated, and thoroughly indoctrinated with Communism. They equip them with beautiful literature and send them around the villages to deceive the people by offering them heaven on earth. We do not have thousands, but we do have some hundreds who have a motive to sacrifice in the fight against Communism. Communism is the enemy of their God, their Christ, and their freedom. Because of this, they are willing to go to their people and warn them of the dangers of Communism. You may not approve of their motive, but surely you approve of what they are doing. Yet you are saying, 'We cannot help them because they are Christian.

We cannot help them because they have a motive. Take away their motive so that they won't do it, and then maybe we can help them to do what they won't do.'"

Despite this discouraging response, we determined to accept the challenge and help our Indian Christian friends in their struggle, which is also our struggle. The first edition of this paper was published in August 1959.

Shortly before the publication of this first edition, crisis hour arrived in Kerala. The Communist government of Kerala was expelled by the central government, and elections were scheduled to take place within six months. The newly born newspaper was thus faced with tremendous responsibility and opportunity. This came about because a group possessed of motivation and knowledge, received the material aid needed to be effective. Within a free society, motivations are multiple and may even appear contradictory. They must be utilized and not destroyed.

My personal motivation is twofold. In the first place I have a wife and family whom I love very dearly. The Communists consider them diseased social animals. At present rates of progress, Communism will have conquered the world within a generation, and as members of the residual diseased bourgeois class, my wife and family will become historically redundant with obvious ugly implications.

In the second place, I have a Christian faith. I believe in God and His love, Christ and His redemption, and the great commission to go into all the world and preach the gospel. Communism is the enemy of God and of Christ and His gospel. These two facts have motivated me to do everything within my power to stay the advance of Communism.

Others share this motivation. A brilliant orthopedic surgeon was faced with the facts about Communism. He said to me, "I wake up every morning and I see one billion people encircling us for our conquest and our destruction. I don't like it, so I assume that it cannot be so and try to put it out of my mind. I have been trained to examine evidence and face facts, and the evidence keeps returning to haunt me. I examine it and I cannot escape It. I then examine my own life. I look at my wife and children and I say, 'What am I doing to preserve their future?' Certainly I am building a good surgical practice, acquiring a good name, getting a good bank balance, but what will that matter if the Communists take over? The only thing that is important is stopping the Communists, and I am not doing anything to do that. I don't know what to do but I intend to find out and when I do find out, I don't care what it costs. By God's grace, I'll do it." He is ready to leave home, country, and economic security to do his duty to his home and country.

If the facts about the Communist advance are true, his attitude is not merely praiseworthy, it is perfectly reasonable and intelligent. The trouble is that most people simply do not believe these facts. They think they do, but actually they do not. If they were convinced, they would be prepared to pay any price and spend any amount of time and money to try and avert the threat. Until our actions match our professed beliefs, onlookers can be forgiven for denying our sincerity and despising our hypocrisy.

KNOWLEDGE

The finest motivation is impotent without adequate knowledge. For generations mothers have longed to be able to protect their children from the scourge of poliomyelitis, but they could not do it because they did not know how. Only out of knowledge acquired from continuing study has a program to combat it emerged. It is possible to hate Communism fervently and simultaneously to serve it faithfully and well. Those who spread poliomyelitis hated it, but that did not prevent their disseminating it. They did not even know they were spreading it. The same kind of thing is happening with

Communism. It is being spread far and wide by people who do not know what they are doing.

When people are found who are motivated and concerned, they must be given knowledge. One way in which this may be done is through literature. The literature on the subject of Communism is extensive. It must be studied. Invaluable training can be gained in study circles where discussion aids in true understanding. There is no substitute for specific knowledge.

Communism should be taught in the schools, but it should be taught with a moral directive. It should not be taught as an alternative economic philosophy, but as a system of tyranny. The object of the teaching should be to protect the students against the deceptive subtleties of Communist dialectics and to promote within them a greater devotion to freedom. It should be taught as a medical school teaches cancer or tuberculosis—as an aid to its elimination.

Teaching that merely compares and contrasts certain features of Capitalist and Communist economics is dangerous indeed. In a free society, the students continuously enjoy the privileges of freedom, and it is difficult for them to conceive of a system where these values do not prevail. Isolated aspects of Communist economics assume a glittering luster when illuminated by the radiance of the star of liberty. In the environment of Communist tyranny, they are tawdry and repulsive.

Khrushchev told the American people that in Russia they are on the verge of abolishing income tax. Within American society that seems a highly desirable goal. To abolish income tax under Communist tyranny is a sham and delusion. The big American corporations do not need to tax their employees. The Communist Party is the monopoly corporation that owns the entire Russian economy. It fixes all wages and prices. It can impose a one hundred percent sales tax without announcing it in any way.

If students are taught that the Communist economy can run without income tax and are not taught the tyrannical role of the Communist Party, great damage is done. At an early age, each student should be taught that the issue is clear-cut—freedom versus slavery. They then should be taught the techniques by which Communism seeks to deceive, conquer, and enslave.

Love without knowledge is frequently impotent. I had been speaking to a church group in California about the necessity for knowledge. Following the message, the minister stood up to give a devotional, apparently in the hope that he could counteract any bad influence I might have had. The theme of his devotional was that love is the greatest force in the world. He said that we are told to love all God's children. Everybody is God's child. The Communists are God's children. We should therefore love the Communists. Khrushchev is God's child. We should love Khrushchev.

After the meeting we fell into conversation. He was apparently conscious that what he had said might have appeared as a rebuttal to what I had stressed, that is, the need for knowledge. He said that this had not been his intention, but that I had seemed to exalt knowledge above love. I told him that as far as I was concerned, he had not said anything, for love cannot operate without knowledge. If a mother spends all her time kissing her child and fails to have it inoculated against polio, has she shown love towards it? Suppose you see an insane hoodlum kicking a little girl to death a hundred yards down the street. Before you can get there, the little girl will be dead. In your hand you have a gun. How do you show love in a situation like that?

What is needed is not pious phraseology, but a loving spirit and the knowledge to apply it in a given situation. Love without knowledge is blind, and knowledge without love may lack dynamic power. We need a synthesis of love and knowledge. Then truth shall prevail.

Program for Survival

Any program to combat Communism must be based on a thorough study of the Communist mind, motives, and techniques. When we understand these, we can see clearly in the murk of the Communist dialectic, detect the tactic of the enemy, and devise a program to abort his plans.

ORGANIZATION

Organization is the genius of Communism. Communism is the triumph of organization over undirected economic and social forces. It is a truism that organization will prevail over disorganization. An anti-Communism program needs organization.

A commonly held view is that unity is the great need in this organized anti-Communism program. An argument such as the following is assured of a tumultuous reception with almost any group of businessmen: "Communism is the universal enemy. It is the enemy of every segment of a free society. It is the enemy of both Management and Labor. It is the enemy of all religions: Protestant, Catholic, Jewish, Hindu, and Muslim. Since it is the enemy of all free political parties, it is the common enemy of Republicans and Democrats. Since it is our universal enemy, it should cause us to submerge our differences and unite ourselves into the struggle against it." Such an argument will be cheered to the echo, yet it ignores the important question of motivation. When groups submerge their differences, they frequently submerge their motivating forces, and the organization so formed is like an automobile without gasoline because the dynamics of action reside in the submerged differences.

Suppose, for example, a joint Catholic-Protestant organization is formed. The liberty of the Catholic conscience necessitates freedom to propagate the doctrines of the faith. The liberty of conscience of an evangelical Protestant depends upon his freedom to preach the gospel of Christ. If the Protestant gets into an organization where he must refrain from preaching the gospel, and the Catholic in that organization must refrain from advancing Catholicism, both are embarrassed and rendered so much less effective. If, however, they are in different organizations where the consciences of both are clear, they can do far more effective work.

The Christian Anti-Communism Crusade held a school for anti-Communists in the educational building of the Tower Grove Baptist church in St. Louis. The school was attended by a considerable number of Catholics. After the school, the Catholics were very eager to form a joint Protestant-Catholic anti-Communist organization. I replied that, should we do so, each would paralyze the effectiveness of the other. Each group has a dominant purpose. The emotional attitudes of the members are tuned to the fulfillment of that purpose. Unless the message is in tune with that purpose, it will not produce the maximum result. Opposition to it may be unconscious, but it will be real nevertheless. If the message against Communism is tuned to the basic purposes of the organization, it will rally the enthusiastic support of the group. When an organization consists of elements with contradictory purposes, it is difficult to mobilize the enthusiastic support of all elements. Maybe this should not be so, in relation to such a universal enemy, but as a practical issue, it is so.

I suggested that the Catholics form a Catholic organization so that they could speak to Catholics without the embarrassment of a Protestant leader. Rather hesitantly, they agreed and formed the Cardinal Mindszenty Foundation. This organization is now doing a most effective work, and its leadership is now convinced of the wisdom of the course pursued. Instead of uniting, Catholic speaks to Catholic, and Protestant speaks to Protestant. Information is shared. Joint projects may be undertaken. But organizational unity is not sought. Neither infringes his conscience. Each has the dynamic of his faith and can be much more effective than if a united organization had been formed.

Organizational unity is a mirage. The great need is multiplicity, not unity. The unity of a free society resides in its diversity. Movements must be formed that conserve the motivating forces within each group and channel them into the struggle for freedom and survival. The Communists understand this very well. That is why they operate through a great number of front organizations, each of which is tuned to some specific motivating dynamic. Every religious, professional, economic, and cultural group should organize an anti-Communist program.

There is always the temptation to try to form a totalitarian organization modeled on Communism. After I had spoken at a school in Eugene, Oregon, I received a letter from one of the students that began, "Dr. Schwarz, you hypocrite! You came to us and you showed us the power of Communist organization, their dedication, their devotion, and their discipline. You told us how the Communist leader can sit and order every individual to do a certain task and how the individual obeys whatever the cost. Then you start an organization with a membership fee of $10 a year and life membership at $100. How will you ever combat them like that? Let's form an organization like that of the Communists where we have discipline and authority and where people do what is necessary at whatever cost to themselves."

I replied that I appreciated the spirit of his letter. I did not object to his calling me a hypocrite, for I often felt that way myself. Yet I was afraid that he did not fully understand the conflict between totalitarian organization and the Christian liberty of conscience. This liberty of conscience itself should direct the individual into unselfish service to fulfill his responsibility towards God and to the preservation of that liberty for all men. Any organization that flouts this principle is anti-libertarian and anti-Christian. Discipline must be largely self-discipline; sacrifice must be voluntary, not compulsory. The mainspring of our organization must be from within the character of free citizens.

I cannot compel you to do anything in this struggle. God Himself renounced His right to compel. It depends upon voluntary choice and free will.

Who will win? The Communists are supremely confident of complete victory. They claim that their victory is assured because of the quality of character in democratic lands. They affirm that the environment generating this character is Capitalism in its dying phase. Since Capitalism is dying, it creates character without survival virtue. They are convinced that the average citizen of the Free World is so intellectually lazy and dishonest, so greedy and selfish, so intoxicated with entertainment, so consumed with his immediate problems that no matter how clear the evidence of impending doom, that evidence will never be acknowledged, and the organizational steps necessary for survival will never be taken.

We categorically reject this claim. We are not the helpless victims of our environment, doomed to destruction. The fault lies not in our environment but in us. The political, judicial, educational, and cultural organizations of a free society can function only when the individual citizens have enlightened minds and are dedicated to the foundations of freedom. The basic responsibility rests on each one. The success of this book can be measured by the number of readers whose attention has been redirected from the responsibility of others to their own responsibility; who are asking the question, "What can I do?" Upon such a foundation, the political, legislative, and cultural programs necessary can be built.

Material forces alone do not determine the destinies of men. The resources of an infinite God can change the balance of material assets. These resources are liberated through the prayer, the sacrifice, and the intelligent organization of people filled with the love of God. Fundamentally, the problem is a moral and spiritual one. The foundations of freedom must be girded with a moral and spiritual revival. As free men humbly seek God and present their bodies, minds, and hearts to their country and the cause of all mankind, we may well believe that tyranny shall not triumph and freedom shall not perish from the earth.

FURTHER STUDY

Klein, Aaron and Brenda J. Elliott. *The Manchurian President: Barack Obama's Ties to Communists, Socialists and Other Anti-American Extremists*. Washington DC, WND Books, 2010.

LaHaye, Tim and David A. Noebel. *Mind Siege: The Battle for Truth in the New Millennium*. Nashville, TN: Word Publishing, 2000. Chapter 15.

Noebel, David A. *Understanding the Times: The Collision of Today's Competing Worldviews*. Revised 2nd Ed. Manitou Springs, CO: Summit Press, 2006.

CHAPTER TWELVE

The Heart, Mind, and Soul of Communism

by
Fred C. Schwarz

In 1917, in a café in Geneva, Switzerland, an intensely ambitious and fanatical man sat writing furiously. He had written there for many years, in exile from his native land of Russia, living in the expectation of the great day of revolution when he would be called to the center of the world's stage. He was the acknowledged leader of a small Marxist sect, the Bolshevik section of the Russian Social Democratic Labor Party. To the majority of Marxists he was an extremist, unduly schismatic, tinged with anarchistic ideas, sincere but dangerous. He had, scattered throughout Russia and the prisons of the world, 40,000 followers, devoted to their leader, equally fanatical, and unreservedly dedicated to the ideas of revolution and world conquest. His name was Vladimir Ilich Lenin.

Suddenly, in February of 1917, the news burst upon the world of a great Russian upheaval. The Czar was dethroned, a parliament was established to guide the steps of a new-born republic, and the Social Revolutionary leader, Kerensky, was called to the helm. Lenin and his scattered followers hastened to the new center of revolution, Petrograd, since renamed Leningrad. Stalin returned from Siberian exile, Trotsky came from a Canadian concentration camp, and Lenin traveled by armored train across embattled Germany to his native land, leaving Geneva, the city of his exile. On arrival Lenin announced to the other non-bolshevik revolutionaries that he alone, supported by his bolshevik fragment, would conquer and rule the vast territories of Russia. They looked at him in amazement and said, "Farewell Lenin the Marxist; welcome Lenin the Anarchist." Zealously, scientifically, and ruthlessly he set to work to make his prediction come true. In April he renamed the Bolshevik section of the Russian Social Democratic Labor Party the Communist Party of Russia. In October the Communists organized a second revolution, overwhelmed the new infant republic, and Lenin became dictator of all Russia.

There then came to pass the modern miracle of the world. An expansive program of conquest was initiated which has been successful beyond the wildest dreams of avarice. History records no movement growing, conquering, consolidating, and expanding as Communism has unceasingly done since that time. The statistics are startling, even terrifying. In 1917, they had 40,000 followers; in 1966 they controlled more than one billion. The number of actual communists is over 43 million. To consummate their dream of world conquest they merely need to multiply the present population under their control by less than 3. Anyone who is not startled and profoundly alarmed by these figures is evidently free from the responsibilities of rational comprehension, satisfied to live a mere animal existence with no thought of the morrow.

How has this tremendous success been accomplished? What tremendous dynamic of power is concealed within the categories of Communism that has driven it forward as an irresistible whirlwind? How has it managed to captivate the mind and imagination of young and old, mobilize the intelligence, loyalty, and capacity to sacrifice of those so captivated, discipline them and transform them into the mold of a Communist Cadre and then send them forth—limitless in enthusiasm, confident of victory, careless of personal death—to lay waste and conquer the earth?

WHAT IS COMMUNISM?

Communism is a religion of promise. It has advanced across the world on the wings of a promise. The promise is two-fold in nature. One aspect of the Communist promise is very well-known, but the other is almost unknown. One aspect appeals to the poor, the ignorant, and the underprivileged; the other aspect appeals to the wealthy, the intellectually superior, and the idealistic reformers.

To the poor of the earth—and they are legion—the servants of Communism go with this message: "Follow me, and I will build a new world for you and your children, a world from which hunger and cold have been forever banished; a world in which war and pestilence are mere historic memories; a world without exploitation of man by man; a world without racial animosity and discrimination; a world of peace and plenty; a world of culture and intellect; a world of brotherhood, liberty, and justice." Can you imagine the appeal of this promise to those millions living in the narrow no-man's land between malnutrition and starvation, never having had the comfortable sensation of retiring to bed after a full and satisfying meal in the knowledge that at least food and raiment for the days ahead are assured? Can you imagine the appeal of this promise to the millions who watch their children die in birth or during their first year, the victims of filth, starvation, and preventable disease carried by flies and mosquitoes? The force of this appeal is multiplied when the messenger is obviously sincere and is willing to leave his own home and the land of his birth, to forsake his family and loved ones to carry this message to these unfortunate poor. Identifying himself with their woes, he lives like them, eats their food, and daily risks his life to bring the message he bears to more and more who stand in dire need. Surely it does not require any great faculty of imagination to understand the tremendous appeal such a program must have in those dark lands of ignorance, illiteracy, hunger, and disease—the lands of the East. That aspect of the Communist promise is widely known and easily understood.

There is a second portion of the promise that is used, not to captivate the poor, but to seduce the rich; not to enlighten the ignorant, but to enlist the educated; not to bribe the cynical, but to ensnare the idealistic. Not only is there to be a new society created, but there is also to emerge a new and finer mankind. Human nature itself is to be transformed into something infinitely finer and more beautiful. Mankind is to be redeemed from vice, depravity, and sin in all its forms. The Methodist hymn well expresses this vision in the following words:

> These things shall be; a mightier race
> Than ere the world has seen shall rise
> With light of knowledge in their eyes

Evangelical Christians, above all others, should be able to understand the appeal of such a promise. They are dedicated to the redemption of man through the Gospel of the Grace of God revealed in Jesus Christ. How they rejoice when a wayward sinner finds his way in repentance and faith to the foot of the Cross of Calvary and rises a new man in Christ Jesus. What a rejoicing there was in Christian circles a few years back when in the Billy Graham campaign a prominent radio announcer and a minor gangster found Christ. The very temperature of the evangelical Christian climate was raised—hearts rejoiced, purses and pocketbooks opened, and many

The Heart, Mind, and Soul of Communism

Christians received a new vision and made a new dedication of their lives to Christ.

Communism is not a program to cure one or two, but to cure all of the sins of the whole world. Its plan is not to reform one drunkard but to eliminate all drunkenness, all crime, all vice, and everything that spoils and mars what man should be. Surely the appeal of such a vison can be well understood. Often during the question time at the conclusion of an address, the following request is made: "Please explain the appeal Communism has to those who have nothing to gain and everything to lose by its success. I can understand its appeal to the poor and ignorant, but please explain to me how it appeals to millionaires, college professors, and ministers of religion. That I cannot understand." Surely this problem presents no difficulty when we see the promise of the creation of a new and redeemed mankind. What nobler vision could any man have? To this mighty task every capacity of body and mind should be dedicated—the task of creating a New Heaven and New Earth wherein the redeemed may dwell. Failure to comprehend this central truth is responsible for some of the most common misconceptions with regard to Communism. How often we used to hear it said, "Communism is all very well in theory, but it won't work because of the weakness of human nature." No Communist ever proposed to establish the Communist society with present sinful nature. Before the social order of Communism can come to pass, the new and redeemed mankind must emerge from the ashes of the destroyed Capitalistic Civilization.

COMMUNISM AND SCIENCE

To promise is one thing; to fulfill is another. How do the Communists propose to bring their promise to pass? By what means will they be enabled to work this incredible transformation? The Communists answer by one word: "SCIENCE."

During the last century a tremendous transformation has been wrought in the material world. How many of us would be willing to return to the condition of life enjoyed—pardon the word—by our great-great-grandparents of that era? Imagine what you would do when punished by a toothache—a visit to the barber who did his best with the assistance of a large pair of forceps and two or three strong helpers. The story of surgery of those days would turn the stomach of the strongest. It was a nightmare of agony, haste, ignorance, dirt, germs, suppuration, and death. It was a world without electricity and all it brings, without modern transportation, without central heating, refrigeration, trash disposal, or even primitive sanitary facilities in populous areas. It was a world without baths, as bathing is a modern habit. It was a world of ignorance, pain, hardship, disease, and premature death. Every baby born had but half the life expectancy of those here today. What has wrought the change? The answer is one word: "SCIENCE."

Consider the world of agriculture, with the quality, variety, and abundance of food products, not to mention the world of beauty and flowers. A mere century or two ago the economist Malthus could mathematically prove that mankind would always be fighting famines by the very nature of things. Animal life, including humans, must always increase more rapidly than their food supply. Yet today the people of this country live in a land of abundance, veritably a paradise of profusion, enjoying food of the highest quality practically unrestricted. What has brought about this profusion of food products? The answer is science, with its application of scientific principles of plant breeding, resulting in the development of species of plants suitable to the individual terrain and the climatic characteristics of the various regions of the country. A whole chapter could be devoted to the study of corn alone—the different varieties, its disease resistance, its special flavors for human consumption, its adaptability to the most specialized features of topical and climatic conditions of any area. Science has transformed the world of agriculture.

A very similar story could be told in the realm of animal husbandry. The domestication of animals; the selective breeding of the most productive strains of poultry, sheep, and cattle; the building of characteristics suitable for peculiar environments—all this has been convincingly accomplished with great benefit to the human race. The Communists propose to use this same science to transform human nature itself. The idea is provocative yet fascinating. How do they propose to apply scientific principles? Let us inquire further.

Science consists of a knowledge of the laws of nature and of an application of the forces of nature, within the framework of those laws, to accomplish a desired purpose. Science is dependent upon the laws of nature; it cannot act independently of them. Let us take the manufacture of steel as a scientific process. Steel cannot be made out of good intentions, by the mere application of industrious, well-intentioned effort: it cannot be created from brotherly love. Steel is the end-product of a scientific sequence of steps. Firstly, the correct raw material must be secured—the coal and iron ore. Then these raw materials must be treated in the appropriate manner, associated together in the correct relationship of temperature and humidity. There is an inescapable sequence of scientific steps before the end product can mature. There can be no steel without the furnace; the heat of the furnace may be searing and terrible, but there is no escaping it. There is a sequence of steps involved in any scientific project, and none of these steps can be eluded because they are distasteful.

Communism acquired great prestige among the intellectuals by reason of its claim to be scientific. Its creators, Marx and Engels, grouped together all preceding Socialists under the heading "utopian." They considered them unrealistic dreamers, unaware of the nature of social and economic laws and the steps necessary to produce a new Communist man. The most famous classical document of Communism is the pamphlet by Engels entitled *"Socialism: Utopian and Scientific."* It has been translated into more languages than the *Communist Manifesto* itself.

Scientific Marxism begins with three basic hypotheses to serve as the foundation for the scientific program. These may be classified as follows:

1. Atheism
2. Materialism
3. Economic Determinism

ATHEISM

Communism clearly enunciates, "There is no God." Karl Marx was an atheist before he was a Communist. Atheism was his first and last intellectual love. His earliest writings were attempts to prove that the German philosopher Hegel was an atheist. From the fiber and texture of his atheism he built his philosophy and program of Communism. His greatest disciple, Lenin, commences his pamphlet on religion with the words, "Atheism is a fundamental portion of Marxism, of the theory and practice of scientific socialism." Communism without atheism is cancer without malignancy, a contradiction in terms. When Communism rejects God, it simultaneously rejects all supernatural moral law, all absolute criteria of truth and error. It abolishes heaven and hell and all absolute values associated with human life. Man is left in a battlefield where the laws are his own to make or break, where all codes of ethics and morality are relative, discretionary, and subject to change. The criterion of moral value becomes objective success; the world becomes a pragmatist's dream.

The Heart, Mind, and Soul of Communism

MATERIALISM

Having disposed of the question of God, the next subject to be considered was the nature of man. Here Communism is equally specific: man is matter in motion and nothing more. The entire universe of which man is a part is entirely material. Thought is a quality of matter; matter thinks; the brain secretes thought as the liver secretes bile. The total life of mankind—thoughts, emotions, sentiments, culture, and religion—are simply the product of the motion of his material constituents. Man is an animal and nothing more. In the dim past ages of antiquity, by some yet unknown materialistic process, a chemical aggregation of molecules took to itself the quality of being matter; a unicellular, proto-plasmic, primordial mass came into being and an evolutionary sequence of events commenced. Reproduction, differentiation, selection, mutation, and countless more materialist phenomena ensued and all life came into being. At the apex of the evolutionary tree there stands man, the first of the animals, yet an animal and no more. He has no spirit, nor yet any soul. As there is no God he obviously cannot have been made in the image of that which does not exist. There is no continuity associated with individual life; there is no heaven to gain or hell to shun. There is no special value associated with every individual life. Each human is an animal; the totality of the individuals comprise the human race; the future of the race is significant, while that of the individuals is insignificant. The race of mankind can be scientifically improved by recourse to the normal laws and techniques of animal husbandry.

ECONOMIC DETERMINISM

The human individual possesses certain characteristics of social and individual life, certain patterns of thought and emotional life. How is the personality and character of each individual derived? What determines what each animal shall think? What emotions shall accompany such thoughts? What shall be the pattern of moral, social, and religious behavior that emerges? It is at this point that Marx makes his greatest contribution to human thought, so we are told. This is the discovery which, according to his great co-worker, Frederick Engels, transformed economics from empiricism to science. In simple language here it is: The entire personality, including thoughts, emotions, religious experiences, family attitudes, sentiments, and artistry is derived from the prevailing mode of economic production. We are the captive creation of the Capitalistic System. It has ordained what we shall think, how we shall feel, and what we shall do in any given situation. The *Communist Manifesto* makes this lucidly plain. It specifically states that the family as we know it—the hallowed relationship of parent and child—is derived from the Capitalistic Economic System and that parental love will vanish with the vanishing of Capitalism. It goes further and specifically states that the concepts of freedom and justice are derivatives of the class struggle, and that when class struggle ceases the concepts will disappear. No one is individually responsible for his character or thought. As his class of social origin has determined, so he thinks, feels, and acts. What is needed to change character and personality is a basic change in the economic system.

It follows logically that all undesirable human characteristics are derived from the prevailing economic system. Communists are realists. They affirm the depravity of human nature; everywhere men and women are lazy, ignorant, self-indulgent, patriotic, and religious—no one could build a Communistic social order from such poor raw material. The first essential is a radical program to purify and perfect mankind. This must be done in a scientific manner. The inescapable sequence of scientific steps is as follows, some of which will be further discussed in more or less detail:

1. Destruction of the Capitalistic System, the root of all evil, by a violent revolution
2. Institution of the Dictatorship of the Proletariat
3. Liquidation of those classes of society incurably diseased by Capitalism and considered dangerously infective
4. Segregation of those diseased but capable of useful work in conditions of isolation
5. Hospitalization of the diseased but curable in "corrective" labor camps
6. Re-education of the total population in new relationships of labor with the emphasis on labor rather than reward
7. The emergence of the young generation with characters uninfluenced by Capitalism and appropriate to a socialist environment
8. The perfection of human nature
9. The withering away of the State; the Dictatorship of the Proletariat
10. The emergence of Communism

THE DESTRUCTION OF CAPITALISM

This must be accomplished by a violent revolution. The Communists have always been perfectly frank on this subject. Beginning with the *Communist Manifesto*, which says, "We openly declare that our ends can be attained only by the forcible overthrow of all existing social conditions," the identical sentiment has been repeated ad nauseam in all the writings of the Communist hierarchy and in official pronouncements of the Comintern and the Cominform. They categorically reject any suggestion that the transition from Capitalism to Socialism can be by the peaceful pathway of reform. One of the principal epithets of abuse in a somewhat extensive vocabulary is the word "reformist," a term of ridicule and contempt. Scientific law has written that the change-over must be both revolutionary and violent. This is determined both from their philosophy of Dialectical Materialism and from a fake evaluation of the economic forces in society. To use a Marxian analogy: Force is the midwife to deliver the Socialist order from the womb of a decadent Capitalism. Originally the transition was to be the operation of spontaneous forces automatically produced by the progress of Capitalism. The maturing of the Capitalistic Society inevitably produced the Proletariat, the propertyless mass of industrial slaves who became the grave-diggers of Capitalism. However, a new twist came to the ideas when Bolshevism was born at the Congress of the Russian Social Democratic Labor Party in 1903. Lenin, the founder of Bolshevism, and thus of Fascism, substituted the idea that the revolution was to result from the scientific planning and execution of the Party, which was the class-conscious vanguard of the Proletariat. He replaced the idea of spontaneity with the idea of a planned conspiracy. Every Party member became a disciplined conspirator dedicated to the goal of the overthrow of the government by force and violence. The action of the government in charging the leading members of the Party with conspiracy to violently destroy constitutional government is soundly based and an excellent demonstration of "government by law" within the framework of a democracy.

In 1917, the party of Lenin achieved the first success in its campaign for world conquest when it organized a violent revolution in Russia, bringing it to absolute power. Beset as he was with incredible difficulties, Lenin nevertheless took the requisite time in 1920 to write a textbook to direct the Communist conspirators of the world in the technique of organizing the violent revolution to seize power in their own respective countries. The book is one of the Communist classics, a "must" in reading for every recruit and is entitled *Left-wing Communism: An Infantile Disorder*. It is the blueprint

The Heart, Mind, and Soul of Communism

for the internal conquest of countries by Communism. It is one of the most cynical, yet Satanically clever, books ever written. Lenin shows how as true scientists, Communists must manipulate the forces in each country from behind the scenes and have millions unconsciously working for them. The key to the program is the word "infiltration"—infiltration of governments, of churches, of sporting bodies, of social clubs; infiltration of institutions of any and every kind, but above all, infiltration of industrial labor unions. All of these named and implied organizations are to be so scientifically manipulated as to bring to pass a violent revolution. Suffice it for our present purposes to say that in 1949, in Australia a mere handful of Communists, just 7,000 in a population of 8,000,000, less than 0.1% of our people following in detail the blue print of Lenin, came close to the conquest of the entire country without receiving one dollar or one man from outside to support them.

THE DICTATORSHIP OF THE PROLETARIAT

The old-fashioned Marxists reasoned thus: Capitalism is the root cause of all human sin; destroy the Capitalistic System and we will destroy sin. They believed that after the revolution they would be able to introduce a form of society in which men would be free and in which they would receive enough for every need. But into this honeymoon of optimism there came the grim voice of the scientific realist, Lenin. In effect he said: My dear friends, you have forgotten something very important. You are really a crowd of idealistic utopian dreamers. Certainly all human frailty, ignorance, and avarice are derived from the Capitalistic System. That is axiomatic. But you say that all we have to do to remove sin is to destroy the Capitalistic System. You try to go too quickly. When we have destroyed the root of all evil, the fruit remains in the characters of the many millions of the earth who are diseased and deformed. It is true that their diseased condition will vary in the different countries, but nevertheless mankind in general remains ignorant, illiterate, indolent, avaricious, class-conscious, patriotic, and religious. Before the true Communistic Society can be created, these disease characteristics, a hangover from Capitalism, must be eliminated. To do this, an intelligently applied scientific program, based on the established principles of animal husbandry, must be implemented. To do this, it is necessary to have a strong and intelligent power to carry out the program. In the progressive quality of its dialectic heart, history has appointed the Communist Party, the self-conscious, enlightened vanguard of the Proletariat, for this role. Therefore, we must establish an absolute dictatorship for this party. We will call it the "Dictatorship of the Proletariat."

Nearly all of the above paragraph is constituted of ideas and thoughts which Lenin expressed to his less-realistic Marxist friends. In his book *Problems of Leninism*, Stalin defines the term "Dictatorship of the Proletariat" as "The rules based on force and unrestricted by law, of the Proletariat over the Bourgeoisie."[1] Put simply this means the rule, based on force and unrestricted by law, of the Communist Party over everyone else. Stalin's definition, as given above, is profoundly interesting. He, along with all other true Communists, rejects two cardinal principles of civilization. The first principle is "The government of law." The power of the Communists is specifically to be unrestricted by law. The second principle is "Government by Consent." The power of the Communists is openly based on force. In this way, the Communists turn back the clock from civilization to barbarism.

Having established the dictatorship of the Communist Party, it now becomes their duty to scientifically implement a program directed to the elimination of the residual Capitalist disease and the building of a new and redeemed race of Socialist men and women so that Communism may ultimately come to pass. The steps of this program will now be considered.

LIQUIDATION OF INFECTIOUS CLASSES

The problem has entered the familiar and well-trodden pathway of animal husbandry. The problem may be presented thusly: The husbandman, the Communist Party, has transferred his herds from the diseased environment of Capitalism to the disease-free environment of Socialism. Unfortunately, the animals bring with them the disease contracted in their old environment. The dominant motive of the husbandman is to breed a new stock, entirely free from this disease. This cannot be done in a day. Obviously he will have to concentrate on the new generation for his finished product and utilize his present stock in the best possible manner to accomplish the necessary work of the new environment, without permitting them to transmit the disease to the young. The virility and infectiousness of the disease varies according to that portion of the old environment the animals inhabited. Certain environmental areas, i.e., certain classes of society, produce a more virulent and infectious disease. Obviously these animals must be eliminated for the well-being of the whole program. There is absolutely no element of reprisal or punishment in this liquidation; it is simply a necessary scientific procedure. The husbandman may presumably be very fond of certain diseased animals, but sentiment has no place in a scientific program; the animal must go. This is entirely logical within the framework of Communist beliefs. Remember, there is no God; man is pure animal; there is no question of soul or spirit, or heaven or hell, to be considered. This is simply scientific human betterment on a mass scale. There is, in general, a complete misunderstanding as to the Communist attitude toward killing in a Socialist Society. I have been a known opponent of Communism for many years, having challenged Communists to debate on any platform in the world. How often friends have said to me, "If the Communists come to power you will be one of the first to be killed." I always pretend innocence and reply, "Is that so? Why?" I am then informed that the Communists will punish me because I have opposed them. I hasten to reply that this reveals a complete failure to understand the very mind of Communism. They do not punish or reward. These are Bourgeois ideas that have no place within a redeemed Communist mind. No enlightened Communist blames me for my opposition to Communism. I am merely the unfortunate victim of my economic environment. Unfortunately I am diseased, and thus a danger to the whole program of human betterment. So I must be liquidated, but no more so than all other members of my social class. Since all personality is derived from our social class, all members of a given class have actually or potentially the dangerous disease of character, and they must be eliminated. The treatment you are to receive should the Communists come to power is entirely unrelated to the attitude you have adopted to them in the past. Opposition begets no penalty, and support begets no reward. A Bourgeois class of origin begets liquidation.

Thus, the mass-murder program of Communism is a logical and inescapable consequence of their basic beliefs. It is science in action. So many have been deceived on this point. They attribute the bestiality and excesses of Communism to the national characteristics of certain races—to Russian imperialism, to Asiatic cruelty, to a Jewish conspiracy of revenge; to anything and everything except the real culprit —that system of ideas and beliefs known as Communism. The murder of millions in Russia was not the excess due to a barbaric past; the liquidation of millions proceeding a pace in China is not an example of Oriental cruelty. It is scientific Communism in action. Anglo-Saxon Communism will be just as scientifically ruthless, just as dehumanized as the Russian and Chinese varieties; it believes the same things, and it is as true today as ever, "As a man thinketh in his heart, so he is."

A short while ago I was in Edinburgh, Scotland, and I became involved in argument with a group of Communists conducting a meeting in the main thoroughfare, Princess Street. In the midst of the argument one Communist asked me, "Well, what is freedom?" I replied, "You might define freedom as the right to live like an American, inhabit a comfortable and centrally heated home, drive your own automobile, own a refrigerator, a washing machine, a radio, a television set, eat all the food you desire, and have an argument like this without the police cutting your throat." He replied, "If I was a policeman, I would cut your throat." I said, "Do you really mean that?" He replied, "I certainly do." I called to the surrounding crowd, "Listen to this; here is a good object lesson." Another Communist intervened, "We've all got to die sometime. What does it matter if you die a little sooner instead of later?" They were not angry; they were not facetious; they were simply stating sound Communistic doctrine. Man is an animal. Individual life is insignificant. In the great and noble task of redeeming mankind, why worry over a few early deaths by the way.

Thus, we see the consistent logic of the Communists. Should you ask them, "You inhuman monsters; do you mean to say you would murder in cold blood millions of people?" they would unhesitatingly reply, "What do you mean by murder? That is a Bourgeois term. Nature has been killing people by countless millions for centuries, killing them by hunger, war, disease, and old age; killing them to no purpose. We have a purpose, and a noble one, and should we hesitate to take the necessary steps because they are unpleasant to our Bourgeois prejudices? How unworthy we would be of the task history has entrusted to us." Cold, inexorable, scientific logic.

Recently I conversed with two very well known men, each of whom had been a member of the American Communist Party for many years. Of both I asked the same question. "What are the plans of the American Communist Party with regard to liquidation in this country?" Both replied in this vein: I often heard it discussed in Party circles. The argument went like this. This character disease is derived from the Capitalistic System. Capitalism in America is more developed than in any other country. Therefore, its imprint in personality is deeper. The percentage to be liquidated here will be correspondingly higher. As a tentative figure, shall we say about one-third of the American people will be marked for liquidation.

From the two similar answers recounted in the preceding paragraph, we learn that the Communists plan to put to death a mere fifty million people, more or less, based on the present population level in the United States. Who are these people to be? The prime factor to be considered is class of social origin. Mrs. Sikorsky gives an official list of classes designated in the rape of Lithuania and Poland in her book *The Dark Side of the Moon*. Of special interest to church people is "Category 13," which includes persons active in parishes, clergymen, secretaries, and active members of religious communities. In Lithuania, the lists for liquidation and deportation included about 700,000 out of a total population of 3,000,000, slightly less than the one-third proposed for America. But Lithuania had not advanced so far in a Capitalistic sense as has America.

Should the Communist menace conquer this country, it may comfort you to know that the hand that condemns you and your family to death is driven not by malicious vindictive hatred, but by scientific necessity.

LABOR CAMPS

Not all those diseased are immediately liquidated by bullet or bayonet. Others go by the slower pathway of overwork

and starvation. Let us return to our animal husbandry analogy. The herd has been transferred to the new environment of
Socialism. In this environment, a great deal of work cries out
to be done, and there is a totally inadequate supply of clean
stock for the purpose. It is therefore reasonable to select diseased animals in whom the disease is not overwhelmingly
contagious, segregate them, and put them to work until they
die. They are not allowed to breed and thus contaminate the
future race, but they can be useful in segregation.

This is done under arduous conditions of climatic
extremes, overcrowding, malnutrition, and frequent death.
Nevertheless, much work useful to Socialism is thus accomplished. Canals and railways are built; salt, coal, gold, and
uranium are mined; lumber is felled for export, and cities are
built in the frozen Arctic wastes. In these conditions of labor
the average time to die takes approximately three years, and
much work is accomplished in that time.

This is what the labor camps are in practice but in theory they are something quite different. They are "personality hospitals" in which the disease due to Capitalism can be
cured. The cause of the disease is the false labor relations
of the Capitalistic Society wherein labor is associated with
profit and reward. The cure consists in being established in
new labor relations where labor is its own reward, where it is
divorced from the degradation of gain. We term these "slave
labor camps," because in them people are forced to labor and
receive nothing in return but the merest minimum of food to
maintain existence. The Communists say our opinion is only
a revelation of our Bourgeois ignorance. The Communists
maintain that these slave labor camps are actually only
"personality hospitals" wherein people can be re-educated,
healed of their grievous Capitalistic disease, and become
fit members of the new Socialistic Society. Were you to say
to a Communist, "You beast! You mean you would send a
twelve-year-old boy to serve ten years in a labor camp?" He

would reply, "If your son was sick would you send him to a hospital?" There is a consistency of logic and an ethical justification for every inhumanity and bestiality Communism commits. This insulates them from the appeals of reason, decency, and humanity. They even provide these "personality hospitals" free. What generous people they are! As the reader retires tonight it would be a profitable theme of meditation to ponder which he would prefer—immediate liquidation or re-education in a labor camp. The alternative may soon emerge from the realm of theory to intensely practical politics.

MASS RE-EDUCATION

While the labor camps provide specialized hospitalization, the less fortunate sufferers are not being overlooked. Re-education is provided for them by a new attitude toward labor. Work is now taught to be the great creative force that built the universe and that it is its own reward. However, work nevertheless must bring with it remuneration appropriate to its measure. Every means of speed-up in industry is introduced; labor is exploited in every possible way. The slogan is: "From every man according to his ability; to every man according to his work." The unions become instruments of the dictatorship for the speed-up of work and a means of discipline over the workers. Strikes are forbidden and any incitement to strike is a capital offense. Every factory has its own jails; late arrival to work is sabotage and absenteeism is treason. Under these ideal working conditions, a new attitude toward labor develops; a new character emerges; the new Socialist man is on the way.

THE EMERGENCE OF YOUNG UNMARRED BY CAPITALISM

Along with this vast program of re-education the much simpler program of the education of the new-born Socialist children comes into being. These have the inestimable benefits of birth into a clean environment. There is no vicious profit motive to despoil them, no patriotism to degrade, and no religion to debauch. All they need is scientific indoctrination and an appropriate conditioning to fulfill all the needs of the most exacting Socialist master. The sin of bygone days becomes an unpleasant memory. The task of the dictatorship is approaching conclusion.

THE EMERGENCE OF COMMUNISM

As the program of science proceeds and the perfection of personality comes to pass, the rigid state of the dictatorship, with its restrictions on human freedom, becomes unnecessary, and the State begins to wither away. Gradually, by imperceptible degrees, the golden age of Communism comes to pass, in which everyone works for the sheer love of working, and everyone gives because it is the glory of his heart so to do. The hand of no man is raised in anger against his brother; the wolf lies down with the lamb; the small child plays on the cockatrice's den, the tuberculous organisms lose their virility; the cancer cells lose their malignity. Everyone takes from the common pool all they need, and men the whole world over brothers are. The slogan of this period is, "From every man according to his ability; to every man according to his need."

This is the dream, the vision that lures men to the Communist hook, the goal at the end of the rainbow. The Communists have achieved portions of it—the violent and destructive revolution, the mass extermination, and the vile labor camps. The rest remains in the realm of pure hypotheses where it is doomed to die with many past Marxian illusions. Every fact of Communist history contradicts the specious optimism that human nature will perfect itself under the Dictatorship of the Proletariat. The evidence against this thesis provided by the Communists themselves is shattering. Take the deterioration that has taken place in the character of leading Communists under the Russian system. In 1917, the Central Committee consisted of 31 members and alternates. The leader, Lenin, attributed the entire success of the Revolution to the sterling characters, undying devotion, and invincible selflessness of this group. Every one of them had suffered much for the cause in prison and out of prison, in exile and out of exile. In torture and imminent danger of death, they remained loyal, devoted, and invincible. It is noteworthy that these fine characters were formed under Capitalism. At long last the golden day of their dreams came to pass and Socialism covered one sixth of the surface of the earth. Freed from the vicious influence of the Capitalist System, what wonderful people they must have become! Let the Communists tell us what happened to them. Lenin and Sverdlov died before Stalin came to power. Alexandra Kollontai lived to die a natural death. The remainder degenerated into such offal, such swine, such treacherous wild beasts, such hyenas using Communist terminology—that every one had to be put to death. When Lenin died in 1924, the Politbureau, the highest body of world Communism, had seven members—Zinoviev, Kamenev, Stalin, Bukharin, Trotsky, Rykov, and Tomsky. Stalin alone survived. All the others degenerated and had to be destroyed. The perfection of character is thus revealed as a delusion; the chain of events breaks down, the golden future fades, and we are left with the intolerable nightmare of the dreadful present: the dictatorship, the extermination program, the labor camp, horror piled on horror, a veritable living hell. Farewell, perfection. The beast is here and here he remains.

Truly the Bible says, "The fool has said in his heart there is no God. They have altogether become corrupt, they have done abominable works; there is none that doeth good." From the tainted source of rebellion against God, the poisoned stream of massacre and slavery flows. At its very source, Communism is the epitome of evil. Unless we see this we have no clear vision of where to attack Communism. It must be rejected in its premises—its atheism, its materialism, and its economic determinism. Just as cancer is evil at its origin because of its rebellion against the authority of the body, and just as its later manifestations of agony, horror, and foul-smelling death spring from the laws of its being, so the later manifestations of Communism are but the scientific derivatives of its evil premises. How many avowed Christian leaders have failed to see this. Not long ago I asked the secretary of a certain council of churches at what point the majority of his members turned against Communism. He replied, "After they invaded Czechoslovakia." I said, "Is that the point at which atheism became wrong?"' Communism is scientific bestiality; it is hellish in origin and execution.

What Can I Do?

Always there arises the question, "What can I do? I would like very much to help in this great battle, but I seem so inadequate. The issues are beyond me. When the problem defies the masterminds of state, college, and church, what hope have I of making any significant contribution?'"There is something everyone can do and it consists in four things: knowledge, courage, faith, and consecration.

Knowledge

Whenever the medical profession endeavors to combat a serious disease, the first essential is a vast program of research into the nature of the disease, its causes, the laws of its development, the conditions favorable to its spread, and wherein its weakness—its "heel of Achilles"—lies, so that it may be attacked and defeated. Understanding is the irreducible minimum of effective counter-action. Ignorant opposition is frequently valuable assistance to the Communist cause. The quality of ignorance and misunderstanding, at all levels of intellect and education, of the nature and mind of Communism is startling. I could amplify this article with illustration after illustration of the most pitiable ignorance revealed to me personally by high military officers, university professors, and ministers of religion. Such statements as the following we hear every day, and they reveal total incomprehension of the nature of Communism. The first statement is, "We must acknowledge the good in Communism and realize it is primarily a reaction to the evils of Capitalistic Society." The good in Communism is like the "good" in tuberculosis, unappreciated by the victim. Again we hear, "It is possible to preserve peace with Communism" when the Communists' very thought processes define the existing state as class war. Or yet again we hear, "We must eliminate social abuses so that Communism may not flourish." Cancer was never cured by improving the general health. Knowledge is the first weapon in our arsenal of defense. The basic Communist texts are available, and these should be studied so that we have an understanding of the Communist laws of thought and their blueprint of conquest. Knowledge is power.

COURAGE

What we discover when we investigate Communism is terrifying. The vastness of the danger oppresses us. We may react in one of two ways. The knowledge may be a "savor of death unto death or life unto life." We may become oppressed and throw in the towel, or we may gird ourselves for the battle, realizing how terrible it will be. Many individuals have to face situations of this nature. They visit their physician to be told they have the dread disease of cancer. They may react in one of two ways—a defeat or a challenge. Some say, "All is finished, life is over," and in despair throw themselves under a train. Others say, "This is grim news, but I will do my best to overcome it," and they make the decisions required, courageously rearrange their life routine, submit to the drastic surgery necessary, pay the heavy cost, and come through triumphantly. Courage transforms the dread knowledge into a challenge, a matchless sacrifice, a heroic endeavor, and a glorious triumph.

FAITH

The Communists say, "There is no God." We know, "In the beginning, God." God has not abdicated from the throne of the universe. He is an active agent in history and makes even the wrath of man praise Him. We have His promises. "When the enemy shall come in like a flood, then will the Spirit of the Lord lift up a standard against him." If we will pray, live righteously, and trust in Him, He will not fail in our hour of need: "If God be for us, who can be against us?"

CONSECRATION

Communism has been able to mobilize the loyalty, discipline, and willingness to sacrifice even unto death of countless millions. In the final analysis, faith can only be matched by faith, devotion by devotion, and consecration by consecration. Are we who name the name of Christ prepared to make equal sacrifices, to serve with equal unselfishness, to manifest like loyalty and devotion as those who name the name of Lenin?

> Rise up, O Men of God,
> Have done with lesser things.
> Give heart and mind and soul and strength
> Unto the King of Kings.
> Rise up, O Men of God!

You Can Still Trust the Communists

CHAPTER THIRTEEN

Worldviews of Destruction

by
David A. Noebel

Beware lest any man [educator, politician, rock star, news anchor-man/woman] take you captive through vain and deceitful philosophy [Naturalism, Postmodernism, Marxism, Pragmatism], after the tradition of men [Marx, Darwin, Nietzsche, Wellhausen, Freud, Dewey, Foucault], after the rudiments of the world [Socialism, Darwinism, Higher Criticism, Humanism, Relativism, Existentialism], and not after Christ.

—Colossians 2:8

Western Civilization in general and the United States in particular have embarked on a hazardous journey of rejecting Christ and replacing Him with any number of mortal men and women along with their ideas. Ideas have consequences, and the 20th century has witnessed the destructive consequences of these utopian schemes and ideas.

Over 120 years ago (1890–1891), James Orr presented the Kerr lectures in Edinburgh, Scotland. He titled his series "The Christian View of God and the World" and argued forcefully for the proposition that biblical Christianity is a worldview. In calling Christianity a worldview (or Weltanschauung in German), he meant that Christianity is more than an emotional two-hour experience on Sunday morning. Rather, Christianity is a 24-hours-a-day relationship with God through Jesus Christ affecting every aspect of life.

In other words, a person who believes that Jesus Christ is the Son of God "is thereby committed to much else besides," says Orr. A Christian is committed to a "view of God, to a view of man, to a view of sin, to a view of redemption, to a view of the purpose of God in creation and history, to a view of human destiny."[1] Added together, these views comprise a worldview.

At the same time another scholar was contemplating the history of ideas and their relationship to the world of religion, philosophy, politics, economics, etc. His name was John Emerich Edward Dalberg-Acton, better known to us as Lord Acton.

Lord Acton's letter to the Anglican bishop of London, Mandell Creighton, contained his famous statement "Power tends to corrupt and absolute power corrupts absolutely." Acton was a scholar and lecturer of the highest order whom Toynbee acknowledged as "one of the greatest minds among Western historians." Acton observed that "no man, no class, no party, no country, no church, not even his own, was wise enough or unselfish enough to be entrusted with unlimited power."[2]

Lord Acton was convinced that twenty or thirty key ideas hold the key to explaining modern history. "The majority of these ideas," he insisted, "were either religions or substitutes for religion."[3] Assembling these twenty or thirty ideas brings us into the world of worldviews. I propose that the 20th century was the century of substitutes for religion.

I define worldview as a bundle or set of ideas that contain a particular perspective regarding each of the following disciplines: theology, philosophy, ethics, biology, psychology, sociology, law, politics, economics, and history.[4]

[248]

Worldviews of Destruction

The most prominent worldviews prancing through the 20th century did indeed speak to these various disciplines with devastating results. At approximately the same time James Orr and Lord Acton penned their works, four other individuals (three men and a woman) were about to emerge on the world's stage and before they finished speaking, writing, and living out their worldviews tens of millions of human beings paid with their lives.

The 20th century is now history. It is a history of incredible advances in many areas—inventions, computers, medicine, technology, transportation, communication, living standards, free states, even expansion of the Christian Gospel. It is also a history of devolution—dictatorships, poverty, illegal drugs, pornography, homosexuality, venereal diseases, AIDS, lawlessness, immorality, teen pregnancy, and abortions. But most disturbing for our study, the 20th century is a history of mass murders and killings unheard of in human history. It is the century of slaughter. More human beings were killed in the 20th century than in all previous centuries combined.

"During the first eighty-eight years of [the 20th] century," says historian R.J. Rummel, "almost 170 million men, women and children have been shot, beaten, tortured, knifed, burned, starved, frozen, crushed or worked to death; buried alive, drowned, hung, bombed, or killed in any other of the myriad ways governments have inflicted death on unarmed, helpless citizens and foreigners. The dead could conceivably be nearly 360 million people. It is as though our species has been devastated by a modern Black Plague. And indeed it has, but a plague of Power, not germs."[5]

When we put the human cost of war and democide together, says Rummel, "Power has killed over 203 million people in [the 20th] century."[6] This figure does not include the slaughter of the innocent through abortion—a foundation stone of the Secular Humanist worldview.

These millions did not die because of James Orr's Christian world view. Most of these millions died at the hands of the three men and one woman whose worldviews were inflicted on the world (and in many ways their legacies continue into the 21st century).

The three men are Benito Mussolini (b. 1883), Adolph Hitler (b. 1889) and Joseph Stalin (b. 1879). The woman is Margaret Sanger (b. 1879).

Mussolini and Hitler represent the 20th century's Fascist/Nazi worldviews. Stalin represents the Marxist/Leninist worldview. Margaret Sanger represents the Secular Humanist worldview. And while the bulk of this book will be charting the Marxist Socialist worldview, it is necessary to understand how Marxism plays its role within the context of the other worldviews.

These are the worldviews primarily responsible for the millions of human beings slaughtered on the altars of Atheism, Naturalism, Dialectical Materialism, Ethical Relativism, beyond good and evil, Libertinism, class morality, biological evolution, social Darwinism, euthanasia, sterilization, infanticide, eugenics, abortion, Collectivism, Statism, Progressivism, dictatorship, new Fascist man, new Aryan man, new Soviet man, new Humanist man, new international child of the future, new social order, new world order, Socialism (national and international), positive law or sociological jurisprudence, and other ideas exploding from the fevered brows of the intelligentsia.[7]

Whoever said ideas have consequences summarized the 20th century. The ideas that moved across and out of the 19th century were fleshed out in the 20th century and the results are obvious for all to see—death, destruction, devastation, heartache, misery—all words and nuances that portray a century ripe for judgment.

As we begin the 21th century we have yet to admit a deep, dark secret to ourselves—the very ideas that brought us a century of terror and slaughter are still being taught in our public institutions of higher education. Ironically, the only worldview not responsible for the slaughter is the only worldview proscribed viz., Christianity. All other world-views have their voices and defenders in our colleges and universities.

For example, "Paul DeMan, who has done more than anyone else to promote deconstruction in the United States, was a Nazi propagandist."[8] Michel Foucault, a major post-modern voice and lecturer at the University of California (Berkeley) was a Maoist[9] and a homosexual who died of AIDS after infecting his lovers on the premise of "inventing new pleasures beyond sex...sex as murder."[10]

And who can deny that both Nietzsche and Heidegger are "back in fashion on university campuses"?[11] Nietzsche was not only a major precursor to Fascism, but is regarded as the father of Postmodernism.[12] Heidegger was "an active, ideologically committed member of the Nazi party."[13]

The Marxist influence on American campuses is also rampant as Arnold Beichman notes in *The Weekly Standard.* America's Communists and former Communists are already taking out full page ads in *The New York Times* seeking to exculpate Communism. Historian Theodore Draper is quoted as saying, "[C]learly an attempt to rehabilitate communism by making it part of the larger family of socialism and democracy" is underway. "No one," he says, "would think of doing this favor for fascism, but communism with even more millions of victims and a much longer life span is the beneficiary of this sustained effort of historical rehabilitation in—of all places—American colleges and universities."[14]

David Horowitz observes, "The situation in the universities was appalling. The Marxists and Socialists who had been refuted by historical events were now the tenured establishment of the academic world. Marxism had produced the bloodiest and most oppressive regimes in human history—but after the fall, as one wit commented, more Marxists could be found on the faculties of American colleges than in the entire former Communist bloc. The American Historical Association was run by Marxists, as was the professional literature association."[15]

In America, the Secular Humanist worldview of Margaret Sanger and John Dewey monopolizes public education. It is the worldview held by thousands and thousands of professors and teachers and entertainers and professional organizations. "The [secular] humanistic system of values has now become the predominant way of thinking in most of the power centers of society," says James C. Dobson and Gary L. Bauer.[16] Dobson specifically mentions the universities, news media, entertainment industry, judiciary, federal bureaucracy, public schools, and Congress. Elsewhere Dobson and Bauer state, "Professors, whose salaries are paid by the taxes and tuition subsidies of millions of hardworking Americans, ridicule capitalism, attack family values, and rewrite American history, so that if it is taught at all, America is always the villain."[17]

The 20th century has been the century in which various humanistic worldviews vigorously and systematically eradicated the biblical Christian worldview from the public square.[18] If this continues, we can expect the same results—heartache, death, and destruction.

NAZISM

What most Christians misunderstand about Nazism is that it is a secular religious worldview or in Lord Acton's terms "a substitute for religion." In fact, most Christians look upon Nazism, Fascism, and Communism as merely political and/or economic movements. And nearly every Christian misses the point that Secular Humanism is a religious worldview. Contrary to the thinking of some German Christians, who insisted that the Nazi State was "a state that once again rules in God's name,''[19] Nazism was never a Christian world-view. None of its ingredients was Christian. Rather, it was pagan with occultish overtones. Dietrich Eckart, for example, a founding member of the Nazi Party was "a dedicated Satanist, a man immersed in black magic and the Thule group of occultists.[20] Himmler, Rosenberg, and Goebbels were dedicated occultists as was Karl Haushofer, who became Hitler's spiritual mentor following Eckart's death. According to Erwin Lutzer, Haushofer took Hitler "through the deepest levels of occult transformation."[21]

While Adolph Hitler historically represents the Nazi worldview, behind him stood a bevy of thinkers, philosophers, and theologians, including Darwin, Marx, Nietzsche, Gobineau,[22] Wagner,[23] Chamberlain, Heidegger, Karl Barth, Paul DeMan, and a who's who of intellectuals amongst Europe's elites. As Gene Edward Veith, Jr. observes, "The intellectual establishment itself is trying to keep hidden the fact that European high culture in its most advanced phase not only was powerless to prevent the construction and implementation of the death camps, but actually provided the ideological base on which the death camps were built.'"[24]

No matter how pagan, occultist, or even anti-Jewish or anti-Christian Nazism may have been, or how Socialistic, collectivistic, or evolutionistic, on Easter Sunday, April 16, 1933, "Protestant pastors across Bavaria delivered an official blessing of Nazism…passed the collection plate on Hitler's birthday, beflagged their churches on state holidays, and even marched in the 1933 May Day Parade for National Labor with swastikas stitched to their Vestments."[25]

In fairness to these pastors it should be noted that in 1918 Marxist Kurt Eisner staged a Communist coup in Munich and held the city for over three months.[26] The Nazis played on this theme and insisted that Christianity and Nazism fight the Red terror together.

What the pastors didn't realize is that Hitler's militant Socialism and Marxist Socialism are blood brothers—one national and one international. They didn't realize that the Nazis were quick to adopt the Soviet methods. They imported from Russia, according to Ludwig von Mises, "the one-party system and the pre-eminence of this party in political life; the paramount position assigned to the secret police; the concentration camps; the administrative execution or imprisonment of all opponents; the extermination of the families of suspects and of exiles; the methods of propaganda....There were nowhere more docile disciples of Lenin, Trotsky and Stalin than the Nazis were."[27]

University of Wisconsin historian Stanley G. Payne summarizes some of the major ingredients of Nazism. These include dictatorship, a new Social Darwinist structure of state and society, a racial revolution, and a state-regulated national Socialism.[28]

A.E. Wilder-Smith in *Man's Origin, Man's Destiny* points up the two major ideas behind Hitler and his Nazi movement: "It is noteworthy that many of our Western intellectuals have socialistic as well as Darwinistic views. Perhaps the two positions may be related. But it is more remarkable that Darwinism is not only the state doctrine of the Communists but was also that of the National Socialists and Fascists."[29]

Anyone reading Hitler's *Mein Kampf* ("My Struggle") realizes "how full Hitler was of Darwinistic thought" and how he based his racial and militaristic policies on the theory of Darwinian evolution. "Darwin's concepts of struggle for existence," says Wilder-Smith, "dominated Hitler's whole thinking and by guiding selection in this struggle Hitler intended to help nature a little."[30]

It is certainly no secret that Darwin's theory of evolution is still taught throughout our nation's colleges and universities. It is also taught at the high school level with absolutely no competition because the US Supreme Court ruled that Creationism is unconstitutional and cannot be taught. The writer of that decision, Judge Brennan, was the court's most vocal Secular Humanist.

This in spite of the fact that Cambridge professor Adam Sedgwick, after reading Darwin's *Origin of Species through Natural Selection or the Preservation of Favored Races in the Struggle for Life*, commented, "If this book were to find general public acceptance, it would bring with it a brutalization of the human race such as it had never seen before."[31]

Can anyone seriously doubt that the 20th century has witnessed the fulfillment of Sedgwick's observation as Hitler, Mussolini, and Stalin glorified struggle and war on the basis of the struggle for life?

Ian T. Taylor in *In the Minds of Man: Darwin and the New World Order* summarizes a number of scholars who "noted the strong connection between evolutionary theory and the German Fuhrer's objectives."[32] Taylor also points out that Werner Maser's study of Hitler found that "Darwin was the general source for Hitler's biology, worship, force, and struggle, and of his rejection of moral causality in history."[33]

Darwin wasn't Hitler's only god, however. Since Nazi means National Socialism it should not surprise anyone that Socialism[34] is as much a part of the Nazi worldview as Darwinism. Then, too, Socialism is consistent with Collectivism or Statism since it requires a dictator to abolish or control private property and decide where and when to produce a pair of shoes.

Friedrich A. Hayek's *The Road to Serfdom* observed the mental collectivizing of students in Germany: "Many a university professor during the 1930s has seen English and American students return from the continent uncertain whether they were Communists or Nazis and certain only that they hated Western liberal (in the traditional sense) Civilization."[35]

Youth flocked to the Nazis and Communist causes and some observed the incredible "susceptibility of university-trained people in Germany to totalitarian appeals."[36] Twenty-five percent of the Nazi SS were PhDs.

It was Germany's intellectual community that prepared the German people and especially the German youth for the "acceptance of some form of militant socialism."[37] Vetterli and Fort quote Hans Kohn and his work *The Mind of Germany* (Harper and Row, 1960) to the effect that "within little more than a decade German intellectuals succeeded in leading German people into the Abyss."[38] Kohn says it was primarily the philosophy of Martin Heidegger, the political theory of Carl Schmitt, and the theology of Karl Barth that convinced German intellectuals that Germany's future was not with the West.

Barth, of course, later joined forces with the anti-Nazi movement and was part of the Barmen Declaration.[39] But as John Robbins notes, while Barth's theological views changed over the decades, his political and economic views did not. Barth admitted that he chose theology because he felt a need to find a better basis for his social action. He was referred to as "Comrade Pastor." Barth claimed that Socialism "is a very important and necessary application of the gospel."[40]

A most revealing Barth comment is this: "If you understand the connection between the person of Jesus and your socialist convictions, and if you now want to arrange your life so that it corresponds to this connection, then that does not at all mean you have to 'believe" or accept this, that, or the other thing. What Jesus has to bring us are not ideas, but a way of life. One can have Christian ideas about God and the world and about human redemption, and still with all that be a complete heathen. And as an atheist, a materialist, and a Darwinist, one can be a genuine follower and disciple of Jesus. Jesus is not the Christian worldview and the Christian worldview is not Jesus."[41] Unfortunately for

Barth and his many defenders, he also ended up praising Communism and even Joseph Stalin. He was the ultimate anti-anti-Communist.[42]

So it wasn't just the teachings of Nietzsche, Fichte, Heidegger, Robertus, Lassalle, and Marx that prepared Germany for Hitler and Nazism. It was also Emanuel Hirsch, a dialectical theologian, Paul Tillich, a Marxist Socialist theologian, Rudolf Bultmann, Karl Barth, Gerhard Kittel, and Friedrich Delitzsch. All played a role in turning the hearts and minds of the German people away from Christ, the Cross, the empty tomb, and biblical Christianity to National Socialism and in some cases Marxist Socialism.

Hirsch and those who basically accepted German Higher Criticism taught that the resurrection of Jesus Christ was "only a spiritual vision" and that the resurrection accounts in the Gospels were later additions. Hirsch thought the idea of a physical resurrection distorted Christianity by focusing attention on the hereafter instead of the present. He stressed the importance of community in the Christian life.[43] Tillich, a member of the Marxist Frankfurt School,[44] was never friendly to biblical Christianity, and Bultmann advocated demythologizing the New Testament.

While space allows only a brief discussion of the Nazi worldview, we need to mention Hitler's and the Nazis' hatred of the Jews (and Bible-believing Christians).

Gene Edward Veith, Jr.'s *Modern Fascism* includes a chapter titled "The Hebrew Disease." He explains why Hitler and the Nazis were anti-Jewish. As he notes, it was more than Jews being considered an "inferior race." Hitler hated the ideas and worldview of the Jews—especially their Monotheism and defense of an absolute moral order based on something apart from the natural order. The Nietzsches and Hitlers of the world rejected a transcendent God who distinguishes right from wrong. Nazis believed that right and wrong are determined by nature, state, community, or human choice. They especially rejected the notion of a God judging man according to His standards. Hitler's anti-Semitism and anti-Bible-believing Christian (these Christians were considered a subset of the Hebrews) were as much theological as biological and racial. There is no doubt that Hitler was an ideological part of the Nietzsche/Wagner/Gobineau/Chamberlain cabal.

Veith also explains why the Christian church in Germany split over Hitler and his Nazi worldview. Those Christians who believed the Bible generally rejected Hitler; those softened up by German Higher Criticism of the Bible generally went with the German church collaborating with Hitler. Hitler referred to these Christians as "positive Christians."

How much have we learned from this portion of history? Not much according to historian Franklin Littell: "The lessons to be learned from the Church Struggle and the Holocaust have hardly penetrated our Protestant seminaries, our liberal Protestant press, our church literature, the thinking and writing of even our ablest older theologians.... American Liberal Protestantism is sick, and the theological form of its sickness can be summarized by saying that it stands solidly on ground but lately vacated by the 'German Christians'...who collaborated with Nazism."[45]

FASCISM

Fascism is a secular religious worldview in the same vein as Nazism. It was a pagan religion with worship of the state and its Duce on its list of major ingredients.

"Fascism," says Stanley G. Payne, "was above all a product of the new culture and intense international Social Darwinism of the early twentieth century, normally (though not in every instance) wedded to war and fundamental international changes. Its pagan warrior mentality sometimes conflicted with the norms and processes of modernization, but fascist states eagerly incorporated major functions of rationalization and modern development."[46]

Evolution was as important to Mussolini as it was to Hitler. A.E. Wilder-Smith states that both "Hitler and Mussolini glorified struggle and war on the basis that the fittest would survive and the race would be thus cleansed."[47] Both sought to assist nature in the inevitable progress of mankind.

Elsewhere Wilder-Smith says that Mussolini found "evolutionary doctrine a real windfall, in fact, a godsend."[48] It gave Mussolini the excuse to enslave whole peoples, or wipe them out—especially if they were less highly evolved than his own people. The whole concept of evolution, says Wilder-Smith, "justifies the terror of fascism, communism and other types of tyranny."[49]

According to Veith, the major elements of the Fascist worldview emerged from three sources: Romanticism, Darwinism, and Existentialism. He says these were mainstream Western thought patterns and were the basic assumptions of the intellectual elite of the 1930s. Because Fascist Totalitarianism sought to control all of life, it was a worldview, and since it sought to establish a new religion, it was a religious world view. Says Veith, "This new worldview defined itself against the existing spiritual framework— that of the Jews and their Bible. In rejecting not only the Bible but objective meaning, transcendent morality, and the authority of language itself, the fascists arrayed themselves against the Word."[50]

As with Hitler, who personally failed the lower grades of high school but had his quiver full of intellectuals, so too Mussolini. "Some of the greatest modern writers," says Stephen Spender, "sympathized with fascism."[51] These included Ezra Pound, D.H. Lawrence, W.B. Yeats, George Bernard Shaw, Wyndham Lewis, T.E. Hulme, Roy Campbell, and the early T.S. Eliot. Also, says Spender, "Avant-garde artistic movements—Vorticists, Italian Futurists, German Expressionists—included many devotees of fascism."[52]

George Bernard Shaw, a darling of every leftist and a founder of the Socialist British Fabian Society, character-ized the Jews as "the real enemy, the invader from the East, the Druze, the riffian, the oriental parasite, in a word the Jew."[53] Henri Bernstein, the French Jewish writer, sarcas-tically referred to Shaw as "dear socialist, multimillionaire and anti-Semite."[54] Shaw's advice to the Nazis on the Jewish question was to "[f]orce the Jews to wed Aryans" and thus the Jewish question would be solved.[55]

Shaw's fascistic bent was also coupled with an intense "sympathy for the communist world," says Dobbs. "All totalitarianisms fascinated him since they fitted into his plans for a rigid collectivism." Therefore, he could announce to the world, "We, as socialists, have nothing to do with lib-erty. Our message, like Mussolini's, is one of discipline, of service, of ruthless refusal to acknowledge any natural right of competence."[56]

But Shaw's famous definition of Socialism (also true of Fascism, Nazism, Communism, and Fabianism[57]) was, "You would be forcibly fed, clothed, lodged, taught and employed whether you liked it or not. If it were discovered that you had not character and industry enough to be worth all this trou-ble, you might possibly be executed in a kindly manner."[58]

None of these individuals or movements could be con-sidered conservative or right-leaning in any meaningful sense of those words. Fascism, Nazism, and Communism were brutal Socialist dictatorships. Mussolini's father was "a socialist revolutionary,"[59] and Mussolini "chose at first the orthodox Marxian position." In fact, says von Mises, "Nobody could surpass Mussolini in Marxian zeal. He was the intransigent champion of the pure creed, the unyielding defender of the rights of the exploited proletarians, the elo-quent prophet of the socialist bliss to come."[60]

According to both von Mises and Vetterli/Fort, Mussolini was under the influence of Angelica Balbanoff, a trained Communist agent who was later to become the first secretary of the Third Communist International.[61] Mussolini also edited a Socialist newspaper for some time entitled "The Class Struggle" and thought himself to be Nietzsche's rendition of "Superman."

Says Vetterli and Fort, "Fascist theory thus exemplified much of the philosophy of Nietzsche. To Nietzsche, the will to power, the desire to dominate gave meaning to life. Truth is relative. It is freed from moral connotations. Truth is whatever aids the will to power....This superman would be beyond the pale of moral restraint. He would himself create the standard of value. The cult of power was to replace traditional religion and moral values. There is no doubt that Benito Mussolini, (as Hitler after him) believed himself to be the personification of Nietzsche's superman."[62]

Have we learned anything from this portion of history? "Will to power," "Moral Relativism," "truth is relative," "replace traditional religion," "replace moral values" are all fundamental planks of Postmodernism! Postmodernism is the latest rage of the intellectuals on America's colleges and universities.[63]

We have learned nothing!

MARXISM-LENINISM

Like Nazism and Fascism, Marxism likewise is a secular religious worldview. In fact, Marxism is a well-developed atheistic, materialistic, evolutionistic, Socialistic, relativistic worldview.

While I have examined this worldview in detail elsewhere[64] and will summarize it briefly in this section, let's cut directly to the praxis of this worldview and state in no uncertain terms for all the world to hear: Marxism-Leninism has been the greatest killing machine in recorded history. And history has recorded some unbelievable mass killings.[65]

With Hitler given the distinction of eliminating 21 million human beings from the face of the earth—Vladimir Lenin, Joseph Stalin, Mao Tse-tung, and other Communist dictators eliminated millions more.[66] Jung Chang and Jon Halliday in their work *Mao: The Unknown Story*, place Mao's killing spree at 75 million alone![67] *The Black Book of Communism: Crimes, Terror, Repression* places the death toll of Communism over 100 million.[68] The suffering and stark terror of this figure is humanly impossible to comprehend. For a taste of what was involved we recommend Robert Conquest's *Harvest of Sorrows*, the account of Stalin's slaughter in the Ukraine.

But Stalin's basis for such a slaughter was Darwin. "Evolution," said Stalin, "prepares for revolution and creates the ground for it; revolution consummates the process of evolution and facilitates its further activity."[69] The Ukrainians were considered not fit to survive! But before Stalin could move into the high stakes of death and destruction, he needed Marx and Lenin.

Karl Marx wrote *The Communist Manifesto* in 1848 and called for the elimination of the bourgeoisie (property owners). He said, "This person [bourgeois] must, indeed, be swept out of the way, and made impossible."[70] He also said, "[T]he Communists everywhere support every revolutionary movement against the existing social and political order of things."[71] And again, "They [Communists] openly declare that their ends can be attained only by the forcible overthrow of all existing social conditions."[72] Lenin took this one step further and set up the state apparatus to, in fact, eliminate the bourgeoisie. And while Lenin did his fair share of killings, it was Joseph Stalin and Mao Tse-tung who took Marxist's teachings and Lenin's state apparatus to its ultimate extent.

Again, as with Nazism and Fascism, Marxist/Leninist/ Stalinist Communism is based on Darwinism, Socialism, and Statism; it is also based on Atheism, Dialectical Materialism, and proletariat morality. In fact, the millions that perished at the hands of the Communists all perished under the innocent sounding expression of proletariat morality. The bourgeoisie were unfit to live because they believed in God, a created order, transcendent morality, family values, and property ownership.

"It is a commonplace," says Jacques Barzun, "that Marx felt his own work to be the exact parallel of Darwin's. He even wished to dedicate a portion of *Das Kapital* to the author of *The Origin of Species*."[73]

Marx thought he had discovered the evolution of society as Darwin had discovered the evolution of biological life. Both theories brought the world to the bottom of the abyss. The struggle for life and survival of the fittest form the basis of both Darwin and Marx. And thus Stalin, too! Stalin merely put into practice what Marx (and Lenin) taught.

Marx's Atheism, Dialectical Materialism, Darwinism, and Socialism make up the heart of the Communist world-view. These are the ideas put into praxis which brought us the slaughter of the 20th century. Yet, as we enter the 21st century, Marxist ideas are still part of the intellectuals' quiver. Campus Marxists and postmodernists, for example, continue to propagate Atheism, Materialism, Darwinism, Socialism, and Collectivism. Hardly anything has changed! We have allowed history to teach us absolutely nothing. An atheistic evolutionist, for example, has immediate access to America's public educational institutions and stands a good chance of winning recognition and awards. A theistic creationist, on the other hand, is denied access to such educational institutions and considered a Neanderthal or a trilobite. An atheistic evolutionist who is also an advocate of world government has access to all educational institutions and is guaranteed even more awards and foundation grants. Anyone who suggests US military personnel should not be placed under UN control will be denied access and called narrow-minded, intolerant, and unloving. The ways of the left in propaganda and name-calling haven't changed for over a hundred years (see Zygmund Dobb's *The Great Deceit: Social Pseudo-Sciences*) and evidently will not change anytime soon.

Regarding theology, Marxism/Leninism/Stalinism is Atheistic. Lenin, for example, in his "Socialism and Religion" address insisted that Communism is based on the scientific, materialistic view of the world and, therefore, says Lenin, "our propaganda necessarily includes the propaganda of atheism."[74] Elsewhere Lenin says, "Every religious idea, every idea of God, even flirting with the idea of God, is unutterable vileness...vileness of the most dangerous kind."[75]

"For Marx and the classical Marxist authors," says Hans Kung, "in their personal life, in their culture, in their system and in their practice—atheism was and remained of central importance and essentially connected with their theory of society and history."[76] This led Dostoevsky to remark, "The problem of Communism is not an economic problem. The problem of Communism is the problem of atheism."[77]

The philosophy of Marxism/Leninism/Stalinism is Dialectical Materialism. The heart of the philosophy states two things: a) matter is reality, and b) matter behaves dialectically.[78] Dialectical Materialism attempts to explain all of reality—including inorganic matter (the molecular, atomic, and subatomic), the organic world (life, and according to Materialism, mind or consciousness), and social life (economics, politics, etc.). All of nature reflects, illuminates, and illustrates Communist dialectical philosophy. For better or worse, the Marxist philosophy is built primarily on the "science" of Darwinian evolution. Matter behaves in an upward progression from an inorganic to an organic state, from the organic to man, from man to the social level and all responding to certain laws: a) the unity and struggle of opposites; b) the transformation of quantity into quality; and c) the negation of the negation. The dialectical laws manifest a threefold rhythm of equilibrium (thesis), disturbance (antithesis) and re-establishment of equilibrium (synthesis). All good Marxists believe the physical universe acts according to such laws.

Marxist ethics proceeds out of Marxist theology, philosophy, biology, economics, and history. It is an ethics that states an absolute: class morality. Whatever advances the proletariat class, by definition, is good. Or put another way, each act is considered ethically good if it assists the flow of history toward a Communist end. Killing, raping, stealing, and lying are not outside the boundaries of Communist morality. Marxists/Leninists/Stalinists have absolutely no trouble believing that killing evolving materialistic human beings infected with the concepts of God, transcendent morality, and private property is as morally justified as a farmer killing a materialistic evolving cow afflicted with hoof-and-mouth disease. The killing fields of Cambodia, the Ukraine, Russian, and China are the practical results of class morality.

Said one Communist dictator, "Our cause is sacred. He whose hand will tremble, who will stop midway, whose knees will shake before he destroys tens and hundreds of enemies, he will lead the revolution into danger. Whoever will spare a few lives of enemies, will pay for it with hundreds and thousands of lives of the better sons of our fathers."[79]

Marxist/Leninist/Stalinist biology centers on Charles Darwin. Says Marx, "Darwin's [*Origin of Species*] is very important and provides me with the basis in natural science for the class struggle in history."[80] Frederick Engels said, "Just as Darwin discovered the law of evolution in organic nature, so Marx discovered the law of evolution in human history."[81] Few doubt that Darwin's theory of evolution and Marx's theory of Communism fit hand to glove.

The psychology of Marxism centers around materialistic Behaviorism in which man is looked upon as a conditioned evolving animal or as Lenin says, "Matter is primary nature. Sensation, thought, consciousness, are the highest products of matter organized in a certain way. This is the doctrine of materialism, in general, and Marx and Engels, in particular."[82]

Marxist sociology can be summarized quickly: abolish all social structures that reflect a theistic worldview. Or as Marx says in *The Communist Manifesto*, "The Communists disdain to conceal their views and aims. They openly declare that their ends can be attained only by the forcible overthrow of all existing social conditions."[83] The three social institutions fit for overthrow are the family, the church, and the state. Few remember that Marx and Engels called for "an openly legalized community of women" in *The Communist Manifesto*.[84]

Marxist/Leninist/Stalinist law is simply evolutionary law writ large. There are no legal absolutes because mankind is evolving and law is evolving with it. There is no eternal lawgiver since there is no God. Therefore, there are no eternal legal principles. Legal principles that assist man in his evolutionary, Socialistic history are just laws; all others are unjust. Case closed! Marx put it like this: "Law, morality, religion, are to [the proletariat] so many bourgeois prejudices, behind which lurk in ambush just as many bourgeois interests."[85]

Politics is power politics. State terror is part and parcel of the "Dictatorship of the Proletariat." Lenin states, "The art of politics lies in correctly gauging the conditions and the moment when the vanguard of the proletariat [the killing machine] can successfully seize power."[86] Engels is likewise brutal: "In reality, however, the State is nothing more than a machine for the oppression of one class by another."[87] The political machinery put together by the disciples of Marx slaughtered millions of human beings.

The economics of the Marxist/Leninist/Stalinist world-view is Socialism. Karl Marx summarized it this way: "The theory of Communists may be summed up in the single sentence: Abolition of private property."[88] Lenin also summarized the heart of Socialism: "Communist society means that everything—the land, the factories—is owned in common. Communism means working in common."[89] Millions were slaughtered to establish a Socialist utopia. But then one can't have an omelette without smashing eggs. But from a Communist point of view, an evolving human animal is no different than an egg. Unfortunately, this position echoes the Secular Humanist position stated by Oliver Wendell Holmes: "I see no reason for attributing to man a significance different in kind from that which belongs to a baboon or a grain of sand....I don't believe it is an absolute principle...that man is always an end in himself—that his dignity must be respected."[90]

The Marxist/Leninist/Stalinist interpretation of history consists of one major and a few minor ideas. The major idea is the dialectical nature of matter. All history—all reality—is seen as the outworking of this all-encompassing concept. Dialectical matter is eternal. All else follows from this premise. Dialectical matter determines history. Communists believe in nudging history. Joseph Stalin alone was guilty of "the persecution, imprisonment, torture and death of some fifty million human beings."[91]

Have our intellectuals learned anything from this period of history? "Postmodernism [is] a wayward stepchild of Marxism."[92] Some haven't!

SECULAR HUMANISM

Secular Humanism is also a secular religious worldview. John Dewey in *A Common Faith* said, "Here are all the elements for a religious faith that shall not be confined to sect, class, or race. Such a faith has always been implicitly the common faith of mankind. It remains to make it explicit and militant."[93]

Margaret Sanger, recipient of the Humanist of the Year award in 1957, represents an aspect of Secular Humanism that may end up killing more human beings than Nazism, Fascism, and Communism combined.

Sanger is the founder of Planned Parenthood (1939), an organization responsible for the death of millions of unborn human beings. These killings continue 24 hours a day, 7 days a week, 365 days a year with no end in sight.

Secular Humanists have put into practice the slaughter of the innocent in accordance with their desire to further the sexual/social revolution. Sanger, Mary Calderone (1974), and Faye Wattleton (1986) have all been recipients of the Humanist of the Year award. All three were heavily involved in promoting the sexual revolution. "If it is possible for one person to change the very foundations of civilization from a moral one to an immoral one, then Margaret Sanger should rightfully be known as the founder of modern culture because today's culture is characterized precisely by the values she and her admirers taught."[94]

As an advocate and practitioner of free-love, Sanger was part of the Wantley Circle along with Havelock Ellis, Harold Child, and Hugh de Selincourt.[95] H.G. Wells was another of her lovers. He said, "Margaret Sanger made currents and circumstances. When the history of our civilization is written, it will be a biological history and Margaret Sanger will be its heroine."[96]

One of the goals of Planned Parenthood was to help "young people obtain sex satisfaction before marriage.

">
Worldviews of Destruction

By sanctioning sex before marriage, we will prevent fear and guilt."[97] The Planned Parenthood publication *You've Changed the Combination* states, "There are only two kinds of sex: sex with victims and sex without. Sex with victims is always wrong. Sex without is always right."[98]

When Wattleton accepted her Humanist of the Year award, she paid special tribute to the founder of Planned Parenthood, Margaret Sanger. To a great extent Sanger epitomizes the Secular Humanist worldview. Nothing in her teaching or lifestyle falls outside of Humanism in theory or practice.

For example, she founded the publication "The Woman Rebel," whose slogan was "No Gods! No Masters!" As an atheistic worldview, Secular Humanism's slogan could well be the same. In the first edition of "The Woman Rebel" she denounced marriage as "a degenerate institution" and sexual modesty as "obscene prudery."[99] Sanger's hero was Havelock Ellis. Upon reading his massive seven-volume *Studies in the Psychology of Sex*, she told her husband that she needed to be liberated from the strict bonds of marriage. She ultimately deserted her husband to practice free love in Greenwich Village.

Sanger's relationship to the Nazi worldview involves Ernst Rudin, Hitler's director of the Nazi Society for Racial Hygiene. In 1933, the Planned Parenthood Review published Rudin's article "Eugenic Sterilization: An Urgent Need." Later in 1933, it published an article by Leon Whitney defending the Third Reich's racial program.[100]

Sanger called for limiting the number of children for the poorer classes, requiring parents to apply for a license to have a baby, forcibly sterilizing poor people while encouraging the more successful human types to have more children, and a new world order without crime and poverty caused by the birth of genetically inferior children. "But unlike Adolph Hitler, Margaret Sanger successfully encouraged

[269]

peaceful methods of racial 'purification.' Whenever possible she advocated that people should be paid to be sterilized by gifts of money and presents."[101] She referred to people with objectionable traits such as disabilities as "human weeds."

Dr. Lothrop Stoddard, a co-worker of Sanger, wrote *Into the Darkness, Nazi Germany Today* (1940), expressing his admiration for the Germans' "weeding out the worst strains in the Germanic stock in a scientific and truly humanitarian ways."[102]

As George Grant notes, Margaret Sanger was mesmerized by the "scientific" racism of Malthusian Eugenics. She followed her lover Havelock Ellis, who in turn followed Francis Galton who first systemized and popularized eugenic thought. Galton was a cousin of Charles Darwin. Grant says that Sanger's attraction to race was also political: "Virtually all of her Socialist friends, lovers, and comrades were committed Eugenicists—from the followers of Lenin in Revolutionary Socialism, like H.G. Wells, George Bernard Shaw, and Julius Hammer, to the followers of Hitler in National Socialism, like Ernst Rudin, Leon Whitney, and Harry Laughlin."[103]

Although Margaret Sanger is a true representative of Secular Humanism, John Dewey is its most famous and important voice. Dewey's influence on American education has dominated since the 1930s. Secular Humanism is the only worldview allowed in public schools. Humanist Charles Francis Potter in his work *Humanism: A New Religion* says, "Education is the most powerful ally of Humanism, and every American public school is a school of Humanism. What can the theistic Sunday Schools, meeting for an hour once a week, and teaching only a fraction of the children, do to stem the tide of a five-day program of humanistic teaching?"[104]

From kindergarten through graduate school, American students are immersed in the doctrines and dogmas of

Secular Humanism. The US Supreme Court designated Secular Humanism a religion in 1961,[105] yet has made sure that Secular Humanism is still allowed to be taught in the classroom.

How this situation came about is explained in one of the most powerful studies of the 20th century—the Veritas Foundation's *The Great Deceit: Social Pseudo-Sciences* and *Keynes at Harvard*. These studies trace how leftists, Socialists, liberals, and humanists slowly but surely captured the social sciences (sociology, anthropology, history, economics, jurisprudence) and even some pulpits of America.

The Great Deceit is replete with references to John Dewey,[106] including his relationship to the League for Industrial Democracy, America's counterpart to the British Fabian Society. Dewey epitomizes Secular Humanism as an atheist in theology, a naturalist in philosophy, an ethical relativist in morals, an evolutionist in biology, and a Socialist in economics.

To conclude this discussion of Secular Humanism as a destructive worldview, let's look at particular Secular Humanist views in ten disciplines:

Theology—*Atheism*: "Humanism cannot in any fair sense of the word apply to one who still believes in God as the source and creator of the universe."[107]

Philosophy—*Naturalism*: "Naturalistic Humanism…is the Humanism that I have supported through the written and spoken word for some forty years."[108]

Ethics—*Relativism*: "No inherent moral or ethical laws exist, nor are there absolute guiding principles for human society. The universe cares nothing for us and we have no ultimate meaning in life."[109]

Biology—*Evolution*: "Evolution is a fact amply demonstrated by the fossil record and by contemporary molecular biology. Natural selection is a successful theory devised to explain the fact of evolution."[110]

Psychology—*Self-actualization*: "For myself, though I am very well aware of the incredible amount of destructive, cruel, malevolent behavior in today's world—from the threats of war to the senseless violence in the streets—I do not find that this evil is inherent in human nature."[111]

Sociology—*Social "Science"*: "Marriage, for most people, has outlived its usefulness and is doing more harm than good."[112]

Law—*Positive Law*: "No matter how misperceived as natural they may be, rights...are the works of human artifice."[113]

Politics—*Globalism*: "It is essential for UNESCO to adopt an evolutionary approach....The general philosophy of UNESCO should, it seems, be a scientific world human, global in extent and evolutionary in background....Thus, the struggle for existence that underlies natural selection is increasingly replaced by conscious selection, a struggle between ideas and values in consciousness."[114]

Economics—*Socialism*: "A socialized and cooperative economic order must be established to the end that the equitable distribution of the means of life be possible."[115]

History—*Atheistic Evolution*: "The laws of biology are the fundamental lessons of history."[116] "War is one of the constants of history and is the ultimate form of natural selection in the human species."[117]

CONCLUSION

"But sanctify Christ as Lord in your hearts, always being ready to make a defense to everyone who asks you to give an account for the hope that is in you, with gentleness and reverence" (1 Peter 3:15).

Erwin W. Lutzer says every believer "must be able to give a rationale for his or her faith, defending the supremacy of Christ over all other alternatives."[118]

The alternative to the 20th century's destructive humanistic worldviews is Jesus Christ. Lutzer rightly says, "We do not know where all this [the ACLU and liberal left seeking to cleanse the public square of biblical Christianity] will end. What we do know is that we have the high honor of representing Christ in the midst of this ideological mega-shift. Our challenge is to rise to this hour of incredible challenge and opportunity."[119]

Lutzer doesn't think that spending two hours in church on Sunday mornings will meet the challenge. Rather than being couch potatoes, we must live for Christ twenty-four hours a day, seven days a week. This kind of life demands discipline, prayer, witness, study, and confrontation (Acts 17:16*ff*). We must live biblical Christianity in all the disciplines—theology, philosophy, ethics, biology, psychology, sociology, law, politics, economics, and history.[120]

If the 21st century is to turn out differently than the 20th, Christians need to pay attention and learn from the lessons of history that are the subject of this book.

Lutzer, who has studied the surrender of the Christian church under Hitler, gives this advice: "It is time that Christians become leaders in art, education, politics, and law….Let's not make the mistake of the German church and isolate the spiritual sphere from the political, social, and cultural world. Bonhoeffer was critical of the church when its only interest was self-preservation. We should be characterized by giving, not withholding. Since we share this planet with all of humanity, we must reestablish connections in all of those areas where Christians often led the way."[121]

FOR FURTHER STUDY

LaHaye, Tim and David A. Noebel. *Mind Siege: The Battle for Truth in the New Millennium*. Nashville, TN: Word Publishing, 2000.

Nash, Ronald H. *Worldviews in Conflict: Choosing Christianity in a World of Ideas*. Grand Rapids, MI: Zondervan Publishing House, 1992.

Noebel, David A. *Understanding the Times: The Collision of Today's Competing Worldviews*. Rev. 2nd ed. Manitou Springs, CO: Summit Press, 2006.

Noebel, David A., J.F. Baldwin and Kevin Bywater. *Clergy in the Classroom: The Religion of Secular Humanism,* Rev. 3rd ed. Manitou Springs, CO: Summit Press, 2007.

Pearcey, Nancy R. *Total Truth: Liberating Christianity from Its Cultural Captivity*. Wheaton, IL: Crossway Books, 2004.

Veith, Jr., Gene Edward. *Modern Fascism: Liquidating the Judeo-Christian Worldview*. St. Louis: Concordia Publishing House, 1993.

CHAPTER FOURTEEN

Barack Obama's Red Spiritual Advisor

by
David A. Noebel

El Salvador has officially joined the Red regimes of Cuba, Venezuela, Nicaragua, Ecuador, and Bolivia. South America is turning Red, dark Red, and little is being said to alert North Americans of the encroaching Red plague.[1] Perhaps that's because North America is moving in the same direction. The President of the United States, Barack Obama, has surrounded himself with Socialists, and some of those closest to him have had a part in turning South America Red.

According to the Associated Press, Mauricio Funes, the presidential candidate of the left-wing Farabundo Martí National Liberation Front (FMLN), is the new head of the nation of El Salvador. Behind Funes "is a party of former Marxist guerrillas that fought to overthrow U.S.-backed governments in the 1980s and whose rise to power has raised fears of a communist regime in the war-scarred Central American country."[2]

The AP further reported "ex-guerrillas will almost certainly form part of the Funes government, including Vice President-elect Salvador Sanchez Ceren, a rebel commander-turned-congressman."[3]

And then there's the "drug" connection! *Investor's Business Daily* reports that "last May, the FMLN confessed to 'a relationship' with Colombia's drug-trafficking FARC Marxist terrorists after documents found on the computer of dead FARC chieftain Raul Reyes, killed in a 2008 raid, proved it."[4]

Funes, of course, says he'll "govern moderately, more like Brazil 'socialist' President Luiz Inacio Lula da Silva than Venezuela's radical [Communist] Hugo Chavez."[5] Of course, this is what the Nicaraguan Communist Daniel Ortega said, too, before he displayed his Communist "proletariat morality" by hugging Communist dictators Castro and Chavez. Ortega and all his South American pals are hardcore Marxist-Leninists.

While all of this, of course, is relevant to an ardent free-market Capitalist, what really frightens me is that Obama's latest announced "spiritual advisor" has had connections with all these Marxist regimes. And who is the President's latest advisor? The Rev. Jim Wallis!

Front Page Magazine reports, "The most notable of [Obama's] spiritual advisors today is his friend of many years, Rev. Jim Wallis."[6] Rev. Wallis admits that he and Obama have "been talking faith and politics for a long time." He was picked by Obama to draft the faith-based policies of his campaign at the Democratic National Convention in Denver, Colorado in 2008. Why should this alarm us?

First, Jim Wallis has been a major player with the Communist Committee in Solidarity with the People of El Salvador (CISPES).[7]

Second, his "Witness for Peace" was an attempt to defend the Nicaraguan Sandinistas! Wallis, together with the Rev. Jeremiah Wright (Obama's former pastor of 20 years) "rallied support for the communist Nicaraguan regime and protested actions by the United States which supported the anti-communist Contra rebels."[8]

Third, Wallis and his Sojourners community of fellow-travelers believe Fidel Castro's Cuba, Hugo Chavez's Venezuela, Daniel Ortega's Nicaragua, and the other revolutionary forces "restructuring socialist societies" are the Communist paradises the United States needs to emulate in order to establish "social justice." Writing in the November 1983 issue of Sojourners, Jacob Laksin notes, "Jim Wallis and Jim Rice drafted what would become the charter of leftist activists committed to the proliferation of Communist revolutions in Central America."[9]

The ugly truth is Wallis wishes to see the destruction of the United States as a nation and in its place "a radical nonconformist community" patterned after the progressive, Socialist commune he established in Washington, DC, in 1971.[10]

"The Sojourners community," says Laksin, "actively embraced 'liberation theology,' rallying to the cause of communist regimes that had seized power with the promise of bringing about a revolutionary restructuring of society." Clark Pinnock, a disaffected former member of Sojourners, said that the community's members were "100 percent in favor of the Nicaraguan [Communist] revolution."[11]

All this revolutionary activity in spite of the fact that today's Cuba, for example, has to import 84 percent of its food supply due to the Socialistic mess of the agricultural system (150,000 oxen till the ground because tractors represent Capitalism). However, in a move that looks more like Capitalism than Marxism's state farms, "Raul Castro is moving to boost food production by putting more land under the control of private farmers."[12]

It appears that Raul Castro is learning what America's early pilgrims learned back in the 1620s! William Bradford noted in his *History of Plymouth Plantation* that once he canceled the pilgrims' Socialistic experiment and provided each settler with a piece of property to till, starvation was averted. We can hope and pray that Raul Castro continues to implement more Capitalistic policies and will learn firsthand the economic system that has brought more people out of poverty than any other in the history of the world.[13]

Of course, Rev. Wallis should have learned the lessons of Plymouth Plantation early in his education, but may not have because our Secular Humanistic K–12 curricula delete most of the history of the pilgrims and the Mayflower Compact in an attempt to avoid acknowledging its "advancement of Christianity."

For years, Wallis has been in the forefront of the "evangelical" left and has been fêted at numerous evangelical colleges and seminaries. That seems to be the "in" thing right now! His publication *Sojourners* is piled high on these campuses for the reading pleasure of the naïve and foolish.

Unbeknown to these colleges and seminaries is Wallis' Red background. He was the president of the radical Students for a Democratic Society (SDS) while at Michigan State University. The SDS was the youth arm of the League for Industrial Democracy—the American counterpart to the British Fabian Society founded to promote Socialism throughout the West. One of the League's mentors for years was Norman Thomas, who argued that "the American people will never knowingly adopt socialism, but under the name of liberalism, they will adopt every fragment of the socialist program until one day America will be a socialist nation without ever knowing how it happened."[14] Another prominent League mentor was John Dewey, a signatory of the atheistic, Socialistic 1933 *Humanist Manifesto*. The SDS actually merits a chapter in Richard J. Ellis's *The Dark Side of the Left: Illiberal Egalitarianism in America* published by the University of Kansas Press.

In October of 1969, SDS original organizer Tom Hayden directed his followers to "set off on a rampage, smashing windows of parked cars, hurling rocks and bricks through apartment windows, and fighting with police." Hayden blamed the police for his violence even though later his followers "comforted themselves, because theirs was a violence to end all violence, a liberating and righteous violence that would rid the world of a system that deformed and destroyed people. Such glorious ends justified, even ennobled, violent means."[15]

Ellis insists that the language of revolution and violent confrontation was evident throughout the ranks of the SDS. Jim Wallis was part and parcel of this pro-Communist group of radicals and revolutionaries.

Wallis' Sojourners enterprise has been a radical, Socialistic undertaking from the start. *Front Page Magazine* says, "As one of its first acts, Sojourners formed a commune in the Washington, DC neighborhood of Southern Columbia Heights, where members shared their finances and participated in various activist campaigns that centered on attacking the US foreign policy, denouncing American 'imperialism,' and extolling Marxist revolutionary movements in the Third World."[16]

Sojourners contributing editors included the radical Daniel "Plowshares" Berrigan, Walter Brueggemann, James Hal Cone (author of the racist *Black Theology and Black Power* that depicts the white race as devils), Rosemary Radford Ruether (Professor of Feminist Theology, Catholics for Choice, God is the feminine Gaia), Ron Sider, Cornel West,[17] and Garry Wills. Today, *Sojourners'* Board of Directors includes Wallis, Ron Sider, Brian McLaren, and Bart Campolo.

Over the years, Wallis has been pro-Vietcong and actually gloried in America's defeat in Vietnam. He said, "I don't know how else to express the quiet emotion that rushed through me when the news reports showed that the United States had finally been defeated in Vietnam."[18]

However, like Jane Fonda, Wallis said next to nothing about the Communist genocide that followed the wars in Vietnam and Cambodia. In fact, in a typical Communist response, he criticized those fleeing Vietnam by boat as somehow attempting "to support their consumer habits in other lands."[19]

Wallis has been closely associated with Richard Barnet (former contributing editor of *Sojourners*) and the Institute for Policy Studies, a radical left-wing think tank supporting Socialist revolutionaries around the world.[20] Wallis had his book *The Soul of Politics* published by Orbis Books in 1994, a radical left-wing Roman Catholic publishing arm of the radical left-wing Maryknollers and *Sojourner* magazine has been a strong supporter of the Cuban dictator Fidel Castro and, indeed, has supported every left-wing, liberation theology cause around the world.[21]

And yes, Wallis portrays the evangelical right that happens to be pro-American and anti-Communist "as members of the forces of darkness."[22] For Wallis, a good Christian is someone who is pro-Communist and Socialist, while a bad Christian is someone who is anti-Communist and pro-Capitalist. The cry of the Sojourners crowd is "social justice" for the poor and downtrodden—social justice being code for Socialism or the redistribution of wealth.

The Marxist worldview is totally contrary to biblical Christianity, and I document this extensively in my book *Understanding the Times: The Collision of Today's Competing Worldviews*. Furthermore, Communism is directly responsible for the murder of tens of millions of human beings, a slaughter documented in the 1999 publication of *The Black Book of Communism* by Stephane Courtois, et. al., and R.J. Rummel's *Death by Government*. Both books are not on *Sojourner*'s list of must reading!

I will attempt to be as kind and gentle as humanly possible and break the news to the Rev. Wallis and his "spiritual" advisee Barack Obama—Socialism has never lifted the poor out of poverty. It has equally distributed poverty, but it has never been able to create the wealth that is partially responsible for lifting the poor out of poverty. This is more than documented in Peter Bauer's *Equality, the Third World, and Economic Delusion* and Thomas Sowell's *Intellectuals and Society*.

I say "partially responsible" because one's worldview is even more important than wealth in reducing poverty. But Socialism is a flawed idea, and it poisons the worldview of the people it influences. Those on the evangelical left who are concerned with the poor need to read Theodore Dalrymple's *Life at the Bottom: The Worldview That Makes the Underclass*. Although not a Christian, Dalrymple understands the importance of a proper worldview and its role in combating poverty, drugs, crime, and broken families.

Can we admit a hard truth? Christian Capitalist Truett Cathy's Chik-fil-A has done more to fight poverty and help the poor than all the pronouncements of Jim Wallis, Ron Sider, Daniel Berrigan, Brian McLaren, Tony and Bart Campolo, and their entire crew of left-wing sociological and economic friends combined.

Thomas Sowell explains, "It would be devastating to the egos of the intelligentsia to realize, much less admit, that businesses have done more to reduce poverty than all the intellectuals put together. Ultimately, it is only wealth that can reduce poverty and most of the intelligentsia have no interest whatever in finding out what actions and policies increase the national wealth."[23]

In fact, the intellectuals are the very ones who complain about those who do increase wealth. Again, Thomas Sowell speaks to this issue: "Think about the things that have improved our lives the most over the past century—medical advances, the transportation revolution, huge increases in consumer goods, dramatic improvements in housing, the computer revolution. The people who created these things—the doers—are not popular heroes. Our heroes are the talkers who complain about the doers."[24]

In *Intellectuals and Society* Sowell quotes the French writer Raymond Aron to the effect that the European Left are resentful of any economic system that lifts people out of their poverty apart from its "revolutionary code" and "State Interventionism."[25] The fact that India and China have instilled Capitalistic ingredients in their economic policies and have lifted tens of millions out of poverty is considered a downer.

Socialism is built on the slogan "What can government do for me today?" instead of "What can I do to better prepare myself to take care of myself in order to be a better Christian and servant of my Lord?" Preparation involves individual responsibility, traditional family values, education, love of God and neighbor, and compassion for the up-and-outers as well as the down-and-outers.

Socialists stand against nearly every Christian, conservative principle imaginable. Compare the Socialist agenda with Yale professor David Gelernter's summary of the conservative position—"the freedom of every American to make his own way, free speech on the radio and everywhere else, free elections for workers and other people…freedom to acknowledge and celebrate the nation's rootedness in Christianity, Judaism, and the Bible…love of liberty, and love of God."[26]

In 2006, Barack Obama was the keynote speaker at Jim Wallis' Call to Renewal conference, "Building a Covenant for a New America." Following his address, in an interview in the *United Church News*, he cited "the teachings of the UCC (United Church of Christ) as foundation stones for his political work." He said, "Just as my pastor the Rev. Jeremiah Wright from Trinity United Church of Christ in Chicago welcomed me as a young man years ago, UCC churches across the country open their doors to millions of Americans each Sunday…I believe that democracy demands that the religiously motivated translate their concerns into universal values. Social justice and national security are both universal values, values that may originate for some in their religious beliefs, but are shared by us all."[27]

What Americans can look forward to now that Rev. Wallis has the ear of President Obama is what *Sojourners* magazine has been pedaling since 1971—"advocating America's transformation into a socialist nation."[28]

CHAPTER FIFTEEN

The Socialization of America

by
David A. Noebel

In retrospect, we may discover that 1883 was a most significant year. We're familiar with 1848 giving the world *The Communist Manifesto* and 1859 giving us *The Origin of Species by Means of Natural Selection or the Preservation of Favoured Races in the Struggle for Life*, but 1883 gave us three portentous happenings. These seemingly unrelated happenings turned history toward state-sponsored Socialism which today is called Neocommunism, Interventionism, Progressivism, Radical Environmentalism, etc.

1. Karl Marx died on March 14, 1883, and was buried in Highgate Cemetery in London, England. The assumption that Communism died with him was logical since only six people attended his funeral. But the truth is that it had not yet begun its murderous journey through the 20th century.

2. John Maynard Keynes was born on June 5, 1883, in Cambridge, England. His political, economic, and moral influence continues to affect every American.

3. The Fabian Socialist Society was an offshoot of The Fellowship of the New Life, which was born in October 1883 in London, England.

Today's financial events illustrate that America is not exempt from being led toward Socialism. Predictions differ, depending on one's perspective, as to whether this will be a Socialistic paradise or a Socialistic hell. Time will tell. In the meantime, we'd do well to listen to warnings of the past.

Russian thinker and author Fyodor Dostoyevsky offered the following take on Socialism: "The future kingdom of socialism will be a terrible tyranny of criminals and murderers. It will throw humanity into a true hell of spiritual suffering and poverty."[1]

Fabian Socialist George Bernard Shaw added: "You would be forcibly fed, clothed, lodged, taught and employed whether you liked it or not. If it were discovered that you had not character and industry enough to be worth all this trouble, you might possibly be executed in a kindly manner."[2]

That's probably why Margaret Thatcher added that the "problem with socialism is that you eventually run out of other people's money."[3]

Today, we will link the US House of Representatives—and its radical, progressive, Socialistic societies and caucuses—directly to Karl Marx through Keynes and the Fabians.

Before identifying many of the House members caught up in the Socialist web, however, let's first identify the major economic dogma of the early Socialists.

Socialism is the economic system of both the Marxist-Leninist worldview and the Fabian Society's worldview. John Maynard Keynes was a member of the British Fabian Society, whose American counterparts were the Intercollegiate Socialist Society and the League for Industrial Democracy. Their American voices were centered in the ideas of Norman Thomas and John Dewey among others. Dewey, you may remember, was an early signatory of *The Humanist Manifesto* (1933) and its atheistic, Socialist gospel.

The Socialization of America

Socialists are united in their desire to see Capitalism destroyed, either forcefully or gradually, and most would rejoice if Christianity were destroyed along with it. Socialists and liberals generally see in Christians "an infallible marker of mental retardation."[4]

The Christian worldview endorses sound or hard money, fiscal responsibility, saving for a rainy day, deferred gratification, paying off monthly credit card bills, living within one's means, etc. Keynesian economics, on the other hand, argues for consumption, extravagance, and not providing for the future, arguing that "the great vice is saving, thrift and financial prudence."[5] Keynesians love huge national spending and debt and high inflation—anathema to Christians and most conservatives.

Socialists see Capitalism as an evil economic system founded on the concepts of profit, individualism, private property, private business, and freedom to buy and sell products and services. Indeed, a working definition of Capitalism is "the peaceful and free exchange of goods and services without theft, fraud, and breach of contract." Capitalism is tailored to individual initiative rather than groupthink or community initiative. Nearly all inventions that have furthered the Capitalistic enterprise and blessed humanity in the process have been the result of individual initiative rather than committee, group, or government activity.

Marx advanced the Socialist cause by calling for social or public ownership of property and the abolition of private property. He believed that people were best suited to work on state farms, public parks, nationalized banks, or the government bureaucracy rather than for private employers, who would certainly take advantage of their employees, causing them both social and economic harm. Marx, however, was an economic leech on fellow Communist Engels, who supported him with his Capitalistic father's monies.

George Bernard Shaw represented the Fabian point of view by calling for "the socialization of the means of production, distribution, and exchange" to bring about an equal distribution of goods and services to all members of society and to make the State "the ALL of social well-being." The State "subsumes all economic life of the nation."[6]

In other words, Socialism is an economic system that downplays the individual in favor of the group, social order, or the State. It is a system in which the State directs the economic activity of the social order through central planning and by placing economic activity under the jurisdiction of the State. Socialism is also known as Collectivism or Statism and to Marx, Communism.

Today, we call this kind of economic system "Interventionism" or Keynesism. Interventionism is a kind of Socialism or Communism, but without the destruction of the bourgeoisie (which were slaughtered by the millions by Soviet and Chinese Communists).[7] Today's Fabians/Progressives/Radicals allow their Capitalist enemies to create wealth, but acquire it by taxing them instead of slaughtering them (Marx's reign of terrorism on the bourgeoisie). They are then free to distribute the wealth among the economically disadvantaged, the intellectual elites, and the superior governing classes.

Such (re)distribution of wealth ensures the favorable vote of the masses who are being fed, entertained, housed (with sub prime loans) and doctored. ACORN (Association of Community Organizations for Reform Now) and Socialism fit hand-in-glove just as Fannie Mae and Freddie Mac fit Barney Frank, Maxine Waters, and Chris Dodd to a "T."

Most Americans are totally unaware that the US House of Representatives crawls with a large, well-organized assembly of Socialist organizations. These organizations are dedicated to (a) bringing about the destruction of the Capitalist economic system (portrayed as greedy, conservative, religious, and/or filthy rich) and (b) slowly but surely bringing production, education, food, and health care under the complete control and regulation of the federal government.

A prime example of this governmental takeover is the carbon tax currently under discussion. It would punish business and industry's use of gas and oil products (which according to Al Gore will warm the planet by one degree over the next 100 years) by "allow[ing] the federal government to 'control every aspect of our economy,' according to Christopher Horner of the Competitive Enterprise Institute."[8]

The legislators involved in this Socialistic undertaking belong to one or more radical House organizations: the Progressive Democrats of America (6 House members), the Congressional Progressive Caucus (83 House members), the Congressional Black Caucus (42 House members), and the Democratic Socialists of America who do not identify their House members since they consider all members of the Congressional Progressive Caucus part of their membership due to the fact that they both shared operative social democratic politics.

The most prominent national member of DSA is the former AFL-CIO President John J. Sweeney, who could well be the most powerful influence in the House of Representatives.

And for the record, the Chairwoman of the Congressional Black Caucus is Congressional Progressive Caucus member Barbara Lee (CA-9). This is the same Ms. Lee who recently returned from a secretive trip to visit the Communist dictators in Cuba, Raul and Fidel Castro. Of course this shouldn't shock anyone for at least two reasons: (a) Ms. Lee was a staff member for former Rep. Ron Dellums, and (b) according to recently declassified documents from the National Archives, posted to J. Michael Waller's Political Warfare.org blog, Ms. Lee "has been promoting the cause of Caribbean communism since the early 1980s."[9]

The interconnections between these Socialist-based organizations is staggering.

These organizations and their members quite literally comprise a Socialist Red Army within the very contours of the House of Representatives. The Congressional Progressive Caucus (CPC) is the largest partisan caucus in the US House of Representatives and works to advance Socialist causes. The CPC was founded in 1991 by the Senator Bernie Sanders of Vermont. The CPC represents about a third of the House Democratic Caucus. Of the twenty standing committees of the House, eleven are currently chaired by members of the CPC.[10]

When the CPC claimed 64 members in 2006 (now 83 and gaining), the leftist publication *The Nation* boasted, "The largest ideological caucus in the new House Democratic majority will be the Congressional Progressive Caucus, with a membership that includes New York's Charles Rangel, Michigan's John Conyers, Massachusetts's Barney Frank and at least half the incoming chairs of House standing committees."[11]

These current eleven chairs are CPC members: George Miller (CA-9)—Chairman of the House Education and Labor Committee; Henry Waxman (CA-30)—Chairman of the Committee on Energy and Commerce; Bob Filner (CA-51)—Chairman of the House Veterans Affairs Committee; Barney Frank (MA-4)—Chairman of the House Financial Services Committee; John Conyers (MI-14)—Chairman of the House Judiciary Committee; Bennie Thompson (MS-2)—Chairman of the House Homeland Security Committee; Nydia Velazquez (NY-12)—Chairwoman of the House Small Business Committee; Charles Rangel (NY-15)—Chairman of the House Ways and Means Committee; Louise Slaughter (NY-28)—Chairwoman of the House Rules Committee; Bob Brady (PA-1)—Chairman of the House Administration Committee;

The Socialization of America

and Edward J. Markey (MA-7)—Select Committee on Energy Independence and Global Warming.

As of February 20, 2009, the co-chairs of the CPC are Raul M. Grijalva (AZ-7) and Lynn Woolsey (CA-6). The Vice Chairs are Diane Watson (CA-33), Sheila Jackson-Lee (TX-18), Mazie Hirono (HI-2), and Dennis Kucinich (OH-10). Incidentally, the CPC website was hosted by the Democratic Socialists of America until 1999, a group affiliated with the Socialist International which was founded on the ideas of Henri Saint-Simon, Charles Fourier, and Karl Marx!

The Commission for a Sustainable World Society is one of the Socialist International's adjunct organizations. Until President Obama picked Carol M. Browner as his global warming czar, Browner was a member in good standing of the Socialist International. Upon her appointment, her name and biography were removed from its website "though a photo of her speaking June 30 to the group's congress in Greece was still available."[12] We can expect Browner to manipulate and push Socialist legislation to advance the defeat of capitalism and the imposition of more government on the American people. Oil, natural gas, coal, and nuclear energy represent capitalism, and we can expect Congressional Socialists to do everything in their legislative power to thwart their discovery, drilling, usage, and distribution. Socialists promote wind(mill) power because they know it alone cannot meet the energy needs of a Capitalist economy and will, therefore, hasten the death of Capitalism.

Browner will enjoy a great deal of support from the newly appointed Secretary of Labor, Hilda Solis, who is also a member of the Congressional Progressive Caucus. And when Browner needs further help, she can rely on the committee chairs, co-chairs, and vice chairs listed above to assist her in using the global warming/climate change scare to bring the United States of America into a Socialistic world governing body. She can also count on former CPC member Nancy Pelosi (who is already manifesting dictatorial tendencies) to drive the Socialist agenda as fast as humanly possible. Pelosi's San Francisco district (CA-8) is synonymous with Socialism/Progressivism/Collectivism/ Statism/Leftism/Radicalism that in turn are synonymous with Scientific Socialism/Communism/Marxism/Leninism/ Maoism.

We have yet to address the ideological role played by John Maynard Keynes in the demise of American capitalism and Christian influence. Anyone with a Christian, conservative bent fears the reality that the United States is falling headlong off the cliff into socialism and all that this will entail. It is no secret that the radical left is both anti-Capitalist and anti-Christian. Marx would be ecstatic, no doubt, realizing that his life's work of dethroning God and destroying capitalism are about to be accomplished worldwide.

Zygmund Dobbs conducted the research for *Keynes at Harvard* and summarizes the political, moral, and economic slant of Keynes and his friends at Cambridge University:

> Singing the Red Flag, the highborn sons of the British upper-class lay on the carpeted floor spinning out socialist schemes in homosexual intermissions....The attitude in such gatherings was anti-establishmentarian. To them the older generation was horribly out of date, even superfluous. The capitalist system was declared obsolete and revolution was proclaimed as the only solution. Christianity was pronounced an enemy force, and the worst sort of depravities were eulogized as "that love which passes all Christian understanding." Chief of this ring of homosexual revolutionaries was John Maynard Keynes....Keynes was characterized by his male sweetheart, Lytton Strachey, as "a liberal and a sodomite, an atheist and a statistician." His particular depravity was the sexual abuse of little boys.[13]

"The crisis of the Western world," said Whittaker Chambers, "exists to the degree in which it is indifferent to

God."[14] Chambers insisted that the battle within the West was primarily between faith in God and faith in Man, and not only between economic, political or cultural systems. Although elsewhere he did note that in America the lower class was Democrat, the middle class was Republican, and the upper class was Socialist/Communist.[15]

Keynes, like Marx, had a fixation that should have been a clue to his character. Marx practiced phrenology (the study of bumps on one's head), and Keynes practiced chirognomy (the study of people's hands). After studying the hands of Charles Darwin's brother, Sir George, Keynes remarked, "His hands certainly looked as if they might be descended from an ape."[16]

Overall, Keynes despised free or private enterprise, considered homosexuality superior to heterosexuality, sought to replace the gold standard with fiat paper money which was more easily produced by government printing presses, did not believe in the family unit, despised "savings" as a stumbling block against the march of Socialism, and called on the state to control the number of children per family.

The Keynesian economic formula fits all totalitarianisms, including Fascism, Nazism, and Communism. Sir Oswald Mosley, for example, was a Fascist leader and a member of the Fabian Society. Lauchlin Currie, a prominent Keynesian advocate, was a Soviet spy and an economic aid to FDR. Joan Robinson, a Marxist economist, assisted Keynes in some of his economic writings, arguing that "the differences between Marx and Keynes are only verbal."[17]

Keynes also had a strong relationship with the notorious Soviet spy Harry Dexter White. Keynes considered White to be "the central figure in the Keynesian manipulations in the United States." Harry Dexter White just happened to be the Assistant to the Secretary of the US Treasury. Even after White was exposed as a Soviet spy, Keynesians to this day "see nothing wrong in White's Soviet role," a "typical…

attitude of Fabian socialist elements toward the whole coterie of spies and Fifth Amendment communists in the United States."[18]

And it was Keynes himself who admitted that by "a continuing process of inflation, governments can confiscate, secretly and unobserved, an important part of the wealth of their citizens. By this method, they not only confiscate, but confiscate arbitrarily; and while the process impoverishes many, it actually enriches some [e.g., Al Gore]....The process engages all of the hidden forces of economic law on the side of destruction, and does it in a manner that not one man in a million can diagnose."[19]

Thus, it is astounding that Larry Summers, head of President Obama's National Economic Council and former president of Harvard University, when asked by Charlie Rose "what idea, what person has most influenced your thinking on how to deal with this [financial] mess?" without hesitation answered "Keynes."[20]

Following the economic advice of Keynes—huge government spending, debt, and inflation—is kissing the American Capitalist system good night! His advice is what every Socialist would give, even though clear-thinking, common sense Americans know that excessive debt and excessive spending are the main ingredients that created this current financial mess (with the help of Congressional Progressives like Barney Frank hatching Socialist schemes in the House of Representatives).

When Whittaker Chambers took up his sling and aimed his rock at Communism, he admitted that he hit "something else." What he hit "was the forces of that great socialist revolution, which, in the name of liberalism, spasmodically, incompletely, somewhat formlessly, but always in the same direction, has been inching its ice cap over the nation for two decades."[21]

The Socialization of America

That inching is fast becoming a rout with national and international Socialists alike thinking their best opportunity to strike a deathblow to the greatest, freest economic system in all of human history is now.

Because capitalism has raised more human beings out of poverty than all other economic systems combined,[22] we should remember the wisdom of Robert Heilbroner, a former Marxist economist who changed his position before the fall of the Berlin Wall: "The Soviet Union, China, and Eastern Europe have given us the clearest possible proof that capitalism organizes the material affairs of humankind more satisfactorily than socialism: that however inequitably or irresponsibly the marketplace may distribute goods, it does so better than the queues of a planned economy; however mindless the culture of commercialism, it is more attractive than state moralism; and however deceptive the ideology of a business civilization, it is more believable than that of a socialist one."[23]

Little wonder that Winston Churchill painted socialism as "a philosophy of failure, a creed of ignorance, and a gospel of envy whose inherent virtue is the equal sharing of misery."[24]

Of course, it was also Churchill who observed that "Some people regard private enterprise as a predatory tiger to be shot, others look on it as a cow to be milked. Not enough people see it as a healthy horse pulling a steady wagon."[25]

You Can Still Trust the Communists

POSTSCRIPT

by
David A. Noebel

Frederick Charles Schwarz—January 15, 1913 to January 24, 2009—literally lived his own advice: "As free men humbly seek God and present their bodies, minds and hearts to their country and the cause of all mankind, we may well believe that tyranny shall not triumph and freedom shall not perish from the earth."

Dr. Schwarz, the Australian physician, greatly influenced the newly rising conservative movement that ultimately produced leaders such as Ronald Reagan, James Dobson, Norman Geisler, Marvin Olasky, Tim LaHaye, Beverly LaHaye, Phyllis Schlafly, Eleanor Schlafly, Roy Rogers, Dale Evans, Dana Rohrabacher, Mike Antonovitch, Reed Irvine, Robert Dornan, Bill Buckley, Herbert Philbrick, Senator Thomas J. Dodd, Rear Admiral Chester Ward, John Wayne, Pat Boone, George Murphy, Chuck Smith, Robert Schuller, Ralph Wilkinson, Jerry Falwell, and Gary North to name but a few.

Harvard University historian Lisa McGirr's *Suburban Warriors: The Origins of the New American Right* acknowledges that "Fred Schwarz and his Christian Anti-Communism

Crusade helped to reshape the political direction of the nation."[1]

She also notes that Schwarz was "a gifted orator who drew on his medical training in describing the 'evils' of communism, comparing communism to a disease with many symptoms, a disease that would have to be studied, diagnosed and treated."[2]

She reveals that "Ronald Reagan was one of the speakers at the Southern California School of Anti-Communism... with approximately 15,000 in attendance"[3] and includes a picture of the event with Mrs. Reagan and Roy Rogers in the audience.

Clearly Ronald Reagan is among those responsible for the crumbling of the Soviet Union. John O'Sullivan specifically identifies President Reagan, Pope John Paul II, and Prime Minister Margaret Thatcher as the three responsible for its demise in his work *The President, the Pope, and the Prime Minister: Three Who Changed the World.*

Paul Kengor's *The Crusader: Ronald Reagan and the Fall of Communism* makes the case that Reagan certainly deserves recognition for this achievement.

Fred Schwarz, therefore, deserves more acclaim than he has received for his historical effort to make the name "anti-Communist" as respectable as anti-Nazi and anti-Fascist.

I conclude with Dr. Schwarz in his own words as he describes his relationship with Ronald Reagan in his autobiography *Beating the Unbeatable Foe: One Man's Victory over Communism, Leviathan, and the Last Enemy.*

> I did not convert Ronald Reagan to anti-Communism. The Communists had already done this. As president of the Screen Actors Guild he had discerned their duplicity and been subjected to their venomous attack. He attended the Southern California School of Anti-Communism, held in Los Angeles on August 28 to September 1, 1961, and expressed appreciation for the clarity of the messages exposing the pathological nature of Communist doctrines.

Postscript

I take pride in recounting that the man who later became president of the United States, and who enacted programs that led to the downfall of Soviet Communism, once served as a substitute speaker for me. It was in 1962 when he was a lecturer sponsored by the General Electric Corporation. I was scheduled to speak at a luncheon in Omaha, Nebraska, but bad weather delayed my arrival. The meeting was chaired by the mayor of Omaha, and Ronald Reagan held the fort until I arrived.

In due course he became president of the United States of America, and the rest is history. His outstanding role in formulating the programs that led to the downfall of Soviet Communism is undeniable. His place in the pantheon of history is secure.

The influence of my message on his thoughts, statements, and programs was both direct and indirect. The indirect influence resulted from our numerous Schools of Anti-Communism and Anti-Subversive Seminars. In due course many of the students came to occupy responsible positions in government, education, and religion.

Three of them became speechwriters for President Reagan. They were Dana Rohrabacher, Tony Dolan, and Jack Wells.

President Reagan was a great orator. Two of his outstanding speeches were to the British Parliament and to the National Association of Evangelicals in Fort Lauderdale, or the "Evil Empire" speech.

I congratulated Tony Dolan, the speechwriter who helped prepare these speeches, and he replied, "You should have liked it. I took it all from you." He sent me a copy of the "Evil Empire" speech with this note: "I thought you might like to see the oak tree that has grown from the acorn which you planted so many years ago."

As the Bible says, "Cast thy bread upon the waters for thou shalt find it after many days." (Ecclesiastes 11:1)[4]

Thus, although Dr. Frederick Charles Schwarz's life has ended, his influence has not. His understanding of Communism and its Atheism, Dialectical Materialism, Moral Relativism, Socialism, and totalitarianism will serve the present generation as they confront Communism's cousins: Fabian Socialism, Students for a Democratic Society, League for Industrial Democracy, Congressional Progressive Caucus, Democratic Socialists of America, Progressive Democrats of America, Congressional Black

Caucus, Socialist International (founded by Karl Marx), Saul Alinsky's *Rules for Radicals* (dedicated to Lucifer), Commission for a Sustainable World Society, ACLU, MSNBC, *New York Times*, *Rolling Stones*, Pacifica Radio, EPA, Radical Feminism, GLBTQ Studies, Critical Legal Studies, Moveon.org, Hate Crimes, Speech Codes, Diversity Consultants, Planned Parenthood, *Sojourners*, Emergent Church, World Council of Churches, NEA, Liberation Theology, Gay Liberation, Center for American Progress, European Court of Human Rights, United Nations, UN Human Rights Council, Code Pink, Democracy Now, Harvard faculty, New Black Panthers, WHO, UNESCO, Deep Ecology, Optimum Population Trust, PETA, Sustainable Development Commission, Earth First, Green Party, and the left-wing of the Democratic Party—a few among hundreds of other such organizations in the United States and around the world.

Postscript

FURTHER STUDY

Dobbs, Zygmund ed., *The Great Deceit: Social Pseudo-Sciences*. West Sayville, NY: Veritas Foundation, 1964.

Kengor, Paul. *The Crusaders: Ronald Reagan and the Fall of Communism*. New York: Harper Perennial, 2007.

McGirr, Lisa. *Suburban Warriors: The Origins of the New American Right*. Princeton, NJ: Princeton University Press, 2001.

O'Sullivan, John. *The President, the Pope, and the Prime Minister: Three Who Changed The World*. Washington, DC, Regnery Publishing, 2006.

Revel, Jean-Francois. *Last Exit to Utopia: The Survival of Socialism in a Post-Soviet Era*. San Francisco, CA: Encounter Books, 2009.

Schwarz, Fred C. *Beating the Unbeatable Foe: One Man's Victory over Communism, Leviathan, and the Last Enemy*. Washington, DC, Regnery Publishing, 1996.

Watkins, Tim. *In the Face of Evil: Reagan's War in Word and Deed*, DVD Documentary. Baltimore: Leo McWatkins Films, 2005.

You Can Still Trust the Communists

APPENDIX

Is Communism Dead?
You Decide

"In the United States, the working classes are Democrats. The middle classes are Republicans. The upper classes are Communists.'"[1]

—Whittaker Chambers

"Communism is socialism with an international focus and totalitarian methods."[2]

—Thomas Sowell

"Sam Webb, current leader of the Communist Party USA, is the author of *Reflections on Socialism*."[3]

"The founder of *Free Press*, Robert W. McChesney, is a professor at the University of Illinois and former editor of the Marxist journal *Monthly Review*. In February 2009, McChesney urged that capitalism be dismantled… rebuilding the entire society on socialist principles."[4]

"We won't have true 'social justice' until everyone is equal in everybody's house."[5]

—Rev. Al Sharpton

"The Left loves collectivization."[6]

—Phillip Blond

"The cliché that green is the new red is proving all too true. Increasingly, environmental activism promotes utopian hysteria…and exhibits disturbing totalitarian symptoms. Ecocide fits squarely with this emerging zeitgeist."[7]

—Wesley J. Smith

"If totalitarianism was the ugly beast of twentieth century politics, its beauty was admired by the likes of George Bernard Shaw and Thorstein Veblen, and its apologists ranged from Pulitzer Prize-winning journalist Walter Duranty of the *New York Times* to whole armies of fellow-travelers in the media and academic world of their time."[8]

—Thomas Sowell

"The pilgrimages of intellectuals to the lands of the dictators—to Stalinist Russia, Maoist China, or Castro's Cuba—have been among the amazing stories of this [20th] century, as eminent scholars and literary figures have come back to gush over the 'progress' of tyrannies whose own people were making desperate escapes whenever they could. In short, totalitarianism has been an intellectual phenomenon."[9]

—Thomas Sowell

"Visiting the United States in 1933, George Bernard Shaw said, 'You Americans are so fearful of dictators. Dictatorship is the only way in which government can

Is Communism Dead?

accomplish anything. See what a mess democracy has led to. Why are you afraid of dictatorship?"[10]

—Thomas Sowell

"Thomas L. Friedman of *The New York Times* wrote in a September 2009 column that a dictatorship, when 'led by a reasonably enlightened group of people, as [Communist] China is today,' has 'great advantages' over democratic systems."[11]

—Matthew Continetti

"Actor Sean Penn loves Venezuela's communist dictator Hugo Chavez so much he wants journalists who dare to call Chavez a dictator put in prison...Penn also previously called the Chavez-crafted constitution of Venezuela, which gives the president the power to rule by decree, 'a very beautiful document.'"[12]

—Matthew Vadum

"Communist and pro-communist parties rule about a dozen Latin American countries today...World communism was never only an appendix of the USSR. It actually created the USSR, not the other way around."[13]

—Olavo de Carvalho

"I want to warn Americans. As people, you are very naïve about Russia and its intentions. You believe because the Soviet Union no longer exists, Russia now is your friend. It isn't, and I can show you how the SRV [Russia's Foreign Intelligence Service] is trying to destroy the US even today and even more than the KGB did during the Cold War."[14]

—Sergei Tretyakov

"The 'end of communism' proclaimed by the West is a myth. We now see the resurgence of communism...instead of punishing the communists for their crimes the West has extended them a hand, like a sign of apology for defeating them."[15]

—Robert Buchar

"John Sweeney, former president of the AFL-CIO and a member of the Democratic Socialists of America, has removed the bar on known communists holding office in his union. The Communist Party is slowly growing, recolonizing the unions and is strengthening ties to Cuba and China. Democratic Socialists of America is working with both organizations in the unions, in the peace movement and through the Democratic Party's more than 80 strong Congressional Progressive Caucus members."[16]

—Brenda J. Elliott

"Unmentioned in the *Variety* review of Michael Moore's 'Capitalism: A Love Story' is that it ends with an explicit call for socialism and the Bolshevik anthem 'The Internationale' on the soundtrack."[17]

—Kyle Smith

"Harry Bridges [was] arguably the most significant labor leader of the twentieth century, beloved by the workers of this Nation and recognized as one of the most important labor leaders in the world. The International Longshoremen's and Warehousemen's Union [was] the most progressive union of the time."[18]

—Nancy Pelosi

"After the fall of the USSR and the opening of Soviet archives did the truth emerge that [Harry] Bridges had been not merely in the party but a member of the Central Committee of the Communist Party USA."[19]

—Joshua Muravchik

Is Communism Dead?

"Although it was no secret in intelligence circles, the first public mention of Armand Hammer's service as an actual operative of the Soviet Union may have been during the course of a speech given by international journalist Arnaud de Borchgrave in Palm Beach, Fla., in 1980. 'I said that he was a longtime Soviet agent of influence,' recalls de Borchgrave, currently head of United Press International. 'The Soviets had various special categories of agents. Hammer's role was to dispense disinformation to the useful idiots. 'Useful idiots' is the term describing those in Western media, academia, politics and other influential realms who were sympathetic to the Soviet cause.'"[20]

—John Elvin

"American filmmaker Oliver Stone said he deeply admires [Communist] Hugo Chavez…'I admire Hugo. I like him very much as a person….this new documentary 'South of the Border'…is a positive portrayal of a man who Americans do not have access to. He is demonized in the American and European press as a monster.'"[21]

—Ian James

"At the height of Mao's 'cultural revolution' in China—an orgy of intolerant repressions, terror, public humiliations and mass killings [75 million]—Western intellectuals flocked to China and returned to say how wonderful it all was. Mao's little red book of sayings was a hot item in campus bookstores while he subjugated one-fourth of the human race and made them pawns and guinea pigs for his [Communist] vision."[22]

—Thomas Sowell

"Castro is one helluva guy! You people [Harvard Law School] would like him! Most people in Cuba like him."[23]

—Ted Turner

"A revolutionary must become a cold killing machine motivated by pure hate. We execute from revolutionary conviction."[24]

—Ernesto "Che" Guevara

"It is impossible to establish communism as the immediate successor to capitalism. It is, accordingly, proposed to establish socialism as something which we can put in the place of our present decaying capitalism. Hence, communists work for the establishment of socialism as a necessary transition stage on the road to communism."[25]

— John Strachey

"British Prime Minister Gordon Brown is a member of the Fabian Society, the British socialist organization that served as the model for, and incubator of, the Socialist International. Indeed, the SI world headquarters in London and the Fabian Society's London office are but two hands on the same body...the Fabian Society has been a key ally of the communists from Lenin's time to the present, including providing special assistance in covering up Josef Stalin's unspeakable crimes."[26]

—William F. Jasper

"Today [2010], an anti-religious, secular, socialist left is on the offense in the legislatures, the courts and the bureaucracies. From the ACLU crusade against the cross to the Ninth Circuit Court's ruling against 'One Nation under God,' our religious liberty is under attack."[27]

Is Communism Dead?

"I am a Communist, a convinced Communist! For some that may be a fantasy. But to me it is my main goal."[28]

—Mikhail Gorbachev

"The theory of the Communists may be summed up in the single sentence: Abolition of private property."[29]

—Karl Marx

"Berkeley law professor Goodwin Liu is the most radical Obama nominee to date [Ninth Circuit federal appeals court]. Liu has denounced 'free enterprise,' 'private ownership of property,' and 'limited government.'"[30]

"Socialists desire to practice legal plunder, not illegal plunder. Socialists desire to make the law their own weapon."[31]

—Frederic Bastiat

"I see no reason for attributing to man a significance different in kind from that which belongs to a baboon or a grain of sand...I don't believe it is an absolute principle... that man is always an end in himself—that his dignity must be respected."[32]

—Oliver Wendell Holmes

"I am a Bolshevik."[33]

—W.E.B. DuBois

"Kill all the rich people. Break up their cars and apartments. Bring the revolution home. Kill your parents... I'm a radical, leftist, small 'c' communist."[34]

—Bill Ayers

"I went to Communism as one goes to a fresh spring of water…an anti-Communist is a dog."[35]

—Pablo Picasso

"Celebrated film star Vanessa Redgrave was a Trotskyite activist, a co-founder of the Marxist Party and a supporter of the Communist Workers' Revolutionary Party."[36]

—Don Feder

"Howard Zinn is a fellow traveler socialist historian…The Wobblies [Industrial Workers of the World] are singled out for praise and the Communist Party of the United States gets some nice words as well."[37]

—Roger Kimball

"In the summer of 1932, H.G. Wells delivered a major speech at Oxford University to Britain's Young Liberals organization, in which he called for a "'Phoenix Rebirth' of Liberalism" under the banner of 'Liberal Fascism.' Fabian socialism had failed, he explained, because it hadn't grasped the need for a truly 'revolutionary' effort aimed at the total transformation of society…Fabians had failed abolishing private property, achieving a fully planned economy, violently crushing the forces of reaction—they'd have to learn that lesson."[38]

—Jonah Goldberg

"I'm wearing a Chairman Mao badge, that's where it's at. I'm just beginning to think he's doing a good job."[39]

—John Lennon

"'Revolution No. 9,' 'Working Class Hero,' 'Back in the USSR,' 'Power to the People,' Imagine,' Sometime in New York City,' 'Bloody Sunday,' 'Attica State' (now's the time for revolution), 'Angela' (glorifies Communist Angela

Is Communism Dead?

Davis), and 'Piggies' were all written and sung to further the Communist Revolution."[40]

—David L. Brown

"Everywhere I hear the sounds of marching, charging feet, boy. The sound of fear and the time is ripe for rising in the streets, boy...The time is right for violent revolution."[41]

—Mick Jagger

"The experiment of Communism had cost about a hundred million helpless people their lives."[42]

—David Pryce-Jones

"By the 1940s, folk singers had become a ceremonial part of Communist Party meetings. And at nearly all of them, one would find Pete Seeger playing...and a new arrival on the East Coast musical scene, Woody Guthrie."[43]

—Lauren Weiner

"The American descent into Marxism is happening with breath taking speed."[44]

—Stanislav Mishin

"Given thirty years of postmodern relativism in our universities, we were bound to get a postmodern president at some point...He was schooled in the postmodern university and operates on hand-me-down principles from postmodernism. One does not need to read Foucault or Derrida, or to be acquainted with Heidegger, to see how relativism enhances contemporary multiculturalism. Keep that in mind and everything else makes sense."[45]

—Victor Davis Hanson

"After Nationalizing Health Care and Student Loans—
Obama Continues Attack on Private Sector in Weekly
Address."[46]

—Jim Hoft

"We're all known by the company we keep, and Obama
consistently — and deliberately— keeps company with
hard leftists…. He couldn't be more of a Manchurian
candidate if he were auditioning for the role in the movie.
This stuff is just too bizarre for most Americans to process:
an actual Marxist in the White House." [47]

—Sean Hannity

"In 2008 Senator Barack Obama named Cornel West to his
presidential campaign's Black Advisory Council…West, a
member of the Democratic Socialists of America seeks to
transform America into a Socialist country with the help of
the founders of the Maoist Revolutionary Communist Party
USA—Carl Dix and Bob Avakian."[48]

"The New Party was established in 1992 by 'union activist
Sandy Pope and University of Wisconsin professor Joel
Rogers,' USA Today reported on November 16, 1992. The
paper wrote the New Party was 'self-described as socialist
democratic.'"[49]

"Van Jones resigned late Saturday after a simmering
controversy over his past statements ["I was a communist"]
and activism [with the San Francisco Bay-area
Revolutionary Movement (STORM) with Marxist roots."[50]

"Van Jones speaks out in favor of Joel Rogers and his
Center on Wisconsin Strategy (COWS). Van Jones praises
Rogers for his White House connections."[51]

Is Communism Dead?

The latest Marxism-Leninism manifesto titled *The Coming Insurrection* is printed and "Distributed by The MIT Press, Cambridge, Mass." The work calls for a violent revolution of Western Civilization with COMMUNISM being the goal.[52]

—The Invisible Committee

"What distinguished Fascist movements in general from Communist movements was that Communists were officially committed to government ownership of the means of production, while Fascists permitted private ownership of the means of production, so long as government directed the private owner's decisions and limited what profit rates they could receive."[53]

—Thomas Sowell

"Make no mistake: This is a budget [2010-2011] aimed to advance the administration's philosophy and ideology. By increasing taxes and letting the country spiral into debt, this budget is a firm step toward transforming America into a collectivist society overseen by a social-welfare state."[54]

—Rep Paul Ryan (R. Wisconsin)

"To fundamentally transform America...level the playing field...spread the wealth."[55]

—Barack Obama

"Barack Obama is the most radical president in American history who oversees a secular socialist machine."[56]

—Newt Gingrich

"Strictly on the numbers, the United States is in the express lane to Declinistan: unsustainable entitlements, the remorseless governmentalization of the economy and individual liberty, and a centralization of power that will cripple a nation of this size."[57]

—Mark Steyn

"There were more self-declared communists on the Harvard faculty than there were Republicans."[58]

—Ted Cruz

"If you asked the Harvard faculty to vote on whether this nation should become a socialist nation, 80 percent of the faculty would vote yes and the 10 percent would think that was too conservative."[59]

—Ted Cruz

"To avoid being mistaken as such a sellout, I chose my friends carefully: The more politically active black students; the foreign students; the Chicanos; the Marxist professors."[60]

—Barack Obama

"Hillary Clinton was offered an internship by her hero Saul Alinsky—famed author of *Rules for Radicals*—about whom she wrote her thesis: 'There Is Only the Fight: An Analysis of the Alinsky Model.' In an unprecedented move, Wellesley sequestered the thesis in 1992, even refusing to divulge the title until the Clintons left the White House."[61]

—Jonah Goldberg

"Hillary Clinton was offered a summer internship in the Berkeley, California, law offices of Robert Treuhaft, one of [Black Panther Bobby] Seale's lawyers, who had cut his teeth fighting for the Stalinist faction in the California labor movement."[62]

—Jonah Goldberg

Is Communism Dead?

"Barack Obama, for years a Chicago community organizer, was trained by Alinsky's disciples."[63]

—Jonah Goldberg

"Black liberation theology is a product of the dreary leftist politics of the twentieth century, the very vehicles employed by the left to advance statism."[64]

—Jeffrey Schmidt

"And, guess what this liberal will be all about? This liberal will be about socializing…uh, will be about, basically taking over and the government running all of your companies."[65]

—Rep. Maxine Waters, (D. California)

"There ain't no rules here [the U.S. House of Representatives], we're trying to accomplish something… All this talk about rules…when the deal goes down…we make 'em up as we go along."[66]

—Rep. Alcee Hastings (D. Florida)

"I would think that if you understood what communism was, you would hope, you would pray on your knees, that we would someday become communists."[67]

—Jane Fonda

"Harvard-educated economist Barack Obama, Sr., was a committed communist."[68]

—Glenn Beck

"Barack Obama's teenage mentor was Frank Marshall Davis, black poet and communist with an FBI file."[69]

—Glenn Beck

"In 1988, the Center for Labor Education and Research (CLEAR) at the University of Hawaii—West Oahu produced a documentary about the life of Frank Marshall Davis...To understand the way the progressive media work, consider this: The documentary makes not one single mention of Davis's undeniable communist affiliations, his pornographic writings, or—to be sure—his flirtation with pedophilia."[70]

—Jack Cashill

"Science will become materialistic, hence truly scientific; God will be banished from the laboratories as well as from the schools."[71]

—William Z. Foster

"The press, the motion picture, the radio, the theatre, will be taken over by the government."[72]

—William Z. Foster

"The churches will remain free to continue their services, but their special tax and other privileges will be liquidated. Their buildings will revert to the State. Religious schools will be abolished and organized religious training for minors prohibited. Freedom will be established for anti-religious propaganda."[73]

—William Z. Foster

"We've got to establish a socialist economic structure that will limit private profit-oriented businesses. Whether the transition is peaceful depends on the way our present government leaders react. We must commit our lives to this transition...we should be very proud of our new breed of soldier...It's not organized but it's mutiny, and they have every right."[74]

—Jane Fonda

Is Communism Dead?

"Communism is one of the options that can improve people's lives."[75]

—Tom Hayden

"President Obama's Chicago neighbor and friend William Ayers, a high-ranking [Communist] Weatherman, famously told *The New York Times* on September 11, 2001, 'I don't regret setting bombs [and] I feel we didn't do enough.'"[76]

"Each Postmodernist included in this work (Foucault, Derrida, Barthes, Lyotard, Baudrillard, Rorty, etc.) is theologically atheist, philosophically skeptical, ethically relativist, biologically evolutionist, psychologically soulless, legally pragmatist, and politically leftist."[77]

—David A. Noebel

"Nobody ever believed that Mikhail Gorbachev had ceased or would ever cease to cherish and promote his own Grand Design, the Leninist-Marxist plan."[78]

—Malachi Martin

"Two of my favorite philosophers are Mao tse Tung and Mother Teresa—two people I turn to most."[79]

—Anita Dunn

"I am a Leninist. Lenin wasn't afraid to dirty his hands. If you can get power, grab it...we need Marx more than ever."[80]

—Slavoj Zizek

"You would be forcibly fed, clothed, lodged, taught and employed whether you like it or not. If it were discovered that you had not character and industry enough to be worth all this trouble, you might possibly be executed in a kindly manner."[81]

—George Bernard Shaw

"I am for socialism, disarmament, and ultimately for abolishing the State itself as an instrument of property, the abolition of the propertied class and sole control by those who produce wealth. Communism is the goal. It sums up into one single purpose—the abolition of the system dog-eat-dog under which we live, and the substitution by the most effective non-violence possible of a system of cooperative ownership and use of all wealth."[82]

—Roger Baldwin

"President Jimmy Carter awarded Roger Baldwin the Metal of Freedom on January 16, 1981."[83]

"The goal of socialism is communism."[84]

—Vladimir Lenin

"Our program necessarily includes the propaganda of atheism."[85]

—Vladimir Lenin

"Stuart Chase, representing the Fabian socialists in the United States proposed Keynes as the socialist ideal long before Keynes wrote the *General Theory* in 1936. Chase outlined the Keynesian principles of abandoning the gold standard in 1932…Chase called his book *A New Deal*. It was written in 1931 and published in 1932. Franklin D. Roosevelt borrowed this socialist slogan as a label for his administration."[86]

—Zygmund Dobbs

Is Communism Dead?

"Keynesian leftists…are confident that a great national debt and continuing inflation plus enormous internal and foreign commitments assure the continuance of Keynesian operations for generations to come regardless who is in power."[87]

—Zygmund Dobbs

"Margaret Cole, English Fabian revolutionary, has stated: 'We Socialists used Keynes and the U.S.S.R. as touchstones.'"[88]

—Zygmund Dobbs

"The simple fact is that when I took up my little sling and aimed at Communism, I also hit something else. What I hit was the forces of that great socialist revolution, which, in the name of liberalism, spasmodically, incompletely, somewhat formlessly, but always in the same direction, has been inching its ice cap over the nation for two decades."[89]

—Whittaker Chambers

"Communism restores man to his sovereignty by the simple method of denying God."[90]

—Whittaker Chambers

"As humanism in its development became more and more materialistic, it made itself increasingly accessible to speculation and manipulation, at first by socialism and then by Communism."[91]

—Alexsandr Solzhenitsyn

"It takes a long time to do the necessary administrative steps that have to be taken to put the legislation [ObamaCare] together to control the people."[92]

—Rep. John Dingell (D. Michigan)

"Democrats are trying to impose a 'secular-socialist machine.'"[93]

—Newt Gingrich

"The faith to which Obama actually clings is neocommunism. It is a leftism of the most insidious kind: secular and uncompromising in its rejection of bourgeois values, but feverishly spiritual in its zeal to tear down the existing order, under the banner of its all-purpose rally cry: 'social justice.'"[94]

—Andrew C. McCarthy

"Neocommunism is leftism liberated by the collapse of the Soviet Union."[95]

—Andrew C. McCarthy

"What neocommunists are for is a set of abstractions— 'social justice,' 'equality,' 'redistributive rights,' the 'rule of law,' and of course, 'our values.'"[96]

—Andrew C. McCarthy

"Remember the history of the world is communism, socialism, totalitarianism, statism."[97]

—Rush Limbaugh

"We can't expect the American people to jump from Capitalism to Communism, but we can assist their elected leaders in giving them small doses of Socialism until they awaken one day to find that they have Communism."[98]

—Nikita Khrushchev

"Antonio Gramsci, the Marxist thinker who became the guru of the former sixties radicals who are now entrenched among the elites, promoted the idea that Western society could be overturned by capturing the citadels of the

Is Communism Dead?

culture—the universities, schools, churches, media, civil
service, professions—and subverting its values."[99]

—Melanie Phillips

"Communists are that part of mankind which has recovered
the power to live or die—to bear witness—for its faith.
And it is a simple, rational faith that inspires men to live
or die for it. It is not new. It is, in fact, man's second oldest
faith. Its promise was whispered in the first days of the
Creation under the Tree of the Knowledge of Good and
Evil: 'Ye shall be as gods.' It is the great alternative faith
of mankind...The Communist vision is the vision of Man
without God. It is the vision of man's mind displacing God
as the creative intelligence of the world...It is the vision
of man, once more the central figure of the Creation, not
because God made man in His image, but because man's
mind makes him the most intelligent of the animals."[100]

—Whittaker Chambers

You Can Still Trust the Communists

[322]

ENDNOTES

PREFACE 2010

1. R.J. Rummel, *Death by Government* (New Brunswick, NJ: Transaction Publishers, 1994).
2. Van Jones was finally relieved of his White House duties in September 2009. After he was let go, he was promptly rehired by the radical, George Soros-funded Center for American Progress. See "Van Jones Rejoins CAP to Lead Green Opportunity Initiative," *Center for American Progress* (February 24, 2010), http://www.americanprogress. org/issues/2010/02/van_jones.html.
3. Kathy Shaidle, "Van Jones, 'Green Jobs Czar,' a Self-Described 'Communist' Arrested during Rodney King Riots," *Conservative Politics Examiner* (July 17, 2009), http://www.examiner.com/examiner/ x-722-Conservative-Politics-Examiner~y2009m7d17-Van-Jones-Green-Jobs-Czar-a-selfdescribed-communist-arrested-during-Rodney-King-riots.
4. Roger Kimball, "A Maoist in the White House," *Pajamas Media* (October 16, 2009), http://pajamasmedia.com/rogerkimball/2009/10/16/ a-maoist-in-the-white-house/. Ms. Dunn was former Obama White House Communications Director. This quote was in a speech Dunn delivered to a group of high school students in June 2009.
5. Tony Pierce, "Fidel Castro to Congressional Black Caucus Members: 'How Can We Help President Obama?'" *The Los Angeles Times*, (April 7, 2009), http://latimesblogs.latimes.com/washington/2009/04/ congressional-caucus-members-meet-with-the-castro-cousins-in-cuba. html. Rep. Barbara Lee (D-CA) is also a member of the Congressional

Progressive Caucus.

6. Barack Obama, *Dreams from My Father: A Story of Race and Inheritance* (New York: Three Rivers Press, 2004), 100.

7. Marvin Olasky, "All Together Now," *WORLD Magazine* 24, no. 22 (November 7, 2009): 25.

8. Ibid.

9. Barack Obama, "Barack Obama: My Spiritual Journey," *Time* (October 16, 2006), http://www.time.com/time/magazine/article/0,9171,1546579,00.html.

10. Cliff Kincaid, "Controversial New Video of Obama's Pastor," *Accuracy in Media* (November 1, 2009), http://www.aim.org/aim-column/controversial-new-video-of-obamas-pastor/. The video shows Wright "praising Marxism and discussing his ties to Communists in El Salvador and Nicaragua and the Libyan government." Wright is introduced by Marxist Robert W. McChesney, co-founder of Free Press.

11. Brian Ross and Rehab El-Buri, "Obama's Pastor: God Damn America, US to Blame for 9/11," *ABC News* (March 13, 2008), http://abcnews.go.com/Blotter/story?id=4443788.

12. Jennifer Rubin, "Obama and the Woods Fund," *Pajamas Media* (July 7, 2008), http://pajamasmedia.com/blog/obama-and-the-woods-fund/.

13. US Senate Committee on the Judiciary, *The Weather Underground: Report of the Subcommittee to Investigate the Administration of the Internal Security Act and Other Internal Security Laws of the Committee on the Judiciary, United States Senate, Ninety-fourth Congress, First Session* (Washington, DC: US Government Printing Office, 1975), 1–2, 11–13.

14. Bill Ayers, *Fugitive Days: A Memoir* (New York: Penguin, 2003), 70.

15. See the Code Pink website: http://www.codepink4peace.org/article.php?list=type&type=3.

16. Jonathan Martin, "Code Pink Co-founder Is Obama Bundler," Politico (June 11, 2008), http://www.politico.com/blogs/jonathanmartin/0608/Code_Pink_cofounder_is_Obama_bundler.html.

17. Kristinn Taylor and Andrea Shea King, "Obama Funder Jodie Evans Provokes Crisis in Egypt over 'Hamas-Aid' Event, Obama Pals Ayers and Dohrn in Cairo with Code Pink," *Big Government* (December 31, 2009), http://biggovernment.com/taylorking/2009/12/31/obama-funder-jodie-evans-provokes-crisis-in-egypt-over-hamas-aid-event-obama-pals-ayers-and-dohrn-in-cairo-with-code-pink/. Also "Hamas Terrorists Guaranteed Code Pink's Safety in Gaza," (January 12, 2010), http://biggovernment.com/taylorking/2010/01/12/hamas-terrorists-guaranteed-code-pinks-safety-in-gaza/. Also, Ryan Mauro, "Code Pink's Support for the Enemy," *Front Page Magazine* (January 21, 2010), http://frontpagemag.com/2010/01/21/code-pink's-support-of-

Endnotes

the-enemy/.

18. Catherine Moy, "Code Pink 'Bundles' for Barack," *Human Events* (April 14, 2008), http://www.humanevents.com/article.php?id=25997.

19. See the video interview by Charlie Rose, "A Conversation with Reverend Jim Wallis" (June 21, 2005), http://www.charlierose.com/view/interview/1082.

20. Wallis would agree with the Rev. Al Sharpton's definition of social justice: "We won't have true social justice until everyone is equal in everybody's house." Sharpton made this statement on May 2, 2010, before a church in Danbury, CT, http://www.youtube.com/watch?v=95bcEb1rV18.

21. Discover the Networks, "Michael Klonsky: Another Communist in Obama's Fringe Promoting 'Progressivism' and His Small Schools" (March 5, 2010), http://romanticpoet.wordpress.com/2010/03/05/mike-klonsky-another-communist-in-obamas-fringe-promoting-progressivism-and-his-small-schools/.

22. Andy McCarthy, "Another Communist in Obama's Orb," *National Review* (October 22, 2008), http://article.nationalreview.com/376079/another-communist-in-obamas-orb/andrew-c-mccarthy.

23. Obama, *Dreams from My Father,* 76–77, 89, 91, 96–98, 134, 145, 171, 220, 277, 330.

24. Cliff Kincaid, "Obama's Communist Mentor." *Accuracy in Media* (February 18, 2008), http://www.aim.org/aim-column/obamas-communist-mentor/.

25. Lamar Alexander, "Why Make Government the Prime Source for Student Loans?" *The Washington Post* (March 7, 2010), http://www.washingtonpost.com/wp-dyn/content/article/2010/03/05/AR2010030502972.html. Also see "Obama to Nationalize $103 Billion Student Loan Industry," *Education News* (January 20, 2010), http://www.educationnews.org/higher_education/32602.html.

26. Phyllis Schlafly, "Community Organizing Explained," *Townhall* (February 3, 2009), http://townhall.com/columnists/PhyllisSchlafly/2009/02/03/community_organizing_explained.

27. Saul Alinsky, *Rules for Radicals: A Pragmatic Primer for Realistic Radicals* (New York: Vintage Press, 1989), 10.

28. Ryan Lizza, "The Agitator: Barack Obama's Unlikely Political Education," *The New Republic* (March 17, 2009), http://www.tnr.com/article/the-agitator-barack-obamas-unlikely-political-education.

29. Barack Obama, "Why Organize? Problems and Promise in the Inner City," in Peg Knoepfle, ed., *After Alinsky: Community Organizing in Illinois* (Springfield, IL: Institute for Public Affairs, 1990), 35–40.

30. Lizza, "Barack Obama's Unlikely Political Education."

31. Richard Poe, "Hillary, Obama and the Cult of Alinsky," *Rense* (January 13, 2008), http://www.rense.com/general80/fon.htm.

32. L. David Alinsky, "Son Sees Father's Handiwork in Convention," *The Boston Globe* (August 31, 2008), http://www.boston.com/bostonglobe/editorial_opinion/letters/articles/2008/08/31/son_sees_fathers_handiwork_in_convention/. .

33. See Barack Obmama's home page: http://www.BarackObama.com.

34. Pamela Geller, "Obama Organizing in High Schools," *Atlas Shrugs* (January 30, 2010), http://atlasshrugs2000.typepad.com/atlas_shrugs/2010/01/atlas-exclusive-obama-organizing-for-communism-and-youth-corps-in-the-public-school-1.html.

35. Ibid.

36. See the New Organizing Institute's home page, http://www.neworganizing.com/.

37. See Zack Exley's March 14, 2010 blog post: http://revolutioninjesusland.com/index.php/2010/03/14/going-back-over-to-zackexleycom/.

38. See the *Revolution in Jesusland* website: http://revolutioninjesusland.com/index.php/about/.

39. Stephanie Block, "Obama, ACORN, and the Churches," *Spero News* (October 7, 2008), http://www.speroforum.com/site/article.asp?id=15363.

40. Abdon M. Pallasch, "Strong, Silent Type: Obama's Legal Career," *Chicago Sun-Times* (December 17, 2007), http://www.suntimes.com/news/politics/obama/700499,CST-NWS-Obama-law17.article.

41. Bud White, "Wade Rathke: ACORN'S Founder, Ayers' Compatriot," *No Quarter* (February 2, 2009), http://www.noquarterusa.net/blog/2009/02/02/wade-rathke-acorns-founder-ayers-compatriot-2/.

42. James Simpson, "Cloward-Piven Government," *American Thinker* (November 23, 2009), http://www.americanthinker.com/2009/11/clowardpiven_government.html.

43. Ibid.

44. Richard Henry Lee, "Obama and the Woods Fund of Chicago," *American Thinker* (July 7, 2008), http://www.americanthinker.com/2008/07/obama_and_the_woods_fund_of_ch.html.

45. Rubin, "Obama and the Woods Fund."

46. Ibid.

47. James Simpson, "Barack Obama and the Strategy of Manufactured Crisis," *American Thinker* (September 28, 2008), http://www.americanthinker.com/2008/09/barack_obama_and_the_strategy.html. Also see Abdon M. Pallasch, "Obama's Legal Career," *The Chicago Sun-Times* (December 17, 2007), http://www.suntimes.com/news/politics/obama/700499,CST-NWS-Obama-law17.article.

48. Simpson, "Cloward-Piven Government."

49. "The faith to which Obama actually clings is neocummnism. It is a leftism of the most insidious kind: secular and uncompromising in it

Endnotes

rejection of bourgeois [middle class] values, but feverishly spiritual in its zeal to tear down the existing order, under the banner of its all-purpose rally-cry: "social justice." Andrew C. McCarthy, *The Grand Jihad: How Islam and the Left Sabotage America* (New York: Encounter Books, 2010), 12.

50. For an updated exposé of Progressivism see Bradley C.S. Watson, "Darwin's Constitution: Why Progressives Took It upon Themselves to Purify Our Founding Charter of Its Meaning," *National Review* (May 17, 2010), 28*ff*. Progressivism is based on: a) Social Darwinism and b) Pragmaticism. Both lead to "the Constitution as a living, breathing, evolving document." The team players: John Dewey, William Graham Sumner, Lester Frank Ward, William James, Herbert Croly, and W.E.B. DuBois.

51. See Goldberg's work by the same name: Jonah Goldberg, *Liberal Fascism: The Secret History of the American Left, from Mussolini to the Politics of Meaning* (New York: Doubleday, 2007).

52. Jill S. Sprik, "Stealing Capitalism: The Crime of the Century," *American Thinker* (March 28, 2010), http://www.americanthinker.com/2010/03/stealing_capitalism_the_crime.html.

53. Quoted in Robert C. Cottrell, *Roger Nash Baldwin and the American Civil Liberties Union*, (New York: Columbia University Press, 2000), 228–29.

54. See Joseph Klein, "The Wrong Prescription," *Front Page Magazine* (September 22, 2008), http://www.frontpagemag.com/readArticle.aspx?ARTID=32427. This interview is available online: http://www.youtube.com/watch?v=niJAkR_6tKQ.

55. Quoted from "Biography for Jane Fonda," *The Internet Movie Database*, http://www.imdb.com/name/nm0000404/bio.

56. Ibid.

57. Vladimir Lenin, *Collected Works*, 45 vols., vol. 30 (Moscow: Progress Publishers, 1978), 107.

58. "Quotes from the Marxist World" (March 8, 2010), http://www.targetofopportunity.com/political_quotes_marxist.htm.

59. "Gorbachev Interview: I Am an Optimist," *Time* (June 4, 1990), http://www.time.com/time/magazine/article/0,9171,970249,00.html. Also see Dusko Doder and Louise Branson, *Gorbachev: Heretic in the Kremlin* (New York: Penguin, 1991).

60. William Z. Foster, *Toward Soviet America* (New York: International Publishers, 1932), 137.

61. Ibid., 131.

62. Ibid., 113.

63. Ibid., 268.

64. Ibid., 269.

65. Ibid., 273.

66. Ibid., 275.

67. Ibid., 341. Foster insists that the Communist society will "speed up the very evolution of man himself, his brain and body. Capitalism has checked the evolution of the human species." One plank of the Communist worldview is Darwinian evolution.

68. W. Cleon Skousen, *The Naked Communist* (Salt Lake City, UT: Ensign Publishing Company, 1958), 259*ff.*

69. See the Communist Party USA home page: http://www.cpusa.org/.

70. Jonathan Derbyshire, "Interview with Slavoj Zizek," *The New Statesman* (October 29, 2009), http://www.newstatesman.com/ ideas/2009/10/today-interview-capitalism.

71. See the video interview with Slavoj Zizek on the Democracy Now web site: http://www.democracynow.org/2009/10/15/slovenian_ philosopher_slavoj_zizek_on_the. Zizek again says "I am a Communist" and yes, "nationalize all the banks." *Harper's Magazine* (October 2009) also carried an article by Zizek entitled "To Each According to His Greed," http://harpers.org/archive/2009/10/0082658. Lastly, Encyclopedia.com refers to Zizek as an "academic star" and the "Elvis of cultural studies," http://www.encyclopedia.com/ doc/1G2-2699800184.html.

72. Derbyshire, "Interview with Slavoj Zizek."

73. Stanislav Mishin, "American Capitalism Gone with a Whimper," *Pravda* (April 27, 2009), http://english.pravda.ru/opinion/ columnists/107459-0/.

TRUST THE COMMUNISTS?

1. While Russia and Eastern Europe are no longer within the Communist orbit, China, North Korea, Cuba, Venezuela, Nicaragua, Ecuador, Bolivia, El Salvador, and Brazil are anxious to join. For the most up-to-date reporting on Communist strength throughout the world, see The Maldon Institute's two latest reports: "International Communism and Related Activities: 2008" and "Problems of the Revolution in Latin America and the Marxist-Leninist Communist Party of Ecuador." The Maldon Institute, PO Box 25526, Washington, DC 20027-8526, (410) 366-2531, maldon@tmigroup.org.

2. Communist China was seated in the United Nations on October 25, 1971. They were also granted membership on the United Nations Security Council.

3. *Korea*, vol. 25, (Pyongyang, Democratic People's Republic of Korea: Foreign Languages Publishing House, 1958).

4. Liu Shao-chi, *How to Be a Good Communist* (Peking: Foreign Languages Press), 55–56.

5. William C. Bullitt, "A Talk with Voroshilov," printed in *The Great*

Endnotes

Pretense, prepared and released by the Committee on Un-American Activities, US House of Representatives, Washington, DC (May 19, 1956), 18–19.

6. See William Z. Foster, *Toward Soviet America* (New York: International Publishers, 1932), chapter 5.
7. Romans 1:21–25, KJV.

THE RECRUITING OF A COMMUNIST

1. "There were more self-declared communists on the Harvard [Law] faculty than there were Republicans," see Marvin Olasky, "All Together," *WORLD Magazine* 24, no. 22 (November 7, 2009): 25. This article is available online: http://www.worldmag.com/articles/16016.
2. Social Credit originated from the writings of C.H. Douglas, a British engineer and originator of the Social Credit movement (1876–1952).
3. See such works as the following: Thomas Sowell, *Inside American Education: The Decline, The Deception, The Dogmas* (New York: The Free Press, 1993); B.K. Eakman, *Cloning of the American Mind: Eradicating Morality through Education* (Lafayette, LA: Huntington House Publishers, 1998); and James Davison Hunter, *The Death of Character: Moral Education in an Age without Good or Evil* (New York: Basic Books, 2000).
4. Liu Shao-chi, *How to Be a Good Communist* (Peking: Foreign Languages Press, 1949), 37–38.
5. See R.J. Rummel, *Death by Government* (New Brunswick, NJ: Transaction Publishers, 1994); Stephane Courtois, ed., *The Black Book of Communism: Crimes, Terror, Repression* (Cambridge, MA: Harvard University Press, 1999).
6. See William Z. Foster, *Toward Soviet America* (New York: International Publishers, 1932), chapter 5.

THE MOLDING OF A COMMUNIST

1. Vladimir Lenin, *Selected Works of Vladimir Lenin*, One-Volume ed. (Moscow: Foreign Languages Publishing House, 1952), 21.
2. Liu Shao-chi, *How to Be a Good Communist* (Peking: Foreign Languages Press), 50.

THE COMMUNIST AT WORK

1. Vladimir Lenin, *Left-Wing Communism, an Infantile Disorder* (Moscow: Foreign Languages Publishing House, 1950), 120–21.
2. See Robert M. Miller, *Harry Emerson Fosdick: Preacher, Pastor, Prophet* (New York: Oxford University Press, 1985), 474. Daniel Bell

observed that more ministers were on the "sucker list" of Communist Party fronts than any other group. One Methodist Episcopal bishop, G. Bromley Oxnam, was painted as serving God on Sunday and Communist Party fronts the rest of the week.

3. See Anthony Kubek, *How the Far East Was Lost: American Policy and the Creation of Communist China, 1941–1949* (Washington, DC: Regnery Publishing, 1963).

4. See David B. Richardson, "Marxism in US Classrooms," *US News & World Report* (January 25, 1982): 42–45. Herbert London notes, "The strides made by Marxism at American universities in the last two decades are breathtaking." Herbert London, "Marxism Thriving on American Campuses, *The World and I* (January 1987), 189. David Horowitz in *Unholy Alliance: Radical Islam and the American Left* (Washington, DC: Regnery Publishing, 2004) refers to Howard Zinn's *A People's History of the United States* as a "raggedly conceived Marxist caricature" that has been "embedded by leftist academics in the collegiate and secondary schools' curricula."

TECHNIQUES FOR SEIZING POWER

1. Vladimir Lenin, *The State and Revolution* (Moscow: Foreign Languages Publishing House), 35.

2. Vladimir Lenin, *The Proletarian Revolution and the Renegade Kautsky* (Moscow: Foreign Languages Publishing House, 1952), 23–24.

3. Lenin, *The State and Revolution*, 32–33.

4. Lenin, *The Proletarian Revolution*, 27.

5. Vladimir Lenin, *Left-wing Communism: An Infantile Disorder* (Moscow: Foreign Languages Publishing House, 1950), 65.

6. "The Alliance of Certain Racketeer and Communist Dominated Unions in the Field of Transportation as a Threat to National Security." A report by the Subcommittee to Investigate the Administration of the Internal Security Act and Other Internal Security Laws to the Committee on the Judiciary, United States Senate, 85th Congress, Second Session, December 17, 1958, United States Government Printing Office, Washington, DC, 1958, 28–30.

CONSOLIDATION OF POWER

1. Jung Chang and Jon Halliday, *Mao: The Unknown Story* (New York: Anchor Books, 2006).

2. See William Z. Foster, *Toward Soviet America* (New York: International Publishers, 1932).

3. Joseph Stalin, *Problems of Leninism* (Moscow: Foreign Languages Publishing House, 1953), 51.

Endnotes

ALLIES OF COMMUNISM

1. Liberation Theology, Orbis Books publishers, Sojourner's Community, and the World Council of Churches are all examples of Dr. Schwarz's important point.
2. See Eugene Lyons, *Workers' Paradise Lost: Fifty Years of Soviet Communism—A Balance Sheet* (New York: Funk & Wagnalls, 1967).
3. *US News & World Report* (October 5, 1949): 95. Excerpts from a discussion between Nikita Khrushchev and American labor leaders at a meeting in San Francisco, September 21, 1959.
4. See Dinesh D'Souza, *What's So Great about America* (Washington, DC: Regnery Publishing, 2002) and Arthur Brooks, *Who Really Cares: The Surprising Truth about Compassionate Conservatism—Who Gives, Who Doesn't and Why It Matters* (New York: Basic Books, 2006).
5. Liu Shao-chi, *How to Be a Good Communist* (Peking: Foreign Languages Press, 1949), 87.
6. Ibid., 41.

BRAINWASHING

1. Eugene Kinkead, *In Every War but One* (New York: W.W. Norton), 1959.
2. Communists and their Socialist/Progressive cousins in the United States are masters at this brainwashing technique. See Dr. Mary Grabar, *Introduction without Apology: Social Studies Teachers Share Strategies on How to Mold Students* (Owings, MD: America's Survival, 2010), "If anyone doubts that indoctrination takes place in our schools, he should attend the annual National Council for the Social Studies conference." Its keynote speaker at their 2009 conference in Atlanta, Georgia was Columbia historian Eric Foner, "an apologist for communism." According to John Earl Haynes and Harvey Klehr in their book *In Denial: Historians, Communism, and Espionage*, (San Francisco, CA: Encounter Books, 2003), "The subsequent decomposition of communism taught him nothing, and in *The Story of American Freedom*, published in 1998…Foner made the American Communist Party into 'a heroic organization' that profoundly changed American history for the better, the center of gravity for a broad democratic upsurge."

THE DIFFICULT, DEVIOUS, AND DANGEROUS DIALECTIC

1. For an in-depth look into this issue see J.P. Moreland and William Lane Craig, *Philosophical Foundations for a Christian Worldview* (Downers Grove, IL: InterVarsity Press, 2003), 228*ff*.
2. Mao Tse-tung, *On Contradiction* (Beijing: Foreign Languages Press,

1950), 16.

3. Nancy Pelosi referred to Harry Bridges' union—The International Longshoremen's and Warehousemen's Union—as "the most progressive union of the time." Bridges was a member of the Central Committee of the Communist Party USA. See Joshua Muravchik "Pelosi's Favorite Stalinist," *The Weekly Standard* 12, no. 39 (June 25–July 2, 2007), http://www.weeklystandard.com/Content/Public/Articles/000/000/013/783zfoqh.asp.

4. Liu Shao-chi, *How to Be a Good Communist* (Peking: Foreign Languages Press, 1949), 38.

5. Karl Marx and Frederick Engels, *Communist Manifesto* (Moscow: Foreign Languages Publishing House, 1957), 79–80.

6. Today called the Three Self Patriotic Movement.

7. Mao, *On Contradiction,* 1.

8. Vladimir Lenin, *History of the Communist Party of the Soviet Union (B), Short Course*, English ed. (Moscow: 1950), 133.

9. These words were written in italics by Stalin.

10. Joseph Stalin, *Problems of Leninism.* (Moscow: Foreign Languages Publishing House, 1953), 342–43.

11. See Stephane Courtois, ed., *The Black Book of Communism: Crimes, Terror, Repression* (Cambridge, MA: Harvard University Press, 1999).

The Heart, Soul, and Mind of Communism

1. Joseph Stalin, *Problems of Leninism* (Moscow: Foreign Languages Publishing House, 1953), 43.

Worldviews of Destruction

1. James Orr, *The Christian View of God and the World* (Edinburgh, UK: Andrew Elliot, 1897), 4.

2. Robert Schuettinger, *Lord Acton: Historian of Liberty* (LaSalle, IL: Open Court, 1976), 187.

3. Ibid., 174.

4. David A. Noebel, *Understanding the Times: The Religious Worldviews of Our Day and the Search for Truth* (Eugene, OR: Harvest House Publishers, 1991). This work has been updated in *Understanding the Times: The Collision of Today's Competing Worldviews*, Rev. 2nd ed. (Manitou Springs, CO: Summit Press, 2006).

5. R.J. Rummel, *Death by Government* (New Brunswick, NJ: Transaction Publishers, 1994), 9.

6. Ibid., 13. "Democide" is a term coined by Rummel to include "the murder of any person or people by a government including genocide, politicide, and mass murder."

Endnotes

7. For a devastating critique of the role of intellectuals in this mix of ideas see Thomas Sowell, *Intellectuals and Society* (New York: Basic Books, 2009).

8. Gene Edward Veith, Jr., *Modern Fascism: Liquidating the Judeo-Christian Worldview* (St. Louis: Concordia Publishing House, 1993), 137.

9. Arthur Herman, *The Idea of Decline in Western History* (New York: The Free Press, 1997), 349.

10. Ibid., 357.

11. Ibid., 79.

12. See Lawrence E. Cahoone, ed. *From Modernism to Postmodernism: An Anthology*, Rev. 2nd ed. (Cambridge: Blackwell Publishers, 1996), 12–13.

13. Ibid., 174.

14. Arnold Beichman, "Workers of America, Unite?" *The Weekly Standard* (March 9 1998): 35.

15. David Horowitz, *Radical Son: A Journey through Our Times* (New York: The Free Press, 1997), 405. For those interested in further study in this particular area, see Martin Jay, *The Dialectical Imagination: A History of the Frankfurt School and the Institute of Social Research 1923–1950*, (Berkeley, CA: University of California Press, 1996). Also note that the work by Marxist Theodor W. Adorno is still continually used to paint conservatives as Fascists and Nazis: Theodor W. Adorno, *The Authoritarian Personality* (New York: Harper, 1950).

16. James C. Dobson and Gary L. Bauer, *Children at Risk: The Battle for the Hearts and Minds of Our Kids* (Dallas, TX: Word, 1990), 22.

17. Ibid., 182. Also see John A. Stormer, *None Dare Call It Education: What's Happening to Our Schools & Our Children?* (Florissant, MO: Liberty Bell Press, 1998) on why Capitalism is ridiculed, family values attacked, and American history rewritten. Also, B.K. Eakman, *Cloning of the American Mind: Eradicating Morality through Education* (Lafayette, LA: Huntington House Publishers, 1998).

18. Richard John Neuhaus, *The Naked Public Square: Religion and Democracy in America* (Grand Rapids, MI: Eerdmans Publishers, 1984), 6. "In the late nineteenth century [ca 1893] England, several small groups of scientists and scholars organized under the leadership of Thomas H. Huxley to overthrow the cultural dominance of Christianity—particularly the intellectual dominance of the Anglican church. Their goal was to secularize society, replacing the Christian worldview with scientific naturalism, a worldview that recognizes the existence of nature alone." Also see Nancy R. Pearcey and Charles B. Thaxton, *The Soul of Science: Christian Faith and Natural Philosophy* (Wheaton, IL: Crossway Books, 1994), 19. The British Fabian Society was also heavily involved in replacing Christianity with Socialism.

"Socialism was demonstrably conceived as an universal 'religion' and 'faith'...based on the religion of scientific humanism." M. Margaret McCarran, *Fabianism in the Political Life of Britain, 1919–1931* (Chicago: The Heritage Foundation, 1954), 50.

19. David C. Large, *Where Ghosts Walked: Munich's Road to the Third Reich* (New York: W.W. Norton, 1997), 245.

20. Erwin W. Lutzer, *Hitler's Cross* (Chicago: Moody Press, 1995), 61.

21. Ibid.

22. For an excellent summary of Gobineau's ideas on race, see Herman, *The Idea of Decline in Western History*, 46–75.

23. Lutzer noted that Hitler used to say, "Whoever wants to understand National Socialist Germany must know Wagner." Lutzer, *Hitler's Cross*, 80.

24. Veith, *Modern Fascism*, 140.

25. Large, *Where Ghosts Walked*, 245–46.

26. Ibid., 76*ff.*

27. Ludwig von Mises, *Socialism: An Economic and Sociological Analysis* (Indianapolis, IN: Liberty Classics, 1981), 530.

28. Stanley G. Payne, *A History of Fascism, 1914–1945* (Madison: The University of Wisconsin Press, 1995), 484.

29. A.E. Wilder-Smith, *Man's Origin, Man's Destiny* (Minneapolis: Bethany Fellowship, 1968), 187.

30. Ibid., 190. For greater detail on this relationship between Darwin and Hitler see Richard Weikart, *From Darwin to Hitler: Evolutionary Ethics, Eugenics, and Racism in Germany* (New York: Palgrave Macmillan, 2006).

31. Wilder-Smith, *Man's Origin, Man's Destiny*, 190–191.

32. Ian T. Taylor, *In the Minds of Men: Darwin and the New World Order* (Toronto: TFE Publishing, 1984), 409.

33. Ibid.

34. For a complete understanding of Socialism, see von Mises, *Socialism*. For those interested in a Marxist interpretation of Socialism, see John Strachey, *The Theory and Practice of Socialism* (New York: Random House, 1936).

35. Friedrich A. Hayek, *The Road to Serfdom* (Chicago: University of Chicago Press, 1944), 28.

36. Richard Vetterli and William E. Fort, Jr., *The Socialist Revolution* (Los Angeles: Clute International, 1968), 88.

37. Ibid., 87.

38. Ibid.

39. Veith, *Modern Fascism*, 59*ff.*

40. John Robbins, "Karl Barth," *The Trinity Review* (February 1998): 4.

41. Ibid.

42. Ibid.

Endnotes

43. For an excellent summary of the role of theologians in the rise of Hitler's National Socialism, see Veith, *Modern Fascism*, 61*ff.*

44. Jay, *The Dialectical Imagination*, 24–25. For an insightful look at Tillich, see Hannah Tillich, *From Time to Time* (New York: Stein and Day, 1973). Tillich was not only a radical Marxist theologian, but also a libertine. Surprisingly, Tillich is also considered a key theologian to at least one conservative religious denomination. See H. Ray Dunning, *Grace, Faith, and Holiness: A Wesleyan Systematic Theology* (Kansas City, MO: Beacon Hill Press, 1988).

45. Franklin H. Littell and Hubert G. Locke, ed., *The German Church Struggle and the Holocaust* (Detroit: Wayne State University Press, 1974), 24. Quoted in Veith, *Modern Fascism*, 71.

46. Payne, *A History of Fascism, 1914–1945*, 485–86.

47. Wilder-Smith, *Man's Origin, Man's Destiny*, 191.

48. Ibid., 186.

49. Ibid.

50. Veith, *Modern Fascism*, 17.

51. Ibid., 20. Also see Jonah Goldberg, *Liberal Fascism: The Secret History of the American Left from Mussolini to the Politics of Meaning* (New York: Doubleday, 2007), 25–52.

52. Ibid.

53. Zygmund Dobbs, ed., *The Great Deceit: Social Pseudo-Sciences* (West Sayville, NY: Veritas Foundation, 1964), 143.

54. Ibid.

55. Ibid.

56. Ibid., 144.

57. The American counterpart to the British Fabian Society was the League for Industrial Democracy (LID) headed for years by the Socialist John Dewey, father of Secular Humanist education in the United States. Among the League's participants was Morris Hillquit, head of the Socialist Party in the 1920s and "a militant defender of the Bolshevik Revolution and a vociferous supporter of the Communist International." Dobbs, *The Great Deceit*, 26. Sponsors of the LID included Senator Jacob Javits, Senator Paul H. Douglas, Senator Wayne Morse, among others.

58. George Bernard Shaw, *The Intelligent Woman's Guide to Socialism and Capitalism* (New York: Brentanosx, 1928), 470.

59. Vetterli and Fort, *The Socialist Revolution*. 57.

60. von Mises, *Socialism*, 525.

61. Ibid. Also see Vetterli and Fort, *The Socialist Revolution*, 58.

62. Ibid., 68.

63. Gene Edward Veith, Jr., *Postmodern Times: A Christian Guide to Contemporary Thought and Culture* (Wheaton, IL: Crossway Books, 1994). Dennis McCallum, ed., *The Death of Truth: What's Wrong with*

Multiculturalism, the Rejection of Reason and the New Postmodern Diversity (Minneapolis: Bethany House Publishers, 1996). Cahoone, *From Modernism to Postmodernism.*

64. Noebel, *Understanding the Times* (1991) (2006) editions.

65. Rummel, *Death by Government*, 46. "This ancient capital of Khorassan in Persia was then a scene of a carnival of blood scarcely surpassed even in Mongol annals…Separate piles of heads of men, women, and children were built into pyramids; and even cats and dogs were killed in the streets. An utterly fantastic 1,747,000 human beings reportedly were slaughtered."

66. Ibid., 8.

67. Jung Chang and Jon Halliday, *Mao: The Unknown Story* (New York: Anchor, 2006).

68. Stephane Courtois, ed., *The Black Book of Communism: Crimes, Terror, Repression* (Cambridge, MA: Harvard University Press, 1999).

69. Joseph Stalin, *Works,* 13 vols., vol. 1 (Moscow: Foreign Languages Publishing House: 1952), 304. Cited in Wetter, *Dialectical Materialism*, 325. Also see "What Happened When Stalin Read Darwin?" *Answers Research Journal* 13, no. 4 (September 1988): 23. This article is available online: http://www.answersingenesis.org/creation/v10/i4/stalin.asp.

70. Karl Marx, *The Communist Manifesto* (Chicago: Henry Regnery Company, 1954), 30.

71. Ibid., 53.

72. Ibid., 54.

73. Jacques Barzun, *Darwin, Marx, Wagner: Critique of a Heritage* (Garden City, NY: Doubleday, 1958), 8.

74. Vladimir Lenin, *Collected Works*, 45 vols., vol. 10 (Moscow: Progress Publishers, 1978), 86.

75. Ibid., vol. 35, 122.

76. Hans Kung, *Does God Exist? An Answer for Today* (Garden City, NY: Doubleday, 1980), 257.

77. Whittaker Chambers, *Witness* (New York: Random House, 1952), 712.

78. For a full accounting of Dialectical Materialism, see *Understanding the Times* (1991), chapter 7.

79. Nikita Khrushchev, "*Ukrainian Bulletin*," August 1–August 15, 1960, 12. Cited in James Bales, *Communism and the Reality of Moral Law* (Nutley, NJ: Craig Press, 1969), 121.

80. Karl Marx and Frederick Engels, *Selected Correspondence* (New York: International Publishers, 1942), 125.

81. Frederick Engels, *Selected Works*, vol. 2 (1950), 153. Cited in R.N. Carew Hunt, *The Theory and Practice of Communism* (Baltimore: Penguin Books, 1966), 64.

82. Vladimir Lenin, *Materialism and Empirio-Criticism* (New York:

Endnotes

International Publishers, 1927), 34.

83. Marx, *The Communist Manifesto*, 54.

84. Ibid., 33.

85. Karl Marx and Frederick Engels, *Collected Works*, 50 vols., vol. 6 (New York: International Publishers, 1975), 494–95.

86. Lenin, *Selected Works*, vol. 10, 91–92.

87. Karl Marx, *Civil War in France* (New York: International Publishers, 1937), 19.

88. Marx, *The Communist Manifesto*, 21.

89. Vladimir Lenin, *Selected Works*, 12 vols., vol. 9 (New York: International Publishers, 1937), 479.

90. William D. Gairdner, *The Book of Absolutes: A Critique of Relativism and a Defense of Universals* (Montreal: McGill-Queen's University Press, 2008), 41.

91. Malachi Martin, *The Keys of This Blood: Pope John Paul II Versus Russia and the West for Control of the New World Order* (New York: Simon & Schuster, 1990), 177.

92. Cahoone, *From Modernism to Postmodernism*, 10.

93. John Dewey, *A Common Faith* (New Haven, CT: Yale University Press, 1934), 87. For 63 exhibits proving that Secular Humanism is a religion, see David A. Noebel, J.F. Baldwin and Kevin Bywater, *Clergy in the Classroom: The Religion of Secular Humanism*, Rev. 3rd ed. (Manitou Springs, CO: Summit Press, 2007). One of the exhibits is the *Harvard University Gazette* newspaper (July 9, 1993) which admits that Secular Humanism is a religion, and its Humanist chaplain at Harvard is Thomas Ferrick. Exhibit 63 identifies the American Humanist Association listed by the Internal Revenue Service as a 501(c)3 tax-exempt organization "classified as a church." Its Federal identification number is 94-6168317. Exhibit 26 contains the US Supreme Court decision identifying Secular Humanism as a religion along with Buddhism, Taoism and Ethical Culture. Exhibit 60 contains the United States Court of Appeals for the Seventh Circuit labeling Atheism as a "religion for the purposes of the First Amendment."

94. Elasah Drogin, *Margaret Sanger: Father of Modern Society* (New Hope, KY: CUL Publications, 1986), 9.

95. Ibid., 87.

96. Ibid., 38.

97. Lena Levine, "Psycho-Sexual Development," *Planned Parenthood News* (Summer 1953): 10.

98. Sherri Tepper, *You've Changed the Combination* (Denver: Rocky Mountain Planned Parenthood, 1974).

99. George Grant, *Grand Illusions: The Legacy of Planned Parenthood* (Brentwood, TN: Wolgemuth and Hyatt, 1988), 49.

100. Ibid., 96.

101. Drogin, *Margaret Sanger*, 10.
102. Lothrop Stoddard, *Into the Darkness: Nazi Germany Today* (New York: Duell, Sloan & Pearce, 1940), 190–91.
103. Ibid., 94–95. For those interested in Margaret Sanger and Planned Parenthood, which is still funded by the United States government, we strongly recommend George Grant's *Grand Illusions*.
104. Charles Francis Potter, *Humanism: A New Religion* (New York: Simon & Schuster, 1930), 128.
105. "Among religions in this country which do not teach what would generally be considered a belief in the existence of God are Buddhism, Taoism, Ethical Culture, Secular Humanism and others." US Supreme Court, *Torcaso v. Watkins*, decided June 19, 1961.
106. From John Dewey through George Counts, Harold Rugg, and Benjamin Bloom and on to Brock Chisholm and Chester Pierce see Stormer, *None Dare Call It Education*.
107. Paul Kurtz, *The Humanist Alternative* (Buffalo, NY: Prometheus Books, 1973), 177.
108. Corliss Lamont, "Naturalistic Humanism," in *The Best of Humanism*, ed. Roger E. Greeley (Buffalo, NY: Prometheus Books, 1988), 149.
109. William Provine, "Scientists, Face It! Science and Religion Are Incompatible," *The Scientist* (September 5, 1988): 10.
110. Carl Sagan, *The Dragons of Eden: Speculations on the Evolution of Human Intelligence* (New York: Random House, 1977), 6.
111. Carl Rogers, "Notes on Rollo May," *Journal of Humanistic Psychology* (Summer 1982): 8.
112. Lawrence Casler, "Permissive Matrimony: Proposals for the Future," *The Humanist* (March/April 1974): 4.
113. Delos B. McKown, "Demythologizing Natural Human Rights," *The Humanist* (May/June 1989): 24.
114. Julian Huxley, "A New World Vision," *The Humanist* (March/April 1979): 35.
115. *Humanist Manifesto I* (Buffalo, NY: Prometheus Books, 1980), 10.
116. Will and Ariel Durant, *The Lessons of History* (New York: Simon & Schuster, 1968), 18.
117. Ibid., 81.
118. Lutzer, *Hitler's Cross*, 205.
119. Ibid., 201.
120. For a defense of the Christian worldview see David A. Noebel, *Understanding the Times* (1991, 2006); J.P. Moreland and William Lane Craig, *Philosophical Foundations for a Christian Worldview* (Downers Grove, IL: InterVarsity Press, 2003); Norman L. Geisler, *Christian Apologetics* (Grand Rapids, MI: Baker Book House,1997); Norman L. Geisler and Thomas Howe, *When Critics Ask* (Grand Rapids, MI: Baker Book House, 1992); Norman L. Geisler and Ron

Endnotes

Brooks, *When Skeptics Ask: A Handbook on Christian Evidences* (Grand Rapids, MI: Baker Book House,1996); Norman L. Geisler, *Christian Ethics: Options and Issues* (Grand Rapids, MI: Baker Book House, 1990); Norman L. Geisler and Frank Turek, *Legislating Morality* (Minneapolis: Bethany House Publishers, 1998; and Norman L. Geisler, *Systematic Theology,* Vols. 1–4 (Minneapolis: Bethany House, 2002).

121. Lutzer, *Hitler's Cross*, 204.

BARACK OBAMA'S RED SPIRITUAL ADVISOR

1. See Alex Newman, "Resurgent Communism in Latin America," *The New American* (March 29, 2010): 20*ff.* Also see Alex Newman "Latin Communism, Incorporated," by Alex Newman, *The New American* (March 29, 2010): 27*ff.* Newman quotes Olavo de Carvalho (author and leading Brazilian philosopher): "Communist and pro-communist parties rule about a dozen Latin American countries today. This fact, by itself, is enough to prove that the 'end of communism' is a myth."

2. Associated Press, "Salvadoran Leftist President Promises Moderation," *Fox News* (March 16, 2009), http://www.foxnews.com/wires/2009Mar1 6/0,4670,LTElSalvadorElections,00.html.

3. Associated Press, "New Salvadoran President Compares Message of Change to Obama's," *Fox News* (March 17, 2009), http://www. foxnews.com/story/0,2933,509438,00.html.

4. "Salvador Swings Left," *Investor's Business Daily* (March 17, 2009), http://www.investors.com/NewsAndAnalysis/Article.aspx?id=471356.

5. Ibid.

6. "Barack Obama's Newest Spiritual Advisor," *Front Page Magazine* (March 17, 2009), http://www.frontpagemag.com/readArticle. aspx?ARTID=34385.

7. Ibid.

8. "Sojourning Socialists," *Investor's Business Daily* (September 09, 2008), http://www.investors.com/NewsAndAnalysis/Article. aspx?id=459224.

9. Jacob Laksin, "Sojourners: History, Activities and Agendas," *Discover the Networks* (2005), http://www.discoverthenetworks.org/Articles/ Sojournershistory.html. Also see Ronald H. Nash, *Why the Left Is Not Right: The Religious Left — Who They Are and What They Believe* (Grand Rapids, MI: Zondervan Publishing House, 1996, 56*ff.*

10. Laksin, "Sojourners," *Discover the Networks*.

11. Ibid.

12. Blake Hurst, "Dirt Poor in the Workers' Paradise," *The Weekly Standard* 14, no. 26 (March 23, 2009): 13. This article is available online: http://www.weeklystandard.com/Content/Public/

Articles/000/000/016/273yeccg.asp.

13. See Rodney Stark, *The Victory of Reason: How Christianity Led to Freedom, Capitalism, and Western Success* (New York: Random House, 2005) and Thomas Sowell, *Intellectuals and Society*, (New York: Basic Books, 2009).

14. Joseph Farah, "The Day Socialism Comes to America," *World Net Daily* (February 17, 2008), http://www.wnd.com/index. php?pageId=56620. In 1961, Ronald Reagan addressed Thomas's statement while speaking out against socialized medicine. Reagan's comments are available online: http://www.youtube.com/watch?v=AYrlDlrLDSQ.

15. Richard J. Ellis, *The Dark Side of the Left: Illiberal Egalitarianism in America* (Lawrence, KS: Kansas University Press,), 137.

16. "Barack Obama's Newest Spiritual Advisor," *Front Page Magazine*.

17. Cornel West is presently associating himself with the founder of the Revolutionary Communist Party USA. See "A Riveting Exchange Between Cornel West and Carl Dix," *Revolution* #170 (July 19, 2009), http://www.rwor.org/a/170/CWCD_event-en.html. This exchange was sponsored by Revolution Books (a pro-Communist organization) and was a fundraiser for the organization as well as the Prisoners Revolutionary Literature Fund.

18. Nash, *Why the Left Is Not Right,* 58.

19. Ibid., 59. This comment, more than most of Wallis' comments, identifies him as a hardened radical leftist.

20. For a full exposé of this pro-Communist organization, see S. Steven Powell, *Covert Cadre: Inside The Institute for Policy Studies* (Ottawa, IL: Green Hill Publishers, 1986).

21. See Nash, *Why the Left Is Not Right*, chapter 5.

22. Ibid., 66, 71.

23. Thomas Sowell, "The Crusade against Walmart," *Capitalism Magazine* (May 9, 2005), http://www.capitalismmagazine.com/markets/business/4224-The-Crusade-Against-Walmart.html. Sowell covers this area in great depth in Thomas Sowell, *Intellectuals and Society (*New York: Basic Books, 2009).

24. Thomas Sowell, "Talkers Versus Doers," *Town Hall* (June 9, 2004), http://townhall.com/columnists/ThomasSowell/2004/06/09/talkers_versus_doers.

25. Sowell, *Intellectuals and Society*, 105.

26. David Gelernter, "What 'Republican' Should Mean," *National Review* 61, no. 4 (March 23, 2009), 32.

27. "UCC Memeber Sen. Barack Obama Disucusses Faith and Politics," *United Church of Christ News* (June 29, 2006), http://www.ucc.org/news/exclusiveucc-member.html.

28. *Accuracy in Media Research Report* (May 1983), Section 19.

Endnotes

THE SOCIALIZATION OF AMERICA

1. Richard Vetterli and William E. Fort, Jr., *The Socialist Revolution* (New York: Clute International, 1968), xi.
2. George Berard Shaw, *Intelligent Woman's Guide to Socialism* (New York: Brentanno, 1928), 470.
3. Margaret Thatcher, interviewed by Llew Gardner, *This Week*, Thames Television (February 5, 1976). A transcript of this interview is available online: http://www.margaretthatcher.org/speeches/displaydocument. asp?docid=102953.
4. William Voegeli, "The Roots of Liberal Condescension," *Claremont Review of Books* (Winter 2008/09), 6. This article is available online: http://www.claremont.org/publications/crb/id.1594/article_detail.asp.
5. Zygmund Dobbs, *Keynes at Harvard: Economic Deception as a Political Credo* (West Sayville, NY: Veritas Foundation, 1964), 63.
6. Margaret Cole, *The Story of Fabian Socialism* (Palo Alto, CA: Stanford University Press, 1961), 197.
7. Stephane Courtois, ed., *The Black Book of Communism: Crimes, Terror, Repression* (Cambridge, MA: Harvard University Press, 1999).
8. Michael Goldfarb, "Obama's Global Warming Straddle," *The Weekly Standard* (March 16, 2009), 17. This article is available online: http://www.weeklystandard.com/Content/Public/ Articles/000/000/016/254xxzyp.asp.
9. "Lee's Cuban Dream," *The Washington Times* (April 9, 2009), http:// www.washingtontimes.com/news/2009/apr/09/editorial-lee39s-cuban-dream/.
10. See the Congressional Progressive Caucus website: http://cpc.grijalva. house.gov/index.cfm?ContentID=166&ParentID=0&SectionID=4 &SectionTree=4&lnk=b&ItemID=164. Also see Brenda J. Elliott, "Loudon: The Real 'Secret' of American Communism," *The Real Barack Obama* (January 3, 2009), http://therealbarackobama.wordpress. com/2009/01/03/loudon-the-real-"secret"-of-american-communism/.
11. John Nichols, "The Crowded Progressive Caucus," *The Nation* (November 12, 2006), http://www.thenation.com/blog/crowded-progressive-caucus.
12. Stephen Dinan, "Obama Climate Czar Has Socialist Ties," *The Washington Times* (January 12, 2009), http://www.washingtontimes. com/news/2009/jan/12/obama-climate-czar-has-socialist-ties/.
13. See Dobbs, *Keynes at Harvard*, addendum.
14. Whittaker Chambers, *Witness* (New York: Random House, 1952), 17.
15. Ibid., 616.
16. Dobbs, *Keynes at Harvard,* 68. Also see Mark Skousen, *The Making of Modern Economics: The Lives and Ideas of the Great Thinkers* (Armonk, NY: M.E. Sharpe, 2001), 433.
17. Ibid., 330.

18. Dobbs, *Keynes at Harvard*, 83.
19. "Keynes on Inflation," http://www.pbs.org/wgbh/commandingheights/shared/minitextlo/ess_inflation.html. Theses are excepts pulled from John Maynard Keynes, *The Economic Consequences of the Peace*, (London: Macmillan, 1919), 235–48.
20. Larry Summers, interviewed by Charlie Rose, *The Charlie Rose Show*, PBS (February 18, 2009). This interview is available online: http://www.charlierose.com/view/interview/10092.
21. Chambers, *Witness*, 741.
22. Thomas Sowell, *Intellectuals and Society*. (New York: Basic Books, 2009), 105.
23. Henryk Skolimowski, "Education for the Real World," *New Renaissance* (1990), http://www.ru.org/14educat.html.
24. From Winston Churchill's speech at Perth, Scotland on May 28, 1948, *The Churchill Centre and Churchill War Rooms, London*, http://www.winstonchurchill.org/component/content/article/16-quotes/474.
25. From Winston Churchill's speech at Woodford Green, Essex on October 29, 1959, *The Churchill Centre and Churchill War Rooms, London*, http://www.winstonchurchill.org/component/content/article/33-datelines/864-datelines-fh-138.

POSTSCRIPT

1. Lisa McGirr, *Suburban Warriors: The Origins of the New American Right* (Princeton, NJ: Princeton University Press, 2001), 53.
2. Ibid., 61.
3. Ibid., 64.
4. Fred C. Schwarz, *Beating the Unbeatable Foe: One Man's Victory over Communism, Leviathan, and the Last Enemy* (Washington, DC: Regnery Publishing, 1996).

APPENDIX: IS COMMUNISM DEAD? YOU DECIDE

1. Whittaker Chambers, *Witness* (New York: Random House, 1952), 616.
2. Thomas Sowell, *Intellectuals and Society* (New York: Basic Books, 2009), 91.
3. See the Communist Party USA home page: http://www.cpusa.org/.
4. "Obama 'Internet Czar' Linked to 'Net Neutrality' Effort," *World Net Daily* (May 5, 2010), http://www.wnd.com/?pageId=150185.
5. Al Sharpton made this statement on May 2, 2010, before a church in Danbury, CT, http://www.youtube.com/watch?v=95bcEb1rV18.
6. Phillip Blond, "Shattered Society," *The American Conservative* (June 1, 2010): 9. This article is available online: http://www.amconmag.com/article/2010/jun/01/00006/.

Endnotes

7. Wesley J. Smith, "Ecocide: A Crime against Peace?" *The Weekly Standard* 15, no. 32 (May 10, 2010): 17. This article is available online: http://www.weeklystandard.com/articles/ecocide-crime-against-peace.

8. Thomas Sowell, *Is Reality Optional? And Other Essays* (Stanford, CA: Hoover Institutional Press, 1993), 75–76.

9. Ibid.

10. Sowell, *Intellectuals and Society*, 11.

11. Matthew Continetti, "Blame Americans First," *The Weekly Standard* 15, no. 23 (March 1, 2010): 10. This article is available online: http://www.weeklystandard.com/articles/blame-americans-first.

12. Matthew Vadum, "Communist-loving Sean Penn Goes off the Deep End," *News Real Blog* (March 9, 2010), http://www.newsrealblog.com/2010/03/09/communist-loving-sean-penn-goes-off-the-deep-end/. Bill Ayers is also a devotee of Hugo Chavez. See Aaron Klein and Brenda J. Elliott, *The Manchurian President: Barack Obama's Ties to the Communists, Socialists, and Other Anti-American Extremists* (Washington, DC: WND Book, 2010), 212.

13. Alex Newman, "Olavo de Carvalho on Communism in Latin America," *The New American* (March 15, 2010): 27. This article is available online: http://www.thenewamerican.com/index.php/world-mainmenu-26/south-america-mainmenu-37/3119-latin-communism-incorporated.

14. Quote from Sergei Tretyakov, *Comrade J*, as cited in Jamie Glazov, "The 'Collapse' of Communism," *Front Page Magazine* (April 29, 2010), http://frontpagemag.com/2010/04/29/the-"collapse"-of-communism/.

15. Ibid., Quote from Robert Buchar.

16. Brenda J. Elliott, "Loudon: The Real 'Secret' of American Communism," *The Real Barack Obama* (January 3, 2009), http://therealbarackobama.wordpress.com/2009/01/03/loudon-the-real-"secret"-of-american-communism/.

17. Kyle Smith, "Michael Moore Film Ends with Communist Anthem," *Kyle Smith Online* (September 8, 2009), http://kylesmithonline.com/?p=4539.

18. Joshua Muravchik "Pelosi's Favorite Stalinist" *The Weekly Standard* 12, no. 39 (June 25–July 2, 2007), http://www.weeklystandard.com/Content/Public/Articles/000/000/013/783zfoqh.asp.

19. Ibid.

20. John Elvin, "Gore Family Ties," *Insight* (May 22, 2000): 12–13. Also see Edward Jay Epstein, *Dossier: The Secret History of Armand Hammer* (New York: Random House, 1996).

21. Ian James, "Stone: Film an Intro to Chavez and His Movement," *ABC News* (May 28, 2010), http://abcnews.go.com/Entertainment/wireStory?id=10775895.

22. Sowell, *Intellectuals and Society*, 42. Also see John Earl Haynes and Harvey Klehr, *In Denial: Historian, Communism and Espionage* (New York: Encounter Books, 2003), 13. "The number of apologists for the former Soviet Union and its mass murderers dwarfs the handful of aberrant pro-Nazi academics in America. Sympathy for the Communist project and distaste for attacking it are today fully accepted in American higher education."

23. Humberto Fontova, "Ted Turner Lies about Cuba," *American Thinker* (December 18, 2008), http://www.americanthinker.com/2008/12/ted_turners_lies_about_cuba.html.

24. Ibid.

25. John Strachey, *The Theory and Practice of Socialism* (New York: Random House, 1936), 121.

26. William F. Jasper, "The Grasp of Socialist International," *The New American* (March 1, 2010): 23. This article is available online: http://www.thenewamerican.com/index.php/world-mainmenu-26/europe-mainmenu-35/2947-the-grasp-of-socialist-international.

27. Newt Gingrich, "How I'd Create a New 'Contract with America,'" *Newsmax* (February 2010): 63. This article is available online: http://w3.newsmax.com/a/feb10/gingrich/.

28. Esther B. Fein, "Upheaval in the East: Soviet Union; Baltic Separatists' Efforts Anger a Frayed Gorbachev, *The New York Times* (December 23, 1989), http://www.nytimes.com/1989/12/24/world/upheaval-east-soviet-union-baltic-separatists-efforts-anger-frayed-gorbachev.html?scp=1&sq=%22I+am+a+Communist%22+Gorbachev&st=nyt. Also see Dusko Doder and Louise Branson, *Gorbachev: Heretic in the Kremlin* (New York: Penguin, 1991).

29. Karl Marx and Friedrich Engles, *The Communist Manifesto* (London: Verso, 1998), 52.

30. Ed Whelan, "Goodwin Lui's Cheap Attack on the Roberts Nomination," *National Review* (May 3, 2010), 8. This article is available online: http://www.nationalreview.com/bench-memos/49244/goodwin-lius-cheap-attack-roberts-nomination/ed-whelan.

31. Claude Frederic Bastiat, *The Law*, trans. Dean Russell (Irvington, NY: Foundation for Economic Education [1850], 2007), 14.

32. William D. Gairdner, *The Book of Absolutes: A Critique of Relativism and a Defense of Universals* (Montreal: McGill-Queen's University Press, 2008), 41.

33. Meyer Weinberg, ed., *The World of W.E.B. DuBois: A Quotation Sourcebook* (Westport, CT: Greenwood Press, 1992), 11.

34. Aaron Klein and Brenda J. Elliott, *The Manchurian President: Barack Obama's Ties to Communists, Socialists and Other Anti-American Extremists* (Washington, DC: WND Books, 2010), 7, 13.

35. *National Review*, March 8, 2010, 51.

Endnotes

36. Don Feder, "Tinseltown's Marxist Anti-Semite," *Front Page Magazine* (July 14, 2004), http://www.frontpagemag.com/readArticle.aspx?ARTID=12227.

37. Roger Kimball, "Professor of Contempt," *National Review* (February 22, 2010), http://article.nationalreview.com/423758/professor-of-contempt/roger-kimball.

38. Jonah Goldberg, *Liberal Fascism: The Secret History of the American Left from Mussolini to the Politics of Meaning* (New York: Doubleday, 2007), 134.

39. Jann S. Wenner, *Lennon Remembers: The Full Rolling Stone Interviews from 1970* (London: Verso, 2000), 41.

40. David L. Brown, "The Unholy Legacy of the Beatles," http://logosresourcepages.org/Music/beatles.htm.

41. The Rolling Stones, *Street Fighting Man* from Beggars Banquet album, London Records (December 1968).

42. *National Review* (March 8, 2010): 51.

43. Lauren Weiner, "Where Have All the Lefties Gone?" *First Things* (January 2010): 31.

44. Stanislav Mishin, "American Capitalism Gone with a Whimper," *Pravda* (April 27, 2009), http://english.pravda.ru/opinion/columnists/107459-0/.

45. Victor Davis Hanson, "A Postmodern Presidency," *Pajamas Media* (April 4, 2010), http://pajamasmedia.com/victordavishanson/a-postmodern-presidency/.

46. Jim Hoft, "After Nationalizing Health Care & Student Loans–Obama Continues Attack on Private Sector in Weekly Address" *First Things* (March 27, 2010), http://gatewaypundit.firstthings.com/2010/03/obama-continues-attack-on-private-sector-bashes-banks-middlemen-in-weekly-address/.

47. Sean Hannity, *Conservative Victory: Defeating Obama's Radical Agenda* (New York: Harper, 2010), 40.

48. See "A Riveting Exchange Between Cornel West and Carl Dix," *Revolution* #170 (July 19, 2009), http://www.rwor.org/a/170/CWCD_event-en.html. Also see David Horowitz, "Obama's Professor and America's Cultural Crisis," *The Fillmore Gazette* (April 22, 2010), http://thefillmoregazette.com/politics-government/american-culture-under-attack.

49. Erick Erickson, "Obama and the New Party," *Human Events* (June 10, 2008), http://www.humanevents.com/article.php?id=26913. Also see Klein and Elliott's *The Manchurian President*, 81–88. The founders of the New Party were all Marxists, including Noam Chomsky, Carl Davidson, Elaine Bernard, Frances Fox Piven, Bill Fletcher, Cornel West, Barbara, Ehrenreich, and Quentin Young.

50. Scott Wilson and Garance Franke-Ruta, "White House Adviser

Van Jones Resigns Amid Controversy over Past Activism," *The Washington Post* (September 6, 2009), http://voices.washingtonpost.com/44/2009/09/06/van_jones_resigns.html. "Today the Center for American Progress announced that Van Jones is rejoining the center as a Senior Fellow and leader of the Green Opportunity Initiative, a new CAP project," see See "Van Jones Rejoins CAP to Lead Green Opportunity Initiative," *Center for American Progress* (February 24, 2010), http://www.americanprogress.org/issues/2010/02/van_jones.html. Also see Klein and Elliott's *The Manchuraian President*, 152*ff* for a summary of Van Jones Communist background and his role in the Obama administration.

51. "Van Jones Praises Joel Rogers," posted online: http://www.youtube.com/watch?v=bfy7Pz-6OPU. Van Jones made these comments at the January 2009 Mayor's Innovation Project Conference.

52. The Invisible Committee, *The Coming Insurrection* (Cambridge, MA: MIT Press, 2009), 16–17, 103*ff*. Calling themselves "The Invisible Committee," the authors chose to remain anonymous.

53. Sowell, *Intellectuals and Society*, 93. Also see Edward Lee Pitts, "The Quiet Weapon," *WORLD Magazine* 25, no. 10 (May 22, 2010): 31*ff*. This article is available online: http://www.worldmag.com/articles/16688.

54. Robert Costa, "Ryan: 'Two Futures,'" *National Review* (February 1, 2010), http://corner.nationalreview.com/post/?q=YWU5ZmEzNGI0OTNhYTQ3NDE3ZDE5YjAyMzEwZjdiMGI.

55. Glenn Beck, "Obama, in His Own Words," *Fox News* (September 22, 2009), http://www.foxnews.com/story/0,2933,553880,00.html.

56. "Gingrich Calls Obama 'Most Radical President in American History,'" Fox News (April 9, 2010), http://www.foxnews.com/politics/2010/04/08/gingrich-calls-obama-radical-president-american-history/.

57. Mark Steyn, "Tattered Liberty," *National Review* (January 25, 2010), http://article.nationalreview.com/428996/tattered-liberty/mark-steyn.

58. Marvin Olasky, "All Together Now," *WORLD Magazine* 24, no. 22 (November 7, 2009): 25. This article is also available online: http://www.worldmag.com/articles/16016.

59. Ibid.

60. Glen Beck, "Barack Obama's Foundation," *Fox News* (April 6, 2010), http://www.foxnews.com/story/0,2933,590513,00.html.

61. Goldberg, *Liberal Fascism*, 323.

62. Ibid., 322.

63. Ibid.

64. Jeffrey Schmidt, "The Real Agenda of Black Liberation Theology," *American Thinker* (March 19, 2008), http://www.americanthinker.com/2008/03/the_real_agenda_of_black_liber.html.

Endnotes

65. See Joseph Klein, "The Wrong Prescription," *Front Page Magazine* (September 22, 2008), http://www.frontpagemag.com/readArticle. aspx?ARTID=32427. This interview is available online: http://www. youtube.com/watch?v=niJAkR_6tKQ.

66. Newt Gingrich, "This Will Not Stand: Newt on the Passage of Obamacare," *Human Events* (March 22, 2010): 12. This article is available online: http://www.humanevents.com/article.php?id=36142.

67. Quoted from "Biography for Jane Fonda," *The Internet Movie Database*, http://www.imdb.com/name/nm0000404/bio.

68. Beck, "Barack Obama's Foundation," *Fox News*. Also see Andrew C. McCarthy, *The Grand Jihad: How Islam and the Left Sabotage America* (New York: Encounter Books, 2010), 189, 196.

69. Ibid. Also see Klein and Elliott, *The Manchurian President*, 156 for additional information on Davis. Also see McCarthy, *The Grand Jihad*, 205.

70. Jack Cashill, "Decrypting Obama's 'Pop,'" *American Thinker* (February 28, 2010), http://www.americanthinker.com/2010/02/ decrypting_obamas_pop.html.

71. William Z. Foster, *Toward Soviet America* (New York: International Publishers, 1932), 317. Foster was General Secretary of the Communist Party USA, as well as a member of the Socialist Party of America and Industrial Workers of the World (IWW, Wobblies).

72. Ibid.

73. Ibid., 316.

74. Fonda made this statement at the University of Texas in 1971. Karen Elliott, *Dallas Morning News* (December 11, 1971).

75. *The New York Times* (April 18, 1975).

76. Brian Faughnan, "Bill Ayers Speaks about the Weather Underground," *The Weekly Standard* (April 17, 2008), http://www.weeklystandard. com/weblogs/TWSFP/2008/04/bill_ayers_speaks_about_the_we_1.asp.

77. David A. Noebel, *Understanding the Times: The Collision of Today's Competing Worldviews*, Rev. 2nd ed. (Manitou Springs, CO: Summit Press, 2006), 9.

78. Malachi Martin, *The Keys of This Blood: Pope John Paul II Versus Russia and the West for Control of the New World Order* (New York: Simon & Schuster, 1990), 650.

79. Roger Kimball, "A Maoist in the White House," *Pajamas Media* (October 16, 2009), http://pajamasmedia.com/rogerkimball/2009/10/16/ a-maoist-in-the-white-house/. Ms. Dunn was former Obama White House Communications Director. This quote was in a speech Dunn delivered to a group of high school students in June 2009.

80. *New Statesman*, October 29, 2009. This speech is available online: http://www.youtube.com/watch?v=HiBDpL2dExY.

81. George Bernard Shaw, *Intelligent Woman's Guide to Socialism and*

Capitalism (New Brunswick, NJ: Transaction Publishers, 1984), 470.
82. Quoted in Robert C. Cottrell, *Roger Nash Baldwin and the American Civil Liberties Union*, (New York: Columbia University Press, 2000), 228–29.
83. See the Jimmy Carter Library & Museum website: http://jimmycarterlibrary.org/documents/jec/medal.phtml.
84. Vladimir Lenin, *Collected Works*, 45 vols., vol. 30 (Moscow: Progress Publishers, 1978), 107.
85. Lenin, *Collected Works*, vol. 10, 86.
86. Zygmund Dobbs, *Keynes at Harvard* (West Sayville, NY: Veritas Foundation, 1962), 78–79.
87. Ibid., 77.
88. Ibid., 60.
89. Chambers, *Witness*, 741.
90. Ibid., 10.
91. Aleksandr Solzhenitsyn, "A World Split Apart," 1978 Harvard University graduation address, http://www.columbia.edu/cu/augustine/arch/solzhenitsyn/harvard1978.html.
92. Peter B. Chowka, "Rep. Dingell: It's Taken a Long Time to 'Control the People,'" *American Thinker* (May 6, 2010), http://www.americanthinker.com/blog/2010/03/rep_dingell_its_taken_a_long_t.html.
93. Newt Gingrich, "Gingrich: Democrats Want to Impose 'Secular-Socialist Machine,'" *Fox News* (May 16, 2010), http://www.foxnews.com/politics/2010/05/16/gingrich-democrats-want-impose-secular-socialist-machine/.
94. Andrew C. McCarthy, *The Grand Jihad: How Islam and the Left Sabotage America* (New York: Encounter Books, 2010), 12.
95. Ibid., 13.
96. Ibid., 14.
97. Rush Limbaugh, *The Rus Limbaugh Show* (August 14, 2009).
98. For an audio version of this quote in context, see http://www.socialists.com/.
99. Melanie Phillips, *The World Turned Upside Down* (New York: Encounter Books, 2010), 343–44.
100. Chambers, *Witness*, 9.

BIBLIOGRAPHY

Aikman, David. *The Delusion of Disbelief.* Carol Stream, IL: Tyndale Publishers, 2008.

Anderson, Martin. *Imposters in the Temple: American Intellectuals Are Destroying Our Universities and Cheating Our Students of Their Future.* New York: Simon & Schuster, 1992.

Bales, James D. *Communism: Its Faith and Fallacies.* Grand Rapids, MI: Baker Book House, 1962.

Barrow, John D. and Frank J. Tipler. *The Anthropic Cosmological Principle.* New York: Oxford University Press, 1986.

Barton, David. *Original Intent: The Courts, the Constitution and Religion.* Aledo, TX: WallBuilder Press, 1997.

Barzun, Jacques M. *Darwin, Marx, Wagner: Critique of a Heritage.* New York: Barzun Press, 2008.

Bauer, P.T. *Equality, the Third World, and Economic Delusion.* Cambridge, MA: Harvard University Press, 1981.

Beckwith, Francis J. and William Lane Craig and J.P. Moreland, eds. *To Everyone An Answer: A Case for the Christian Worldview.* Downers Grove, IL: InterVarsity Press, 2004.

Behe, Michael J. *Darwin's Black Box: The Biochemical Challenge to Evolution.* 10th Anniversary ed. New York: The Free Press, 2006.

————. *The Edge of Evolution: The Search for the Limits of Darwinism.* New York: The Free Press, 2007.

Berlinski, David. *The Devil's Delusion: Atheism and Its Scientific Pretensions.* New York: Crown Forum, 2008.

Bethel, Tom. *The Noblest Triumph: Property and Prosperity Through the Ages.* New York: St. Martin's Press, 1998.

Black, Edwin. *War against the Weak: Eugenics and America's Campaign to Create a Master Race.* New York: Thunder's Mouth Press, 2003.

Bibliography

Black, Jim Nelson. *Freefall of the American University: How Our Colleges Are Corrupting the Mind and Morals of the Next Generation.* Nashville, TN: Thomas Nelson, 2004.

———. *When Nations Die: America on the Brink—Ten Warning Signs of a Culture in Crisis.* Wheaton, IL: Tyndale House Publishers, 1994.

Bonner, William and Addison Wiggin. *The New Empire of Debt: The Rise and Fall of an Epic Financial Bubble.* New York: John Wiley & Sons, 2009.

Brooks, Arthur C. *The Battle: How the Fight between Free Enterprise and Big Government Will Shape America's Future.* New York: Basic Books, 2010.

Buchanan, Patrick J. *The Death of the West.* New York: St. Martin's Press, 2002.

Budziszewski, J. *What We Can't Not Know.* Dallas, TX: Spence Publishing Company, 2003.

Burnham, James. *Suicide of the West: The Definitive Analysis of the Pathology of Liberalism.* New Rochelle, New York: Arlington House, 1975.

Campbell, John Angus and Stephen C. Meyer. *Darwinism, Design, and Public Education.* East Lansing, MI: Michigan State University Press, 2003.

Carson, D.A. *The Gagging of God: Christianity Confronts Pluralism.* Grand Rapids, MI: Zondervan Publishing House, 1996.

Chambers, Whittaker. *Witness.* New York: Random House, 1952.

Chandler, Robert. *Shadow World: Resurgent Russia, the Global Left, and Radical Islam.* Washington, DC: Regnery Publishers, 2008.

Collier, Peter and David Horowitz. *Destructive Generation: Second Thoughts about the '60s.* New York: Summit Books, 1989.

Colson, Charles and Nancy Pearcey. *How Now Shall We Live?.* Wheaton, IL: Tyndale House Publishers, 1999.

Conquest, Robert. *The Great Terror: A Reassessment.* 40th Anniversary ed. Oxford: Oxford University Press, 2007.

———.*The Harvest of Sorrow: Soviet Collectivization and the Terror-Famine.* Oxford: Oxford University Press, 1987.

Coulter, Ann. *Godless: The Church of Liberalism.* New York: Crown Forum, 2006.

———. *Treason: Liberal Treachery.* New York: Crown Forum, 2003.

Bibliography

Courtois, Stephane, ed. *The Black Book of Communism: Crimes, Terror, Repression.* Cambridge: Harvard University Press, 1999.

Dalrymple, Theodore. *Life at the Bottom: The Worldview That Makes the Underclass.* Chicago: Ivan R. Dee, 2001.

———. *Our Culture, What's Left of It.* Chicago: Ivan R. Dee, 2005.

Davies, Paul. *Cosmic Jackpot: Why Our Universe Is Just Right for Life.* New York: Houghton Mifflin Company, 2007.

Day, Vox. *The Irrational Atheist: Dissecting the Unholy Trinity of Dawkins, Harris, and Hitchens.* Dallas, TX: Benbella Books, 2008.

Dembski, William A. *Uncommon Dissent: Intellectuals Who Find Darwinism Unconvincing.* Wilmington, DE: ISI Books, 2004.

Dobbs, Zygmund. *The Great Deceit: Social Pseudo-Sciences.* West Sayville, NY: Veritas Foundation, 1964.

———. *Keynes at Harvard: Economic Deception as a Political Creed.* West Sayville, NY: Veritas Foundation, 1962.

D'Souza, Dinesh. *What's So Great about Christianity.* Washington, DC: Regnery Publishing, 2007.

Durant, Will. *Caesar and Christ: A History of Roman Civilization and of Christianity from Their Beginnings to A.D. 325.* 11 vols. Vol. 3, The Story of Civilization. New York: Simon & Schuster, 1944.

Ellis, Richard J. *The Dark Side of the Left: Illiberal Egalitarianism in America.* Lawrence, KS: University Press of Kansas, 1998.

Evans, M. Stanton. *Blacklisted by History: The Untold Story of Senator Joe McCarthy and His Fight against America's Enemies.* New York: Crown Forum, 2007.

———. *The Theme Is Freedom: Religion, Politics, and the American Tradition.* Washington, DC: Regnery Publishing, 1994.

Flew, Antony. *There Is a God.* New York: HarperOne, 2007.

Foster, William Z. *Toward Soviet America.* New York: International Publishers, 1932.

Gairdner, William D. *The Book of Absolutes: A Critique of Relativism and a Defense of Universals.* Montreal, QC: McGill-Queen's University Press, 2008.

Geisler, Norman L. and Frank Turek. *I Don't Have Enough Faith to Be an Atheist.* Wheaton, IL: Crossway Books, 2004.

Gellately, Robert. *Lenin, Stalin, And Hitler: The Age of Social Catastrophe.* New York: Random House, 2007.

Bibliography

George, Robert P. and Jean Bethke Elshtain. *The Meaning of Marriage: Family, State, Market, and Morals.* Dallas, TX: Spence Publishing Company, 2006.

Gilder, George. *The Israel Test.* New York: Richard Vigilante Books, 2009.

Goldberg, Jonah. *Liberal Fascism: The Secret History of the American Left, from Mussolini to the Politics of Meaning.* New York: Doubleday, 2007.

Grant, George. *Grand Illusions: The Legacy of Planned Parenthood.* Franklin, TN: Adroit Press, 1992.

Hart, David B. *Atheist Delusions: The Christian Revolution and Its Fashionable Enemies.* New Haven, CT: Yale University Press, 2009.

Hayek, F.A. *The Road to Serfdom.* Chicago: The University of Chicago Press, 1994.

Haynes, John Earl and Harvey Klehr. *In Denial: Historians, Communism and Espionage.* San Francisco, CA: Encounter Books, 2003.

Haynes, John Earl, Harvey Klehr and Alexander Vissiliev. *Spies: The Rise and Fall of the KGB in America.* New Haven, CT: Yale University Press, 2010.

Herman, Arthur. *The Idea of Decline in Western History.* New York: The Free Press, 1997.

Himmelfarb, Gertrude. *The Roads to Modernity: The British, French, and American Enlightenments.* New York: Alfred A. Knopf, 2004.

Hollander, Paul. *Anti-Americanism: Irrational and Rational.* New Brunswick, NJ: Transaction Publishers, 1995.

Hooper, Judith. *Of Moths and Men: The Untold Story of Science and the Peppered Moth.* New York: W.W. Norton & Company, 2002.

Horowitz, David. *The Professors: The 101 Most Dangerous Academics in America.* Washington, DC: Regnery Publishing, 2006.

———. *Radical Son: A Generational Odyssey.* New York: The Free Press, 1997.

———. *Unholy Alliance: Radical Islam and the American Left.* Washington, DC: Regnery Publishing, 2004.

Huntington, Samuel P. *The Clash of Civilizations.* New York: Simon & Schuster, 1996.

Hutchinson, Robert J. *The Politically Incorrect Guide to the Bible.* Washington, DC: Regnery Publishing, 2007.

Jay, Martin. *The Dialectical Imagination: A History of the Frankfurt School and the Institute of Social Research 1923–1950.* Berkeley, CA: University of California Press, 1996.

Bibliography

Joad, C.E.M. *The Recovery of Belief: A Restatement of Christian Philosophy*. London, UK: Faber and Faber, 1952.

Johnson, Paul. *Intellectuals: From Marx and Tolstoy to Sarte and Chomsky*. New York: Harper Perennial, 2007.

Joravsky, David. *The Lysenko Affair*. Chicago: University of Chicago Press, 1986.

Kirk, Russell. *The Roots of American Order*. Washington, DC: Regnery Gateway, 1991.

Klehr, Harvey. *The Communist Experience in America: A Political and Social History*. New Brunswick, NJ: Transaction Publishers, 2009.

Klein, Aaron and Brenda J. Elliott. *The Manchurian President: Barack Obama's Ties to Communists, Socialists and other Anti-American Extremists*. Washington, DC: WND Books, 2010.

Koster, John P. *The Atheism Syndrome*. Brentwood, TN: Wolgemuth & Hyatt Publishers, 1989.

LaHaye, Tim and David A. Noebel. *Mind Siege: The Battle for Truth in the New Millennium*. Nashville, TN: Word Publishing, 2000.

Lee, Francis Nigel. *Communism Versus Creation*. Nutley, NJ: The Craig Press, 1969.

Lennox, John C. *God's Undertaker: Has Science Buried God?*. Oxford: Lion Books, 2007.

Levin, Mark R. *Liberty and Tyranny: A Conservative Manifesto*. New York: Simon & Schuster, 2009.

Lewis, C.S. *Christian Reflections*. Grand Rapids, MI: William B. Eerdmans Publisher, 1967.

———. *God in the Dock: Essays on Theology and Ethics*. Grand Rapids, MI: William B. Eerdmans Publishers, 1970.

Limbaugh, David. *Persecution: How Liberals Are Waging War against Christianity*. Washington, DC: Regnery Publishing, 2003.

Markham, Ian S. *Against Atheism: Why Dawkins, Hitchens, and Harris Are Fundamentally Wrong*. Hoboken, NJ: Wiley-Blackwell, 2010.

Martin, Malachi. *The Keys of This Blood: The Struggle for World Dominion between Pope John Paul II, Mikhail Gorbachev and the Capitalist West*. New York: Simon & Schuster, 1980.

McCarthy, Andrew C. *The Grand Jihad: How Islam and the Left Sabotage America*. New York: Encounter Books, 2010.

McCarran, M. Margaret Patricia. *Fabianism in the Political Life of Britain, 1919–1931*. Chicago: The Heritage Foundation, 1954.

Bibliography

McGrath, Alister. *The Dawkins Delusion: Atheist Fundamentalism and the Denial of the Divine*. London: Society for Promoting Christian Knowledge, 2007.

———. *The Twilight of Atheism: The Rise and Fall of Disbelief in the Modern World*. New York: Doubleday, 2004.

McGregor, Richard. *The Party: Secret of China's Communist Rulers*. New York: Harper, 2010.

Meyer, Stephen C. *Signature in the Cell: DNA and the Evidence for Intelligent Design*. New York: HarperOne, 2009.

Milton, Joyce. *The Road to Malpsychia: Humanistic Psychology and Our Discontents*. San Francisco, CA: Encounter Books, 2002.

Milton, Richard. *Shattering the Myths of Darwinism*. South Paris, ME: Park Street Press, 2000.

Montefiore, Simon Sebag. *Stalin: The Court of the Red Tsar*. New York: Alfred A. Knopf, 2003.

Moreland, J.P. and William Lane Craig. *Philosophical Foundations for a Christian Worldview*. Downers Grove, IL: InterVarsity Press, 2003.

Murphy, Robert P. *The Politically Incorrect Guide to Capitalism*. Washington, DC: Regnery Publishing, 2007.

Nash, Ronald H. *Life's Ultimate Questions: An Introduction to Philosophy.* Grand Rapids, MI: Zondervan Publishing House, 1999.

Nicholi, Armand M. *The Question of God.* New York: The Free Press, 2002.

Noebel, David A. *Understanding the Times: The Collision of Today's Competing Worldviews.* Rev. 2nd ed. Manitou Springs, CO: Summit Press, 2006.

Noebel, David A., J.F. Baldwin and Kevin Bywater. *Clergy in the Classroom: The Religion of Secular Humanism,* Rev. 3rd ed. Manitou Springs, CO: Summit Press, 2007.

Pearcey, Nancy R. *Total Truth: Liberating Christianity from Its Cultural Captivity.* Wheaton, IL: Crossway Books, 2004.

Pearcey, Nancy R. and Charles B. Thaxton. *The Soul of Science: Christian Faith and Natural Philosophy.* Wheaton, IL: Crossway Books, 1994.

Phillips, Melanie. *The World Turned Upside Down.* New York: Encounter Books, 2010.

Pipes, Richard. *Communism: A History.* New York: The Modern Library, 2001.

———. *The Russian Revolution.* New York: Vintage, 1991.

Bibliography

Quigley, Carroll. *Tragedy and Hope: A History of the World in Our Time*. New York: The Macmillan Company, 1966.

Richards, Jay. *Money, Greed, and God: Why Capitalism Is the Solution and Not the Problem*. New York: HarperOne, 2009.

Romerstein, Herbert and Eric Breindel. *The Venona Secrets: Exposing Soviet Espionage and America's Traitors*. Washington, DC: Regnery Publishing, 2000.

Rummel, R.J. *Death by Government*. New Brunswick, NJ: Transaction Publishers, 1994.

Sanford, John C. *Genetic Entropy and the Mystery of the Genome*. Lima, New York: Ivan Press, 2005.

Schaeffer, Francis A. *A Christian Manifesto*. Wheaton, IL: Crossway Books, 1981.

Schmidt, Alvin J. *The Menace of Multiculturalism: Trojan Horse in America*. Westport, CT: Praeger Publishers, 1997.

Schwarz, Fred C. *Beating the Unbeatable Foe: One Man's Victory over Communism, Leviathan, and the Last Enemy*. Washington, DC: Regnery Publishing, 1996.

Shafarevich, Igor. *The Socialist Phenomenon*. New York: Harper & Row, 1980.

Short, Bruce N. *The Harsh Truth about Public Schools.* Vallecito, CA: Chalcedon Foundation, 2004.

Skousen, Mark. *The Making of Modern Economics: The Lives and Ideas of the Great Thinkers.* 2nd ed. Armonk, NY: M.E. Sharpe, 2009.

Skousen, W. Cleon. *The Naked Communist.* Salt Lake City, UT: The Ensign Publishing Company, 1961.

Spetner, Lee. *Not by Chance: Shattering The Modern Theory of Evolution.* New York: The Judaica Press, 1997.

Sowell, Thomas. *A Conflict of Visions: Ideological Origins of Political Struggles.* New York: Basic Books, 2002.

———. *Black Rednecks and White Liberals.* San Francisco, CA: Encounter Books, 2005.

———. *Intellectuals and Society.* New York: Basic Books, 2009.

———. *Inside American Education: The Decline, the Deception, the Dogmas.* New York: The Free Press, 1993.

Stark, Rodney. *For the Glory of God: How Monotheism Led to Reformations, Science, Witch-Hunts, and the End of Slavery.* Princeton, NJ: Princeton University Press, 2003.

Bibliography

————. *The Victory of Reason: How Christianity Led to Freedom, Capitalism, and Western Success*. New York: Random House, 2005.

Steyn, Mark. *America Alone: The End of the World as We Know It*. Washington, DC: Regnery Publishing, 2006.

Stove, David. *Darwinian Fairytales: Selfish Genes, Errors of Heredity, and Other Fables of Evolution*. New York: Encounter Books, 1995.

Taylor, S.J. *Stalin's Apologist: Walter Duranty, the New York Times' Man in Moscow*. New York: Oxford University Press, 1990.

Vetterli, Richard and William E. Fort, Jr. *The Socialist Revolution*. New York: Clute International Corporation, 1968.

Von Kuehnelt-Leddihn, Erik. *Leftism Revisited: From deSade and Marx to Hitler and Pol Pot*. Washington, DC: Regnery Gateway, 1990.

Von Mises, Ludwig. *The Anti-Capitalistic Mentality*. South Holland, IL: Libertarian Press, 1972.

————. *Socialism*. Indianapolis, IN: Liberty Classics, 1981.

Wells, Jonathan, *Icons of Evolution: Science or Myth?* Washington, DC: Regnery Publishing, 2000.

Weikart, Richard, *From Darwin to Hitler: Evolutionary Ethics, Eugenics, and Racism in Germany*. New York: Macmillan, 2004.

Westacott, Michael J. and John F. Ashton. *The Big Argument: Twenty-four Scholars Explore Why Science, Archaeology and Philosophy Haven't Disproved God.* Sydney, AS: Strand Publishing, 2005.

Wetter, Gustav A. *Dialectical Materialism: A Historical and Systematic Survey of Philosophy in the Soviet Union.* London, UK: Routledge and Kegan Paul, 1958.

Wiggershaus, Rolf. *The Frankfurt School: Its History, Theories, and Political Significance.* Cambridge, MA: The MIT Press, 1998.

Wiggin, Addison. *The Demise of the Dollar: And Why It's Even Better for Your Investments.* Hoboken, NJ: John Wiley & Sons, 2005.

Windchy, Eugene G. *The End of Darwinism: And How a Flawed and Disastrous Theory Was Stolen and Sold.* Bloomington, IN: Xlibris Corporation, 2009.

Woods, Jr., Thomas E. *Meltdown: A Free-Market Look at Why the Stock Market Collapsed, the Economy Tanked, and Government Bailouts Will Make Things Worse.* Washington, DC: Regnery Publishing, 2009.

Wurmbrand, Richard. *Marx and Satan.* Bartlesville, OK: Living Sacrifice Book Company, 2003.

INDEX

Index

Dix, Carl, 312
Dobbs, Zygmund, 264, 292, 318, 319
Dobson, James C., 252, 297
Dodd, Chris, 288
Dodd, Thomas J., 297
Dohrn, Bernardine, 3, 4, 5
Dolan, Tony, 299
Dornan, Robert, 297
Dostoyevsky, Fyodor, 264, 286
Dreams from My Father, 2
Dubois, W.E.B., 309
Dunn, Anita, 317
Duranty, Walter, 304
Dzerinski, Felix, 117
Earth Liberation Front, 4
Eckart, Dietrich, 253
Economic Determinism, 228, 229
Eisenhower, Dwight, 68
Eisner, Kurt, 253
Eliot, T.S., 259
Elliott, Brenda J., 306
Ellis, Havelock, 268, 269, 270
Ellis, Richard J., 278
Elvin, John, 307
En-lai, Chou, 34
Engels, Frederick, 34, 55, 96, 227, 230, 287
Eugenics, 270
Evans, Dale, 297
Evans, Jodie, 4
Exley, Zack, 7
Fabian Socialism, 260, 285, 299
Falwell, Jerry, 297
Fascism, 232, 250, 252, 258, 260
Feder, Don, 310
Feuerbach, Ludwig, 181, 182, 184
Fichte, Johann, 257
Filner, Bob, 290
Fonda, Jane, 9 280, 315, 317
Foster, William Z., 10, 81, 98, 316
Foucault, Michel, 247, 251, 311, 317
Fourier, Charles, 291

Frank, Barney, 288, 290
Frankfurt School, 257
Free Press, 303
Freud, Sigmund, 247
Friedman, Thomas L., 305
Funes, Mauricio, 275
Furet, Francois, 307
Galton, Francis, 270
Geisler, Norman, 297
Gelernter, David, 282
German Higher Criticism, 257
Gingrich, Newt, 313, 320
Goebbels, Joseph, 253
Goldberg, Jonah, 9, 310, 314, 315
Goldblatt, Louis, 100
Gorbachev, Mikhail, 10, 309, 317
Graham, Billy, 224
Gramsci, Antonio, 314, 320
Grant, George, 270
Grijalva, Raul M., 291
Guevara, Ernesto "Che", 308
Halliday, Jon, 2, 262
Hammer, Armand, 307
Hannity, Sean, 312
Hanson, Victor Davis, 311
Harvard Law School, 2
Harvard University, 1, 3, 6, 314
Hastings, Alcee, 315
Haushofer, Karl, 253
Hayden, Tom, 278, 317
Hayek, Friedrich A, 255
Healy, Jim, 104
Hegel, Georg W. F., 181, 183, 184, 228
Heidegger, Martin, 251, 256, 311
Heilbroner, Robert, 295
Himmler, Heinrich, 253
Hirsch, Emanuel, 257
History of the Plymouth Plantation, 277
Hitler, Adolf, 250, 254, 259
Hoft, Jim, 312
Holmes, Oliver W., 267, 309
Homosexual, 251, 292

Index

David A. Noebel is president of both Summit Ministries and the Christian Anti-Communism Crusade. He was educated at Grace Bible College, Hope College, the University of Tulsa and the University of Wisconsin. He is a member of the American Philosophical Association and the Evangelical Philosophical Society. Noebel is an author, editor and public speaker and has authored the highly acclaimed worldview classic, *Understanding The Times: The Collision of Today's Competing Worldviews.*